Respectability on the Line

BERKELEY SERIES IN BRITISH STUDIES

Edited by James Vernon

1. *The Peculiarities of Liberal Modernity in Imperial Britain*, edited by Simon Gunn and James Vernon
2. *Dilemmas of Decline: British Intellectuals and World Politics, 1945–1975*, by Ian Hall
3. *The Savage Visit: New World People and Popular Imperial Culture in Britain, 1710–1795*, by Kate Fullagar
4. *The Afterlife of Empire*, by Jordanna Bailkin
5. *Smyrna's Ashes: Humanitarianism, Genocide, and the Birth of the Middle East*, by Michelle Tusan
6. *Pathological Bodies: Medicine and Political Culture*, by Corinna Wagner
7. *A Problem of Great Importance: Population, Race, and Power in the British Empire, 1918–1973*, by Karl Ittmann
8. *Liberalism in Empire: An Alternative History*, by Andrew Sartori
9. *Distant Strangers: How Britain Became Modern*, by James Vernon
10. *Edmund Burke and the Conservative Logic of Empire*, by Daniel I. O'Neill
11. *Governing Systems: Modernity and the Making of Public Health in England, 1830–1910*, by Tom Crook
12. *Barbed-Wire Imperialism: Britain's Empire of Camps, 1976–1903*, by Aidan Forth
13. *Aging in Twentieth-Century Britain*, by Charlotte Greenhalgh
14. *Thinking Black: Britain, 1964–1985*, by Rob Waters
15. *Black Handsworth: Race in 1980s Britain*, by Kieran Connell
16. *Last Weapons: Hunger Strikes and Fasts in the British Empire, 1890–1948*, by Kevin Grant
17. *Serving a Wired World: London's Telecommunications Workers and the Making of an Information Capital*, by Katie Hindmarch-Watson
18. *Imperial Encore: The Cultural Project of the Late British Empire*, by Caroline Ritter
19. *Saving the Children: Humanitarianism, Internationalism, and Empire*, by Emily Baughan
20. *Cooperative Rule: Community Development in Britain's Late Empire*, by Aaron Windel
21. *Are We Rich Yet? The Rise of Mass Investment Culture in Britain*, by Amy Edwards
22. *Participant Observers: Anthropology, Colonial Development, and the Reinvention of Society in Britain*, by Freddy Foks
23. *Drag: A British History*, by Jacob Bloomfield
24. *Respectability on the Line: Gender, Race, and Labor along British and Colonial Indian Railways*, by Mattie Armstrong-Price

Respectability on the Line

Gender, Race, and Labor along British and Colonial Indian Railways

Mattie Armstrong-Price

UNIVERSITY OF CALIFORNIA PRESS

University of California Press
Oakland, California

© 2026 by Mattie Armstrong-Price

All rights reserved.

Cataloging-in-Publication data is on file at the Library of Congress.

ISBN 978-0-520-42155-4 (cloth)
ISBN 978-0-520-42156-1 (pbk.)
ISBN 978-0-520-42157-8 (ebook)

GPSR Authorized Representative: Easy Access System Europe, Mustamäe tee 50, 10621 Tallinn, Estonia, gpsr.requests@easproject.com

35 34 33 32 31 30 29 28 27 26
10 9 8 7 6 5 4 3 2 1

For Wren

Contents

Acknowledgments ix

Introduction 1

PART ONE. RAILWAY PATERNALISM AND THE MAKING OF SEXUAL CULTURES OF LABOR, 1840S–1860S

1. Imperfect Technologies of Moralization: Railway Paternalism in Mid-Nineteenth-Century Britain 19

2. Strains of Permissiveness, Fields of Force: Railway Paternalism in Colonial India after 1857 51

PART TWO. MAKING RAILWAY UNIONISM BETWEEN BRITAIN AND COLONIAL INDIA, 1870S–1880S

3. Paternal Figures: The Politics of Race and Gender in Early Railway Unionism 79

PART THREE. MASS MOVEMENTS AND THE MAKING OF SOCIAL LIBERALISM, 1890S–1910S

4. Laboring behind the Curtain: Industrial Unionism and Social Liberal Governance in Britain 111

5. Conveying Grievances in the Vernacular:
   Nationalist-Aligned Unionism and Social Liberal
   Reform in Colonial India   132

Conclusion   161

Notes   171
Bibliography   201
Index   211

Acknowledgments

It has taken more than a decade to write this book. The project has accompanied me for the better part of my adult life. The debts I've accrued over the period of writing are many and varied.

Historical scholarship rests on archivists' labor. Thank you to the archivists at the British Library, where research for this project began, and to those who maintain collections at the National Archives of the United Kingdom, the University of Warwick Modern Records Centre, the Lambeth Palace Library, and the National Archives of India. Archivists at the latter went out of their way to help me find critical indexes, which enabled me to fill out the archival base for the book's final chapter. Elyssa Livergant scanned research materials at the National Archives of the United Kingdom.

Chapter drafts and the book's prospectus have received helpful feedback both from individual readers and in workshop settings. Thank you to the anonymous reviewers of the manuscript for helping me to bring forward the central throughlines of the text. Thank you to Timothy Alborn for constructive feedback on the prospectus. Susan Pedersen, Guy Ortolano, Ren Pepitone, James Stafford, Emily Sohmer Tai, Maria De Longoria, Lennie Hanson, and Saronik Bosu helped organize workshops at Columbia and NYU, where I presented various chapter drafts. Eileen Gillooly, Ritika Prasad, Ren Pepitone, and Judith Walkowitz provided generative comments on these drafts. Thank you to Samuel Rutherford and Tehila Sasson for organizing conference panels at the North

American Conference on British Studies, where I received feedback on research related to this project. Ritika Prasad co-convened a panel at the Annual Conference on South Asia and has provided invaluable support and feedback on the book. I received vital research guidance from Nitin Sinha and Aparajita Mukhopadhyay. Magda Teter served as my faculty mentor at Fordham and provided helpful comments on several chapter drafts.

Many others have mentored me over the years. At Swarthmore, I am grateful to have worked with Mark Wallace, Bakirathi Mani, Nathaniel Deutsch, and Allison Dorsey. Bruce Lincoln, Margaret Mitchell, and Moishe Postone provided mentorship at the University of Chicago. Thank you to committee members at UC Berkeley—Ramona Naddaff, Martin Jay, Michael Wintroub, and Judith Butler—who helped give this project a foundation. Judith also provided research support and showed solidarity in the context of university-based movements. In this project I've tried to take up Judith's advice to frame historical writings with discussions of literature. I'm grateful to those with whom I learned and those with whom I organized in movements for public education in California, including Katy Fox-Hodess, Zachary Levenson, Vanessa Brutsche, Matt Bonal, Zhivka Valiavicharska, Alexandria Wright, Paul Nadal, Katherine Chandler, Suzanne Li Puma, Madeleine Cohen, Blanca Missé, M. Ty, Nar Hawkins Owen, Johanna Rothe, Althea Wasow, Tehila Sasson, Sam Wetherell, Shannon Ikebe, Puck Lo, Jasper Bernes, Christopher Chen, Annie McClanahan, Eric Blanc, Blu Buchanan, Beezer de Martelly, Eli Friedman, Julia Chang, Rachel Lesser, Brenda Medina-Hernandez, Mar Velez, Daniel Gutiérrez, Amrah Salomón, Alexandra Holmstrom-Smith, Juan Garcia, Colleen Lye, Lyn Hejinian, Leslie Salzinger, Michael Cohen, Leigh Raiford, Joshua Clover, Celeste Langan, and Rei Terada.

At the University of Michigan, I learned from colleagues in the Department of History and the Society of Fellows, including Geoff Eley, Kathleen Canning, Mrinalini Sinha, Kira Thurman, Alice Goff, Jericho Jennifer Nelson, Ana Vinea, and Allan Lumba. S. E. Kile and Madhumita Lahiri have offered vital feedback on drafts, helped me prepare for interviews, and supported me in innumerable other ways both professionally and personally. I'm grateful to Ann Arbor colleagues and friends, including Rachel Best, Holice Kil, Daniel Nemser, Loren Dobkin, Brian Whitener, Ana Sabau, Roi Livne, Ashley Bates, Aubrey McCullen, and Austin McCoy.

At Fordham University, I've received support and mentorship from colleagues in the Departments of History; Comparative Literature; Women,

Gender, and Sexuality Studies; and across the disciplines. In particular, I would like to thank Magda Teter, Kirsten Swinth, Christopher Dietrich, David Hamlin, Christopher Maginn, Silvana Patriarca, W. David Myers, Nana Osei-Opare, Asif Siddiqi, Claire Gherini, Samantha Iyer, Uponita Mukherjee, Michele Prettyman, Diane Detournay, Ivelisse Cuevas-Molina, Mark Naison, Tyesha Maddox, Zein Murib, and Maria Farland. Funding for my research trip to Delhi came from the Fordham History Department's O'Connell Initiative for the Global History of Capitalism. I have also received a writing fellowship from the Townsend Center for the Humanities at UC Berkeley and a research fellowship from Fordham University, which bookended the writing process for this project.

For the duration of this project, James Vernon has provided essential editorial feedback, advising, mentorship, and comradeship. The project is unthinkable without his support and guidance. Thank you, James, for welcoming me into the field and for showing me what is possible here. I am also grateful to Niels Hooper, Nora Becker, Julie Van Pelt, and all of the editorial staff at the University of California Press who have helped usher the book through the production process.

I'm grateful to family for sustaining me. Thank you to Munira Lokhandwala and Maryam Arain for comradeship and support in difficult times. Thank you to Jane Spielman for vital guidance when I most needed it. Thank you to my grandfather, John Armstrong, for teaching me about the railways. Thank you to Gary Price, Lanette Price, Joel Price, Lela Patrik, Julia Armstrong, and Stephen Snudden for their unwavering support. Thank you to my parents, John and Shirley, for their formative care and enduring love. Thank you to Alana Yu-lan Price, who has loved me through it all, and to Wren Armstrong-Price, who lights up my days. This project was also sustained by those who helped support Alana and Wren during this process (including during my research trips), such as Daniel Nemser, Eli Conley, Cadelba Lomelí-Loibl, Rachel Best, Holice Kil, Loren Dobkin, Ashley Bates, Kira Thurman, Joel Price, Lanette Price, Gary Price, Munira Lokhandwala, Maryam Arain, S. E. Kile, and Madhumita Lahiri.

Thank you to those who will read the book; I look forward to being in conversation with you.

Introduction

In 1897, William Wedderburn, a Liberal member of Parliament from Banffshire and a member of the Indian National Congress, asked a representative of the colonial state why Indian signal operators were being denied housing allowances. His question subsequently was forwarded to a representative of the colonial state's Public Works Department (PWD), who insisted that because there are "practical difficulties in the way of requiring a Native Signaller, who as a rule is accompanied by his family, to occupy a set of quarters in a block occupied by Europeans and Eurasians," such signalers "have no claim to compensation when quarters are not provided."[1] This stark communication highlights how the governance of railway workforces in colonial India was bound up with the racial hierarchization of populations. Company managers and state officials in colonial India were in the habit of differentiating railway workforces into three racialized groups—which we can characterize as Indian, multiracial Anglo-Indian, and white British—and unequally distributing housing benefits, salaries, and workplace roles among these groups. Railway companies maintained residential "colonies" that were accessible only to British and Anglo-Indian workers and their families.

In 1899, two years after the PWD attempted to justify the discriminatory distribution of housing benefits, Indian signal operators employed by the Great Indian Peninsular Railway (GIPR) struck work, challenging racially discriminatory compensation regimes. The 1899 GIPR strike marked a watershed in the relationship between railway workers and the vernacular press in India, as nationalist editors of vernacular-language periodicals took up the cause of signalers, publishing articles in defense of the strike and helping generate financial support for it. A group of nationalist leaders even pressed the strikers' case with the railway company's London-based Home Board. The editor of the *Hitavadi*, a Bengali-language paper published in Calcutta,[2] suggested that such advocates could have gone further by informing "the Directors how the Railway authorities make a distinction of colour in their treatment of Railway servants."[3] Meanwhile, the editor of *The Samiran*, a Bengali weekly, insisted that better pay and working conditions for railway employees would help draw respectable Indian men into the industry—a change that would benefit the traveling public: "Ill-treatment of passengers by railway employes is so common because those employes are not themselves respectable men and do not, therefore, know how to treat respectable people."[4] *The Samiran*'s translated article here turned the language of railway management against itself, insisting that, rather than assembling respectable workforces, railway managers were employing rough—mostly British and Anglo-Indian—men, and preventing respectable men from entering the service. By the turn of the century then, "respectability" was a contested term, caught up in debates around employment practices in the railway industry.

Respectability on the Line charts the force of this contested cultural concept through an examination of early railway labor history in Britain and colonial India. The book shows how railway managers sought to cultivate respectable workforces, how groups of railway bachelors stretched the parameters of respectability in nonheteronormative households, how workers' representatives claimed the mantle of respectability in organizing trade unions from the 1870s, and finally, how nationalist editors leveraged the language of respectability to challenge discriminatory practices in the railway industry. During the Victorian and Edwardian eras, respectability was a significant cultural concept that carried social and political force. At once a determinant of suffrage rights, a marker of individual comportment and cultivation, and a designation of the domestic ideal, respectability was a multilayered thing, and thus requires different historiographical lenses in order to be adequately grasped. *Respectability on the Line* ultimately tells a social historical story about how compensation regimes in the railway industry allowed a stratum of railway families to approximate—and sometimes to stretch—the domestic ideal; a cultural historical story about how the idealized figure of the "paternal railwayman" circulated across imperial print media and was then shattered by the vernacular press in colonial India; and a political historical story about how trade unionists and nationalist leaders came to assert responsibility for the moral and material uplift of railway communities while also leading movements that threw prevailing regimes of railway governance into crisis on the eve of the Great War. These stories do not simply run along parallel tracks, but rather form relays and cross over each other in sometimes surprising ways. Throughout the journey, we never stray too far from the question of how railway labor was shaped—not only in the shadow of industrial infrastructures but also in relation to dominant Victorian- and Edwardian-era cultural categories—the category of respectability above all. This cultural category, or keyword, was involved in the stabilization of the liberal imperial regime of accumulation, playing a role in the distribution of political citizenship; in the ordering of workforces; and in the social hierarchization of populations along lines of gender, race, and class. The category of respectability was also redeployed by workers' representatives as they challenged prevailing regimes of railway management. *Respectability on the Line* attends both to these stabilizing processes and to these countersystemic interventions as they played out across railway zones, which were strategic sites for the exercise of state power and for the circulation of people and commodities. The book ultimately treats railway zones as microcosms through which to study the wider history of capitalism in the liberal imperial era.

The liberal imperial regime of capital accumulation took shape in the 1840s, was transformed under various pressures in the 1870s, and came into terminal crisis around the time of the Great War. *Respectability on the Line* focuses its study of railway labor history on these three historical turning points. The book charts the making of paternalistic railway labor-management regimes from the 1840s, the emergence of craft unionist projects in the 1870s, and the turn to industrial and anticolonial labor organizing in the first decades of the twentieth century. Mass labor unrest between 1905 and 1907 forced the British and colonial Indian states to take a more active role in the governance of workplace relations. The resultant social liberal reforms ironically accelerated trajectories of labor unrest, signaling a crisis in prevailing regimes of industrial governance. *Respectability on the Line* thus charts the making and unmaking of the liberal imperial *mode of regulation*—that is, the patterned social, cultural, and political arrangements, including systems of labor-management, that helped stabilize a given regime of capital accumulation.[5]

The histories of railway labor in Britain and colonial India described in what follows are built upon original archival research across two countries. The book treats Britain and colonial India at once as mutually entangled sites—co-implicated locales in a wider imperial field—and as places with distinctive histories; it thus engages simultaneously in a comparative and cross-imperial account of railway labor history. For the history pertaining primarily to colonial India, I have relied especially on records of the colonial state's Railway Department, which are held at the National Archives of India; on the so-called native newspaper reports, which were recently digitized as part of the South Asian Open Archives initiative; and on India Office records, which are held at the British Library. These are all English-language sources. For the history pertaining primarily to Britain, I have relied on trade union records held at the Warwick Modern Records Centre; on railway company and Ministry of Trade records held at the National Archives of the United Kingdom; and on copies of the *Railway Service Gazette*. In addition to such archival sources, the book analyzes numerous published literary works. These works allow me to weave a cultural historical layer of analysis throughout—a layer that supplements and helps to frame the social, economic, and political histories that are built upon company, state, and trade union archives.

The work attends above all to the history of labor-management relations on the Great Western Railway (GWR) in Britain and on the East Indian Railway (EIR) in colonial India, which were some of the largest and longest running railways in their respective territories and thus influential in setting sector-wide managerial norms. The EIR was headed by an agent based in Calcutta, who was answerable to the company's London-based Home Board. Below the agent were various departmental superintendents, who coordinated mid-level managers in their areas. The GWR had a similar corporate structure, although the railway's top managers worked more closely with their directors in matters of labor management. In this way, the separation of ownership and management—a key marker of "modern" corporate governance—was more advanced for colonial Indian railway companies than for their metropolitan counterparts.

DOMESTIC LIFE ON THE LINES

The first section of the book seeks to explain how and with what effects executives shaped the compartments, leisure activities, and living conditions of different members of railway communities. In taking up this question, the book reengages with an established literature on company paternalism and working-class respectability.[6] Much of this scholarship is concerned with the question of how, in nineteenth-century Britain, middle-class notions of respectability and norms of domestic life took root among working-class populations. Behind this question is a concern with how working-class political cultures became more quiescent around the mid-century. In part, this process of cultural translation and political neutralization occurred at and around industrial workplaces, where self-consciously paternalistic executives shaped the living conditions of their employees. Railway directors and managers did so in a variety of ways, including through the creation of company towns or railway colonies, through the outfitting of public-facing employees with uniforms, and through the establishment of mechanics institutions and provident funds. In Britain from the 1840s, executives invested in these paternalistic measures partly to retain skilled workers and their families in far-flung locomotive workshop towns and partly to ensure that public-facing workers would be agreeable to middle-class passengers. The aspiration to cultivate workers' "respectability" thus bridged different managerial imperatives, shaping executives' relations to disparate portions of their workforces, including those who daily interfaced with passengers and those who spent their days minding machinery in workshop complexes. For these latter workshop employees, moralizing measures focused less on workplace comportment and more on matters of domestic life and leisure.

In the GWR's locomotive workshop town of Swindon, established in 1842, blocks of terrace housing fanned out from a plaza, in the center of which stood a mechanics institution—a place where classes were held, performances staged, books checked out, baths and meals enjoyed, provident-fund meetings convened, and a covered market frequented. The mechanics institution was a place for the care of the body and the mind, where railwaymen could partake in a host of "improving" activities. In the blocks surrounding the mechanics institution, most company-owned homes were inhabited by railway families, but in a handful of these homes railway widows rented their upstairs rooms to groups of bachelor railwaymen—a boarding arrangement facilitated by railway managers. Interestingly, in each of these sorts of household, female domestic specialists cohabited with breadwinning men, meaning that at least some approximation of the domestic ideal was realized down through the blocks of company-owned terrace housing.

The Great Western Railway, with its company town of Swindon and its provident funds, practiced a variant of company paternalism and formed what Laura Bear has termed a "moralizing bureaucracy." In her study of segregated railway colonies in India—places modeled on both British company towns and colonial military cantonments—Bear highlights some of the ambiguities of moralization in the railway context, ultimately concluding that "moralizing bureaucracies do not create moral orders, but instead create ethical dilemmas for bureaucrats and clients alike."[7] While Bear does not focus on the history of homosexuality, I've followed her general approach in tracing the extent to which the moralizing institutions of railway paternalism ironically created openings for the flourishing of homoerotic intimacies and bachelor subcultures in railway districts—phenomena that seem in most cases to have been tacitly permitted by railway managers. In both British company towns and Indian railway colonies—including the EIR's locomotive workshop colony of Jamalpur—bachelor railwaymen were able to cohabit. In Britain, bachelor cohabitation was enabled by boarding relationships, whereas in the railway colonies of India, racially privileged bachelors were permitted to live together as heads of household in official bungalows, which were maintained by the labor of domestic servants.[8] A remarkable scrapbook kept up by an EIR engineer suggests that some such bachelors formed family bonds with each other—a striking phenomenon that aligns with Sharon Marcus's argument for the elasticity of marriage in the Victorian era.[9]

ORDERING RAILWAY LABOR

With respect to the making of bachelor subcultures in early railway districts, British and colonial Indian histories seem to run along roughly parallel tracks. But if we zoom out from the blocks of company-owned homes in Swindon and Jamalpur—places where respectable railway families were formed, including by sets of bachelor railwaymen—we can begin to see some of the stark differences between these sites in terms of the practices of railway management and the processes of working-class formation. As we ascend above these two railway zones, sprawling workshop complexes come into view, as do surrounding blocks of non-company-owned housing. By the turn of the century, locomotive workshop complexes drew in thousands of workers who were distributed across fifteen or twenty shops. Most of these workshop employees lived beyond the bounds of company-owned housing. In Swindon, newer housing developments for railway families grew up over the second half of the nineteenth century *around* the central blocks of company-owned housing; while in Jamalpur, housing options for Indian employees—who were excluded from the segregated eastern residential colony—were restricted to the western side of the locomotive workshop complex, along winding and notably unsanitary streets.[10]

The different spatial distribution of workers' housing in Swindon versus Jamalpur gives us some purchase on the divergent making of cultures of labor in these places. In Swindon, workplace hierarchies and divisions of labor were somewhat smoothed over by housing and leisure arrangements that drew workers into shared conditions of life. Any workshop employee, for example, could become a member of the mechanics institution—a building that most employees would have passed on their way home from work. In Jamalpur, by contrast, Indian workshop employees entered the factory complex through different gates than those used by British and Anglo-Indian employees, both of whom would have enjoyed comfortable morning walks from their official bungalows or barracks to their places of work. While their commutes were separate, these groups of employees spent their workdays in close quarters. Sergeants were in charge on the shop floor. Below these middle managers, we find a moderately sized group of higher-grade fitters, boilermakers, and mechanics.[11] In Jamalpur, while sergeants were almost invariably British, among this group of higher-grade employees, British and Anglo-Indian fitters worked alongside Indian *mistris*, or mechanics, who played important mediating roles, translating instructions to entry-level, often subcontracted employees.

As Ian Kerr has shown, subcontracting arrangements were central to the construction of the railways in colonial India, and these arrangements persisted in the operation of railway systems.[12] In locomotive workshop complexes such as Jamalpur, a sizeable percentage of the workforce was employed through subcontracting and piece-work arrangements.[13] Insofar as workers were not employed directly by the company, they were categorically ineligible for paternalistic benefits, including membership in the provident fund, which was established on the East Indian Railway in 1868. In Swindon, by contrast, early career workshop employees were employed directly by the company and were eligible for paternalistic benefits, including housing allowances and membership in the company's provident fund. Paternalistic benefits—from housing allowances to membership in mechanics institutions and provident funds—thus played an important role in forming cultures of labor. In Britain, the universal distribution of such benefits tended to draw workers into shared conditions of life, while in colonial India, the discriminatory distribution of social benefits entrenched the racial hierarchization of workforces and populations.

EARLY TRADE UNIONISM

Respectability on the Line aims to link social and political histories of railway labor by showing how paternalistic managerial practices shaped the parameters of political organizing in the sector and how organizing from below reciprocally shaped managerial and state practices. We have already begun to see how managerial practices helped determine the extent to which workers were drawn into shared conditions of life beyond the shopfloor. In Britain, railway paternalism tended to draw workers into shared leisure activities and similar conditions of domestic life, whereas in colonial India, paternalistic interventions separated British and Anglo-Indian employees from their Indian coworkers. These broad patterns were replicated in the early organizing projects of railway labor. Whereas in Britain, the first wave of railway labor organizing, which took shape in the early 1870s, featured a universalist aspiration to organize all workers in the sector, in colonial India, the first wave of labor organizing was restricted to those who lived within railway colonies and featured a white laborist aspiration to keep higher-grade roles closed to Indian workers. This white laborist project collapsed under the weight of its own contradictions by the end of the 1870s. Meanwhile railway trade unionism had gained a stable foothold in the metropole—a difference in organizing fates that partially can be attributed to political factors, as the unionization of railway workers in early 1870s Britain immediately followed the legalization of trade unionism and the enfranchisement of "registered and respectable" working-class men. Economic factors also contributed to the emergence of railway unionism: On the British railways, a period of acute "speedup" in the late 1860s led to a spike in railway accidents, which helped galvanize higher-grade workers to take collective action.

The first railway trade union in Britain, the Amalgamated Society of Railway Servants (ASRS) attempted to organize all workers in the sector, but in practice the union was dominated by guards and other higher-grade workers employed in traffic and, to a lesser extent, locomotive departments. A rival, explicitly craft unionist project took shape in the late 1870s among engine drivers and firemen—employees who worked in locomotive departments. In this way, early railway trade unionism in the metropole was not without its own conflicts and limitations.

What interests me about early ASRS organizers in Britain is the extent to which they expressed an aspiration toward the universal representation of workers across the sector while at the same time engaging in what was effectively a grade-restricted, craft-unionist practice. In parsing this tension, it might help to examine more closely the practices and rhetoric of early railway unionists in light of the history of railway paternalism. As Simon Cordery has observed, company-sponsored provident funds in Britain were organized along "mutualist" lines, meaning that employee representatives filled out provident society boards alongside managerial representatives.[14] Employee delegates engaged in the day-to-day operation of provident funds, collaborating with managers in making bureaucratic decisions about particular benefit claims. Early ASRS benefit funds were modeled on company-sponsored funds and featured some of the same moralizing language directed against female recipients of funds— language stipulating that railway widows could lose access to payments if they were found to have engaged in "immorality." Rulebooks further stipulated that railway widows would lose access to payments in the event that they remarried. These regulations suggest that railway unionists—those who managed benefit funds—imagined themselves as temporary surrogate husbands for railway widows and as surrogate fathers for these women's "orphaned" children. Along these lines, railway unionists tended to frame their activities through a discourse of paternal social responsibility, yoking together a familiar breadwinner politics with claims of acting as paternal caretakers to wider railway communities and traveling publics. Higher-grade, public-facing trade unionists thus can be thought of as having engaged in a bid for hegemony over railway communities, implicitly asserting that their respectable brokering of railway workforces' grievances and managing of benefit funds would help uplift the moral and material conditions of railway communities as a whole. Hence the uneasy combination of universalist rhetoric and craft unionist practice. It wasn't until the early twentieth century that entry level employees, most of whom did not interface with traveling publics, joined the ASRS in substantial numbers, making this union more meaningfully industrial in its composition and orientation. The political activation of entry-level employees at the turn of the century can partially be explained with reference to the slowing of new railway construction, which had the effect of blocking off paths for promotion. Entry-level employees came to understand that their conditions of labor were likely to improve only via collective action, rather than via individual promotion through the ranks.

RHETORICS OF RAILWAY MASCULINITY

Here it is helpful to bring a cultural historical lens to bear on the history of railway labor politics as well, since the association of public-facing railway workers with paternal care was forged not only in trade unionist rhetoric but also through wider literary depictions of railway workers and their family members. In mid-century domestic novels and sensation fiction alike, railway guards appear as caring father figures, looking out for the well-being of traveling publics and for the needs of their own family members. From the mid-century, domestic fiction and improving periodicals helped recast norms of respectable working-class masculinity and femininity for an industrializing world—a world where male breadwinners faced notably unsafe conditions of employment. While working-class men were held responsible for making arrangements to support their family members even in the event of their accidental deaths, working-class women were imagined to be responsible for bearing up in dignified ways and finding alternative, respectable means of support in the wake of a husband's fatal injury. In this way we can see how early railway trade unionists in Britain echoed dominant cultural representations of railway workers and enforced dominant cultural norms against railway widows.

Cultural representations of railway workers circulated across the British imperial world, including through the *Railway Service Gazette*, the print periodical associated with the ASRS—a periodical that, judging by its letters to the editor, had a cross-imperial readership. Perhaps unsurprisingly then, white unionists in colonial India tried to assert their own, more explicitly racialized politics of paternal responsibility. But in colonial India, a counterdiscourse of railway masculinity that effectively contested the romantic vision of public-facing railwaymen as paternal figures circulated in the vernacular press as well. As Ritika Prasad notes, around the turn of the century, reports in the vernacular press "stressed the rising frequency with which European and Eurasian railway employees abducted and molested Indian women. It explained their boldness through the lenient punishment meted out to them.... Consequently, some commentators urged Indian women to defend themselves against the depredations of 'white-skinned railway employees,' the Calcutta *Sanjivani* even urging them to carry scimitars concealed on their person when traveling by train."[15]

Colonial sexual violence perpetrated by racially privileged railwaymen was thus associated with a wider "menace of 'white violence'" in the vernacular press—a menace to which self-defense was taken to be the only viable response.[16] As Manu Goswami has shown, nationalist discourse associated the railways with incarceration—whether with respect to locked third class carriages; segregated waiting areas at railway stations; or, as in some of the more horrific cases of sexual violence, to forcible confinement within office complexes and residential spaces.[17] In this way, sexual violence perpetrated by white railwaymen appeared as an unambiguously political matter, linking together various contexts and forms of colonial violence and calling for collective action.

In Britain, the situation could not have been more different. Sexual violence and associated acts of forcible confinement perpetrated by railway workers against female passengers, while evidently common and openly discussed in railway memoirs, did not similarly become a matter of significant political concern. Rather, cases of violence perpetrated by male *passengers* against women were covered, sometimes widely, in the press. But even in texts written by British women that register rail workers' sexual violence, this violence tends to be construed as exceptional and thus does not effectively undercut what was a wider cultural association of guards and other public-facing railwaymen with a specifically paternal form of care.[18] In colonial India, the vernacular press succeeded in shattering this romantic image, recasting racially privileged rail workers and managers as bearers of gendered colonial violence and as exemplars of an exploitative and confining regime. Labor organizers in colonial India borrowed from and advanced this political frame, highlighting in the vernacular press the overlapping forms of "ill-treatment" endured by Indian railwaymen at the hands of their managers. In Britain, by contrast, railway labor organizers continued to lean on the romantic image of the paternal railwayman into the twentieth century, despite the increasing anachronism of this image in an era when unions were organizing especially among non-public-facing workers. The *cultural* responses of wider publics to rail workers' acts of sexual violence thus helped determine the trajectories railway labor organizing took in Britain and colonial India—trajectories that were also shaped by sector-wide economic factors and by the distinctive systems of railway management in these two sites.

A HISTORY OF LABOR UNDER CAPITALISM

By showing how the different trajectories of railway labor organizing in Britain and colonial India were shaped at once by cultural, social, and economic factors, *Respectability on the Line* offers a multilayered history of labor under capitalism. In their introduction to the journal *Critical Historical Studies*, Manu Goswami, Moishe Postone, Andrew Sartori, and William H. Sewell Jr. argue for the renewed study of histories of capitalism, suggesting that critical historians ought to analyze the "processes by which economic, social, and cultural forms become intrinsically interrelated."[19] There is an interesting tension in this formulation, wherein plural processes seem to produce an interrelation between cultural, economic, and social levels—an interrelation that appears necessary or intrinsic, rather than merely contingent. This formulation perhaps resonates with Stuart Hall's conception of the conjuncture, which he sees as a moment when crises in different levels of historical experience seem to line up, setting the stage for a consequential, multilayered historical transformation. *Respectability on the Line* is framed around several such consequential conjunctures, especially the mid-nineteenth century conjuncture and the pre-WWI conjuncture, which came at the dawn and the dusk of the liberal imperial era of capital accumulation, respectively. These conjunctures were defined by overlapping crises and transformations across different levels of historical experience: Social unrest dovetailed with cultural contestation at moments of economic volatility, giving rise to new modes of regulation. In colonial India during the first decade of the twentieth century, nationalist editors redeployed the cultural category of respectability against railway managers while also collaborating with railway workers to build mass, nationalist-aligned strike movements. These movements, in turn, compelled significant transformations in regimes of railway governance, ultimately signaling the breakdown of the liberal imperial mode of regulation along the lines.

DEMOCRATIZING THE NATIONAL MOVEMENT

The collaborative relations maintained between railway workers and nationalist editors in colonial India—relations first solidified during the 1899 GIPR signalers' strike—not only spurred changes in the mode of railway governance but also helped contribute to a wider democratization of the national movement. In a recent essay on the anti-indenture movement in India, Mrinalini Sinha has outlined the process by which networks of organizers from various backgrounds helped democratize the national movement over the first decades of the twentieth century.[20] She shows how anti-indenture organizers collected "affidavits" of formerly indentured workers that were then published by nationalist editors and how these affidavits broadened readers' circle of concern, thereby helping to forge a new, more democratic conception of *the people*. Her work encourages historians to look to the stories of people drawn into political organizing during this time and to the ways that these politically activated individuals and groups interfaced with nationalist editors and organizers and shaped the agenda of the national movement, affected the form and content of published articles, and established new patterns of organization. In this vein, we can see how newly activated sectors of railway workers engaged with the national movement and its press organs and organizers in order to effectively convey workplace grievances to railway officials and to build networks of support among editors and wider segments of the public.

These networks of support were drawn into strike action following the Partition of Bengal. In the summer of 1906, a strike on the East Indian Railway was supported, and even co-organized, by Swadeshi leaders. While clerks, station masters, and signal operators had initially struck work, Swadeshi organizers travelled down the line to help bring workshop mechanics into the struggle. As Sumit Sarkar notes, this effort to broaden the strike involved an attempt to expand beyond the base of "white collar employees belonging to the fringes of bhadralok society" to include the "proletariat of railway workshops" as well.[21] This opening toward industrial, anticolonial unionism gave a scare to colonial state officials, who heard echoes of the 1905 Russian general strike in the railway yards of West Bengal.[22] Officials involved with the Railway Department of the colonial state sought an antidote to rail strikes after 1907. While briefly attempting conciliation boards along the lines of those Lloyd George had introduced in Britain, officials ultimately settled upon the reform of retirement policies, seeking to make these policies at once less racially exclusionary and more effective at preventing strikes: The rule established by the secretary of state of India in 1911 held that striking could render a worker and his family members ineligible for his retirement bonus.

SOCIAL LIBERALISM BETWEEN METROPOLE AND COLONY

Respectability on the Line considers in its final section how railway labor organizing reciprocally shaped and was shaped by social liberal approaches to governance after 1906. In both Britain and colonial India, the period between 1905 and 1907 was defined by strike organizing on the railways—organizing that drew in entry-level employees on a large scale. While social liberal reforms undertaken after the general election of 1906 were motivated in part by a desire to bring about labor peace, they ultimately had the ironic effect of bolstering labor radicalism in railway districts. In 1913, three British railway trade unions amalgamated into the National Union of Railwaymen. This breakthrough for industrial unionism followed in part from social liberal state interventions in the railway sector. In addition to Lloyd George's 1907 conciliation boards, which helped give unionists a platform for representing workers' grievances to management, the 1911 National Insurance Act (NIA) had the unintended consequence of encouraging union amalgamation. As the NIA was taking shape, trade unionists representing workers set to be covered by the act successfully agitated to have unions recognized as approved societies for administering insurance funds. Through their agitation, unionists asserted their self-conception as respectable comanagers of social welfare programs. The National Insurance Act placed significant bureaucratic obligations on approved societies. The General Railway Workers' Union—a syndicalist union established in 1889—could not afford the administrative staff required to process insurance cards and to manage state-approved funds.[23] Faced with this lack of organizational capacity and inundated by rank-and-file demands for amalgamation in the wake of the 1911 railway strike, representatives of three trade unions opted in 1913 to form the National Union of Railwaymen. Then, in 1914, a "Triple Alliance" was sealed with miners and dockworkers' unions, whose representatives promised to undertake reciprocal sympathy strikes—strikes that would take shape, up to a point, in the wake of WWI.

In colonial India, the reform of railway retirement benefits in 1911 was framed by its architects as a suitably less liberal counterpart to Lloyd George's conciliation boards and to other social liberal reforms in Britain. But the 1911 reform of railway retirement benefits actually prolonged and intensified strikes on the Indian railways, as those withholding labor typically insisted that, before returning to work, they be assured of retaining their retirement bonus. The retirement bonus, or gratuity, amounted to half a month's wages for each year of employment. For employees entitled to provident fund payouts, the gratuity supplemented payouts. But unlike provident fund benefits, which were accessible only to permanent employees who earned more than 15 rupees per month, the service bonus, from the time of the 1911 reform, was accessible to *all* railway workers, including "menials." The gratuity thus was a more universal benefit than were other retirement benefits; but this universal benefit was also uniquely made into a blunt instrument of labor discipline, as, under the terms of the 1911 reform, striking could render a worker ineligible for the service bonus. Many railway families used their service bonuses to help build or purchase a home, which goes some way toward explaining how this seemingly small benefit could become a central flashpoint of labor-management conflict through 1922: To be denied the service bonus was to see one's hopes for a family home melt into air. The Indian railways witnessed a large-scale, syndicalist strike in 1913, as well as a strike wave—linked to the Non-Cooperation and Khilifat movements—that extended from 1919 through 1922. In 1922, rail managers and railway department officials rescinded the no-strikes stipulation of their retirement gratuity policy. The highest levels of the colonial state were involved in making this change. In June of 1922, the viceroy wrote to "impress on" the secretary of state of India "the urgent necessity for a very early decision in this contentious matter. . . . We have been warned twice during the last week by Agent, East Indian Railway, that if we do not settle this matter of gratuity very soon, there is likelihood of another strike on railway."[24]

Six months after the policy had been scrapped, in February of 1923, Labour Member of Parliament (MP) Thomas Griffiths asked the undersecretary of state for India whether he was aware that a group of railway widows in India were being denied their late husbands' service bonuses. The women's husbands had died before the reform went into effect, and these widows had not received their spouses' accrued gratuity payments. The unjust situation faced by railway widows in the summer of 1922 casts into relief key themes of *Respectability on the Line*, which considers how housing, retirement, and other social benefits served as mechanisms through which railway managers ordered workforces from the mid-nineteenth century, and then shows how these benefits became central sites of contestation in railway labor-management relations down through the Great War. The book breaks new ground both in highlighting how the 1911 reform of retirement benefits in colonial India was designed to further an empire-wide shift toward social liberalism and in demonstrating how this reform ironically helped intensify mass strikes into the early 1920s. By telling this story alongside a parallel account of how social liberalism affected railway communities in the metropole, the book provides a way to follow the contours of colonial difference across this volatile period. Social liberalism was notably bifurcated into distinct colonial and metropolitan modes, and this bifurcation impacted how railway labor politics unfolded in Britain and colonial India, respectively. *Respectability on the Line* thus allows for a historically rich reengagement with a problematic that goes back at least as far as W. E. B. Du Bois's "The African Roots of War," an essay that grappled with the question of how nascent social welfare arrangements helped reconstruct colonial capitalist relations in an era wracked by industrial unrest.[25] Du Bois was concerned with how these processes played out in the era of high imperialism—roughly from the 1880s to the Great War. This is the period that forms the focus of the second half of *Respectability on the Line*. But the above formulation—which speaks of nascent social welfare arrangements helping to reconstruct colonial capitalist relations—resonates as well with the transformations of the 1840s through 1860s, when self-consciously paternalistic managers of industrial firms in Britain and colonial India sought to stabilize social relations by drawing at least some of their workers into company towns and provident institutions. This mid-nineteenth-century conjuncture—during which time a new, internally variegated mode of regulation took shape across the British imperial world—forms the focus of the first section of the book, to which we now turn.

PART ONE

Railway Paternalism and the Making of Sexual Cultures of Labor, 1840s–1860s

CHAPTER I

Imperfect Technologies of Moralization

Railway Paternalism in Mid-Nineteenth-Century Britain

We can begin our journey in mid-century Britain. By 1851, railway investment had already passed through two phases of boom and bust. Lines were stitching together a national economy. And the railways employed upwards of sixty-thousand men, many of whom labored under notably unsafe conditions.[1] The reorganization of railway workforces in the 1840s had helped slot these men into clearly defined work roles and had outlined their paths of promotion through the ranks. From 1842 or so, railway company towns had begun to grow up around burgeoning locomotive construction and repair workshops. The everyday life of workers and their family members in such company towns will occupy much of our attention in what follows. But these everyday experiences were shaped by wider social, cultural, and political trends. At the mid-century, workers and their family members, especially those coping with the aftermath of accidental injuries, faced an increasingly ungenerous dispensation across these levels of historical experience. This relatively ungenerous dispensation shaped—sometimes in surprising ways—the domestic lives of those residing within and beyond railway company towns. Let's begin our study of everyday life in early railway districts with a consideration of the aftermath of two mid-century railway accidents—one real and the other fictional.

On 19 April 1853, George Hawkins wrote a circular to his subordinates in response to a certain "melancholy catastrophe."[2] Since becoming traffic manager for the London, Brighton, and South Coast Railway

(LB&SCR) in 1850, Hawkins had issued forty-five such circulars. Some announced revised fares or timetables. Others enumerated a "blacklist" of recently disciplined employees. In these communications, Hawkins typically adopted a matter-of-fact tone. But Circular 46 opened with a bit more pathos: "Sir, I have to call your very serious attention to the fatal accident which befell poor Barnden on the 13th last." Henry Barnden's accident, while atypical in one respect, reveals one of the vulnerabilities faced by passenger guards, including that they sometimes were required to traverse "running boards" on the outsides of moving carriages. The accident report prepared by the Board of Trade (BOT) noted that Henry Barnden had gotten "out upon the step and handed a newspaper to the guard on the carriage in front of him, but as he turned round to get back to the door of the break, he was struck by a piece of timber scaffolding which projected beyond the masonry abutment of a bridge."[3] The BOT inspector took Barnden's accident as an occasion to press LB&SCR managers to expand their railway's "kinematic envelope" (i.e., the space through which trains could safely pass), while George Hawkins took the catastrophe as an opportune time to prohibit Barnden's mates from reading on the job: "The melancholy catastrophe is clearly traceable to the bad practice of reading on the road, which I fear has become a habit with some of you.... Your duties are too important to be trifled with and every energy and attention should be devoted to the due performance of them for your own safety and the traffic generally. I trust the practice of reading on your journeys will be totally discontinued as I must give you notice that any one found disobeying this order will be immediately disciplined."[4] Hawkins's circular highlighted the centrality of attention to the proper performance of railway labor. Railwaymen were to exercise, in the words of one mid-century manual, a "constant watchfulness while on duty."[5] The practice of reading on the rails surely was incompatible with such perceptual discipline—or at least this was the claim to which Hawkins's circular drew its readers' "very serious attention."

On 18 June 1853, approximately two months after Barnden's accident, the first complete edition of Elizabeth Gaskell's *Cranford* was published. The novel's second chapter, which originally had appeared in a December 1851 edition of *Household Words*, depicted a stationmaster being killed by a train following his ill-advised decision to read on the platform. Captain Brown, who recently had been transferred to the fictional Cranford station, was immersed in the latest installment of Dickens's *Pickwick Papers* when a locomotive whistle blew. Looking up, he saw a girl wandering across the tracks. The stationmaster leapt up and pushed the child to safety before being cut down by the onrushing train. *Cranford*'s second chapter concerned itself with the immediate aftermath of Captain Brown's accidental death, showing how Cranford's residents responded in starkly different ways to the melancholy catastrophe that had befallen their town. While some gathered in the street, "listening with faces aghast" to the tale of Captain Brown's death, Miss Jessie, the stationmaster's eldest daughter, effectively wiped from her face any evidence of grief. "Shivering with feelings to which she dared not give way," Jessie asserted that her sister "cannot live many days, and she shall be spared the shock." The care that Jessie showed her terminally ill sister and the labors of discretion she undertook in the wake of her father's death marked her out as an exemplary moral individual. By foregrounding this remarkable character, Gaskell's *Cranford* effectively reframed a workplace accident as an occasion for the display of domestic virtues. Miss Jessie's self-denying acts of sisterly care even retroactively recast her father's actions: For as much as the Captain acted irresponsibly by reading at the station, his leap to rescue a child in danger could appear—within the frame outlined by his daughter—as a dramatic act of paternal sacrifice.

Gaskell's recasting of the railway accident as an occasion for the display of domestic virtues was of a piece with a host of institutional and legal transformations at mid-century, which together drastically remade the life chances of railway widows and other indirect victims of workplace accidents. Mid-century legal and institutional changes combined to render working class families more directly responsible for weathering the economic fallout of accidental injuries and for maintaining a respectable domestic standing in the wake of railway catastrophes. Parliamentary reforms and subsequent judicial interpretations had established by 1851 that neither injured employees nor their surviving family members were entitled to compensation from railway firms—an entitlement that, with the help of radical coroners, some railway widows had been able to realize from the late-1830s through the mid-1840s.[6] This mid-century legal dispossession dovetailed with a sharp curtailment of the insurance payouts available to rail families. In November 1850, the *Railway Passengers' Assurance Company* (which, despite its name, sold policies to higher-grade railway employees) replaced plans that had paid five hundred pounds in the event of fatal injury with plans that paid to a railwayman's designated heir "a fixed total ... benefit of 20 [shillings] per week (maximum £30)."[7] In addition to such institutional retrenchment, a relatively widespread informal arrangement of support for railway families was largely discontinued around the time of the Great Exhibition. During the 1840s, an injured porter or railway widow was not infrequently given permission, as a sort of sinecure, to set up a bookstall in their local railway station. But between 1848 and 1853, some of the largest railway firms in Britain granted W. S. Smith & Son monopoly rights to sell periodicals and books along their lines. In 1853, *The Times* celebrated the subsequent change in the quality of railway bookstalls, noting that: "The rubbish and the dirt have been swept away."[8]

While these legal and institutional changes rendered railway families more precarious, injured employees and their heirs were not left wholly to their own devices. During the late 1840s and early 1850s, railway executives set in place a number of new paternalistic institutions, some of which were designed to support injured railwaymen and their families. Directors established provident funds, savings banks, mechanics institutions, churches, and other moralizing social institutions, while superintendents administered rental units in company towns, often in ways that involved their continued engagement with rail widows as long-term tenants. Mid-century managers conditioned provident-fund payments and housing tenancies on their own or on approved bodies' judgments as to the moral virtues of grieving railway families—virtues modeled by Miss Jessie. The Great Northern Railway's provident society, established in October 1851, stipulated in its rulebook, "The widow of a member against whom it shall be established, to the satisfaction of the Committee, that she has been leading an immoral life . . . shall not be entitled to . . . any benefit from the society."[9] Such stipulations, along with census returns from company towns, suggest that for early railway widows there were essentially three avenues toward continued respectability—and sustained tenancies—in railway districts: 1) they could remarry another railwayman; 2) they could receive, from a provident fund, maintenance payments and a lump sum to secure a teenaged son's apprenticeship; or 3) they could remain single and operate a boarding house for unmarried railwaymen. Widows pursuing each of these three paths, or a combination thereof, appear in 1851 census returns for New Swindon, the Great Western Railway's workshop town. Susan Hendry lived on Oxford Street and was listed as a pauper, living with her seventeen-year-old son, an apprentice boiler smith. Matilda Johnson, aged thirty-nine, lived on Bristol Street with her twenty-nine-year-old fireman husband, her son from a previous marriage, and a nineteen-year-old lodger. And finally, Mary Dalton lived on Bath Street and was listed as a "lodging house keeper" for three workshop employees, whose ages ranged from twenty-two to thirty-eight.[10] Widow-bachelor households such as Mary Dalton's place were important fixtures of railway towns, and the presence of these households offered, for bachelor boarders, an enabling counterweight to the gravitational force of marriage—a counterweight bolstered as well by vibrant bachelors' subcultures, which were sustained within mechanics institutions and in other company-sponsored sites of rational recreation. The chapter to follow will track some of the cultural, political, and social transformations that combined to produce a moralizing form of railway paternalism at the mid-century and then will outline how this managerial form and its defining technologies enabled, perhaps counterintuitively, the emergence of variegated domestic arrangements and sexual cultures in early railway towns.

THE ORIGINS OF RAILWAY PATERNALISM IN BRITAIN

During the late 1830s and early 1840s, when Rebecca riots, Plug Plot strikes, and Chartist risings shook the north and west, railways served as strategic infrastructures of domestic counterinsurgency. Third class carriages were frequently converted into troop trains, carrying military units overland or metropolitan police forces down from the capital. In advance of the second wave of Plug Plot disturbances in 1842, Parliament passed a railway act that obliged companies and their employees to transport troops on the lines when presented with an order "signed by the proper authorities."[11] On 1 August, a mere two days after this act had received royal assent, the chairman of the Grand Junction assured his shareholders that the company's servants had already been doing their part, as "upwards of 7,000 troops had been conveyed on the line during the half-year, and principally within the space of one week."[12] When a second wave of strikes rippled out from Stalybridge two weeks later, the company again had occasion to transport troops. Writing during this second mobilization, Captain Edward Cleather, superintendent of the Grand Junction Railway, conveyed to his counterpart at the London and Birmingham Railway the news that troops had arrived safely in Manchester, where crowds nevertheless managed to pull down an electric telegraph line. Captain Cleather further outlined to Secretary Creed the measures he had taken to establish a police presence at strategic points: "By vigilance and at some expense no doubt, I hope we may succeed in keeping open the line of communication to Crewe."[13]

Since 1840, Crewe had served as a critical point of intersection between the Grand Junction, the Chester and Crewe, and the Manchester and Birmingham railways. During the volatile summer of 1842, troops passing through this strategic station would have looked out onto sprawling construction sites, as new workshops and cottages were going up in this emerging railway town.[14] The following spring, more than two hundred railway families were relocated from the company's cramped facilities in Edge Hill, Liverpool, to rows of freshly built homes in "the juvenile city of Crewe." To celebrate these families' first Christmas in Cheshire, the directors of the Grand Junction hosted a tea and ball in December 1843[15]—a social event that mirrored the paternalistic rituals textile managers were regularly hosting at the time.[16] The railway town of Crewe was constructed on roughly the same timetable as that of Swindon, whose first blocks of employee housing were also opened in the early months of 1843.[17] While such company towns, built around major workshops, formed the locus of paternalistic intervention along the lines, they were supplemented by smaller residential zones adjacent to sheds and terminal stations, and by an archipelago of residential quarters for individual gatekeepers, signalmen, and stationmasters.[18] Such was the dispersed geography of railway paternalism, a managerial form that took shape in the shadow of Chartist strike waves.

The turn to company paternalism in the early 1840s was not particular to the railways but rather occurred across various sectors of the British economy and was bolstered by contemporaneous political and cultural developments. As Richard Price has noted, this was a time when "an extensive literature was churned out, the central theme of which was the paternal reciprocities of duty between worker and employer." Such advice writing distinguished itself from earlier "Benthamite moralizing" insofar as it "[trumpeted] the qualities of responsibility and duty of the upper classes."[19] A touchstone for this mid-century literary canon was Arthur Helps's *The Claims of Labour* (1844), which encouraged managers to provide their workmen with homes "fit for human beings in a civilized country" and to undertake measures to counteract the "cheapening" of working-class people's lives.[20] Helps framed these practical suggestions with general reflections on the qualities of a good paternal manager, encouraging his readers above all to demonstrate sympathy and liberality toward subalterns:

> Another defect which prevents confidence, is a certain sterility of character, which does not allow of sympathy with other people's fancies and pursuits. A man of this character does not understand any likings but his own. He will be kind to you, if you will be happy in his way; but he has nothing but ridicule or coldness for any thing which does not suit him. This imperfection

of sympathy, which prevents an equal from becoming a friend, may easily make a superior into a despot. Indeed, I almost doubt whether the head of a family does not do more mischief if he is unsympathetic, than even if he were unjust. The triumph of domestic rule is for the master's presence not to be felt as a restraint.[21]

This passage, which pressed managers to broaden their sympathies, notably abstained from specifying the sorts of interests that they were to regard with liberality. To an extent, this was the point, as Helps was encouraging his readers to push the limits of their imaginations and to respond generously when surprised by a given subaltern's idiosyncratic likings. But it's hard not to feel that more is at play in this passage's obliqueness, and that perhaps we are brushing up against a certain open secret concerning sexual and gender nonconformity.[22] More on this open secret in a moment, but for now we can consider how and to what extent, over the volatile 1840s, railway executives put into practice Helps's two tangible pieces of advice—namely, to provide employee housing and to take measures against the "cheapening" of working-class life.

One of the first railway towns in Britain that featured employee housing grew up around the Wolverton locomotive works, which were conceived by the London and Birmingham Railway (LBR) in 1836. Five years later, when Isambard Brunel was considering building employee housing at Swindon, the railway town of Wolverton already contained 165 cottages. Brunel solicited information about the management of these cottages from Richard Creed, the aforementioned secretary of the LBR, who informed him that the cottages at Wolverton were rented at a rate of four pounds, nineteen shillings, eight pence per year. While Brunel hoped that the Great Western Railway (GWR) would charge comparable rents from their employees, the GWR directors decided in October 1842 to let their smallest, two-room cottages at nine pounds, two shillings per year in order fully to offset construction-related expenses. While these rates were reduced slightly during the economic slump of the late-1840s, Swindon's relatively high rents helped ensure that boarding arrangements would feature extensively in this railway town and that across the six blocks of cottages built between 1842 and 1847 overcrowding would be endemic.[23] In 1847, Archibald Sturrock, the works manager at Swindon, observed that there were 1,735 residents distributed across 241 homes (which translated to an average of 7.2 people per cottage, half of which contained only two rooms). Sturrock identified 143 of these residents as boarders or as extended family members, meaning that in many houses a railway family might have shared the downstairs room while a group of boarders lived upstairs.[24]

Edward Snell was one such boarder. For much of his peripatetic life, Snell maintained an illustrated diary. The portions of Snell's diaries from 1843 to 1849—during which time he advanced from draughtsman to deputy works manager at Swindon—convey valuable fragments of domestic life from this early railway town. "Rather queer lodgings mine," Snell wrote of his May 1843 accommodations: "At present the house only 1 story high, walls of rough brick inside, and most of the rooms occupied by a barefooted Scots woman and her family." Snell seems to have shared the remaining room of this unfinished cottage with another railwayman, Mister Drye. In one of Snell's pen-and-ink drawings, Drye sits cross-legged, smoking a pipe, while stirring a pot of porridge over the fireplace. Three large bowls rest on the table behind him, a visual detail implying that a third man likely also shared their room.[25] In an earlier, 1841 entry from his time in Bath, Snell depicted himself and a fellow boarder, Zenas Hall, in bed together. The accompanying diary entry had Hall telling Snell to "shut his head" and go to sleep.[26] Snell's domestic vignettes from the early 1840s, which recorded his experiences with fellow boarders, thus featured an interesting blend of roughness and regard, of anonymity and intimacy. That he lived in ten different cottages between 1843 and 1846 further suggests the fleetingness of these domestic bonds and more generally the instability of living arrangements, particularly for bachelors, in the first years of New Swindon's existence.

For as much as housing arrangements in Swindon would evolve over the second half of the nineteenth century, some of the early features of domestic life here would persist throughout the Victorian era. In the 1850s, the company undertook to ameliorate some of the unsanitary conditions around their cottages and to build larger units at the ends of already established blocks.[27] But with employment at the works ballooning during this period of economic expansion, demand for housing far outstripped the company's supply, a problem that was only partially addressed by a combination of speculative private development and cooperative housing ventures.[28] In addition to this chronic shortage of housing stock and consequent overcrowding, boarding relationships continued to feature centrally in the domestic life of New Swindon. In 1861, there were more than one hundred boarders living in Swindon's six blocks of company-run housing, while in 1881, more than seventy unmarried men lived within the same bounds.[29] The persistence of boarding arrangements seems to have been a function not merely of necessity but also, to some degree, of choice. In 1855, contractors finished building a barracks for single men—a construction project that originally had been undertaken by Brunel in 1847 but that was put on hold because of that year's economic slump. The barracks were managed by an inspector of railway police, who began in March 1855 to advertise single-occupancy rooms to railwaymen. He found few takers, and gave up on the endeavor after only a few months.[30] In 1865, the *Swindon Advertiser* gave an explanation for his failure, suggesting that the town's "unmarried men, albeit away from home, clung to the home element in their off-work life, insofar as they could realise it, and preferred living in lodgings with families, to herding together in a barrack."[31] We might qualify this conclusion by noting that, while the barracks would have drawn men together under one roof, it also would have isolated them into cramped rooms with single beds. Boarding arrangements, by contrast, typically involved the clustering of two or three men in relatively open rooms, which were outfitted with fireplaces and with communal furniture. The "home element" for these men thus was equally a matter of living with a proper railway family as it was of sharing a room with their fellow workers.

To understand the persistence of boarding arrangements in Victorian railway towns such as Swindon, we must attend as well to the historical experience of railway widows. Widows frequently managed boarding houses in company towns with the tacit approval of railway superintendents.[32] The cottage at 27 Oxford Street in Swindon was one such widow-run boarding house. According to 1861 census records, the house was inhabited by John and Susan Harding, along with their four children. But in 1881, Susan Harding was listed as the head of household and as lodging house keeper, cohabiting with four unmarried boarders. A few doors down, at 17 Oxford, a similar domestic trajectory seems to have played out over roughly the same time span. In 1861, John and Mary Mays lived with their son and a pair of boarders. Thirty years later, Mary Mays was listed as the head of household, cohabiting with her thirteen-year-old niece and three male boarders. These were not isolated cases. In the 1881 census returns for Swindon, at least twenty widows were listed as heads of household across the six blocks that formed the nucleus of this railway town.[33] From one perspective, such a surfeit of widow-run households would seem to indicate the generosity of the GWR's paternalistic managers, who evidently recognized a continuing obligation to these indirect victims of industry. But if we view widow-run boarding houses from a wider historical vantage, considering how the germ of this domestic form emerged out of the volatile 1830s and '40s, an alternative perspective opens up. From this altered vantage, the *dependency* of railway widows on the discretion of company managers appears at least as salient as the seeming generosity of these paternalistic authorities.

As we have seen, in his 1844 essay *The Claims of Labour*, Arthur Helps encouraged paternalistic managers to provide their employees with housing "fit for human beings in a civilized country" and to take measures to counteract the "cheapening" of working-class life. We have already seen how GWR managers attempted, with mixed results, to carry out the former injunction beginning in the 1840s. In turning now to the question of how and to what extent managers provided forms of support to railway workers and their heirs following accidental injuries, we are entering onto the terrain of Helps's second injunction. Helps's *The Claims of Labour* (1844) was written at the tail end of an anomalous era in the history of workers' compensation in Britain—an era during which railway widows came remarkably close to realizing a right to compensation from railway firms. Between 1838 and 1845, British railway firms compensated the widows of fatally injured railwaymen with growing frequency and on increasingly generous terms. They were effectively obliged to do so by coroners' juries, which not infrequently issued five-hundred-pound deodands against railway companies.[34] The *deodand* was a medieval legal doctrine that compelled the owner of an object involved in a fatal injury to pay compensation to the crown. Until 1838 or so, the doctrine had rarely been used to issue any but the most nominal fines, but in the wake of an 1838 boiler explosion on the steamship *Victoria*, a number of coroners began to encourage juries to issue more substantial deodands against railway and steamship companies. As Elizabeth Cawthon has shown, these deodands, when challenged, were voided by higher courts. The threat that they might be issued and upheld, however, combined with the publicity surrounding coroners' inquests, effectively compelled railway companies to compensate the heirs of fatally injured workers and passengers.[35] These payments steadily increased through 1845, at which point multi-hundred-pound payouts to railway widows were not atypical occurrences. This upward trajectory would be reversed with Parliament's 1846 abolition of the deodand and with the Government's subsequent establishment of a limited right to compensation for railway passengers and their heirs. By 1851, British courts had clarified that this right to compensation would be stratified on the basis of a passenger's income, and that it would not extend to the heirs of railway workers, even when such workers had been found not at fault for the accidents that had cut them down.[36]

The brief revival of the deodand between 1838 and 1845 relied upon, and gave institutional ballast to, the broader culture of radicalism that defined this era. Thomas Wakley, the coroner most associated with the renewal of the deodand, was himself a radical member of Parliament, representing Finsbury from 1835 to 1852, who spoke in favor of Chartism from the floor of the Commons. For radicals like Wakley, rail accidents illustrated the human cost of commercial greed.[37] Railway directors—and the associated "railway interest" in Parliament—were framed in radical discourse as exemplars of "Old Corruption." But even the most strident radicals typically held out the possibility that company executives might show themselves, despite everything, to be aligned with the interests of the people.[38] This two-sided treatment of railway directors appears in a radical 1838 tract, *The Ghost of John Bull: Or, The Devil's Railroad, a Marvellously Strange Narrative*.[39] The tract is dedicated "(without permission) to such members of parliament as may feel inclined to turn their coats, poor law commissioners, and railroad directors in particular."[40] In the "strange narrative" that follows, a representative railway executive—introduced as a "commercial aristocrat"—is put on trial along with other political and economic elites by a spectral incarnation of John Bull.[41] The elites meet on a railway carriage and then find themselves cast by an accident into a mythical valley, to which John Bull has retired in order to escape the rampant corruption of the nation's political institutions. Before turning his ire on a representative MP, pastor, Poor Law commissioner, and theater director, John Bull first excoriates the railway director for the unsafety of his passenger lines and for his company having exhumed an ancestral graveyard to lay sleepers.[42] But after learning from "Old Humanity" that the railway director "make[s] a practice of providing for those that are hurt or worn out in [his] service, which," he reminds the director "is rather an uncommon thing amongst you commercial men," Bull tempers his judgment.[43] Here, as in the wider culture of radicalism from which this tract emerged, accidents along the lines were treated as revelatory occasions—as moments that put on display the role of rail directors in the great melodramatic contest between the people and the forces of Old Corruption.[44] Faced with this charged cultural framework—a framework given institutional weight by coroners' juries—rail directors were effectively pressured to provide generous payouts to widows and to grant sinecures to injured railwaymen or their surviving family members. Railway executives' practice of granting to injured employees and to widows the right to set up bookstalls in local stations can be understood as an attempt to make publicly visible the extent to which they were providing for those "hurt or worn out" in their service. But with the abolition of the deodand in 1846, the collapse of Chartism after 1848, the elimination of five-hundred-pound insurance policies in 1850, and—as we will see in the following section—the rewriting of cultural frameworks for representing railway accidents, directors found themselves by the 1850s with greater room for maneuver in determining how and to what extent they should counteract the cheapening of working-class life.[45] No longer did managers feel compelled to offer substantial, publicly visible forms of support. Instead, over the 1850s, executives at various British railway companies established provident funds, savings banks, and other contributory schemes for their employees. These schemes, while conceived and partially funded by managers, ultimately made employees and their family members more directly responsible for mitigating the economic fallout of accidental injuries. This move toward the "responsibilization" of railway families dovetailed with contemporaneous literary and journalistic representations of railway accidents and of their working-class victims.

MID-CENTURY CONTRIBUTORY SCHEMES AND THE MORALIZATION OF RAILWAY WIDOWS

On 1 March 1853, George Hawkins, the aforementioned traffic manager of the London, Brighton, and South Coast Railway, sent Circulars 37 and 38 to two of his stationmasters, stating in Circular 38: "I enclose you a list of the men at your station who are not yet contributors to the Savings Bank." Hawkins's addressee was himself on the list of nonsubscribers, which prompted the following note: "May I be allowed to hope you will endeavour both by example and precept to extend the benefits of this excellent Institution; the Directors have done a great deal in establishing it and I trust you will shew them you appreciate their kindness."[46] Circulars 37 and 38 illustrate well how bureaucratic processes were utilized to impose contributory schemes on employees. Hawkins evidently had received from the Savings Bank a list of contributors. He then sent along portions of this list to his stationmasters—men responsible for supervising and conveying orders to ticket collectors and other entry-level employees. With his accompanying circulars, Hawkins implied that the appearance of subordinates' names on the list of contributors would help them to retain their positions and perhaps to advance through the ranks. As he indirectly pressured his small army of subordinates to set aside a portion of their wages, Hawkins deployed the same bureaucratic techniques he would have used to revise timetables or to communicate his blacklist.

Railway savings banks, such as the bank created by the LB&SCR Directors, were one species of contributory scheme established at the mid-century by railway managers. Provident funds were another such mid-century scheme. Like savings banks, provident funds were introduced to employees in the paternalistic language of kindness and care. Unlike savings banks though, provident funds involved the pooling of risk on the part of employee contributors and drew at least a portion of these contributors into the day-to-day work of managing the funds. In October 1851, Seymour Clark, general manager of the Great Northern Railway, wrote to his board of governors about the provident fund he was then in the process of establishing. Articulating the rationale for this contributory scheme—and for paternalistic technologies more generally—Clarke remarked, "The officials, etc. of a Railway ought to be regarded by those in authority as a large Parish, and [just] as all the kind considerate plans for their comfort induce . . . Parishioners to look up with affection to their Pastor, so would Railway officials, etc. look up and serve well, those who really took a sincere interest in their welfare. Kindness induces kindness, and kindly feeling would induce them to give more than eye-service."[47]

Seymour Clarke here implicitly registers the challenge managers faced in discerning whether their employees' visible expressions of deference reflected a deeply felt loyalty. While Clarke had only been hired by the GNR as general manager in 1850, he knew well the challenges of railway management, having previously served as traffic superintendent at Paddington Station, the London terminus of the Great Western Railway. In addition to Clarke, in 1850 the directors of the GNR also hired another GWR alumnus, the aforementioned Swindon works manager, Archibald Sturrock.[48] These two men would have been familiar with the operations of contributory funds from their time with the Great Western; in 1838 the Great Western Provident Society was established, and in 1843, a sick fund was established on behalf of those employed in the GWR's locomotive and carriage departments.[49] These early railway funds provided practical models for the dozens of such funds created by British railway companies from the late-1840s through the late-1860s.[50] As Simon Cordery has shown, most of these funds nominally were co-run by representatives of management and of labor, but in practice workers carried out day-to-day administrative responsibilities and made determinations about particular benefit claims.[51] This sort of governing arrangement characterized the GNR Provident Society, which formally began operating in 1852. The rulebook for this society—an early draft of which, marked up with Secretary J. R. Mowatt's edits, has been preserved—stipulated that the society's governing body was to be composed of "three trustees, a treasurer, and a Committee of not less than 9 and not more than 12 members, and a secretary, to be a paid officer. The trustees, treasurer, and one-third at least of the members of the committee, shall be chosen from among the honorary members."[52] "Honorary members" were defined as those who voluntarily had contributed to the fund but who did not enjoy the benefits of membership. The role of honorary member, and the governing structure of the society more generally, thus enabled managers and other patrons to hold veto power over the fund; at the same time, these same gentlemen were not compelled to attend regular meetings. Ordinary members serving on the governing committee, by contrast, could be fined up to five shillings for missing meetings.

The GNR's provident society was relatively ambitious for its time, aspiring to offer benefits for the following: sickness, temporary disablement, retirement due to injury, and funerals.[53] Allowances were also provided for the widows and children of fatally injured members, but Secretary Mowatt's interventions helped ensure that payouts to widows would not be overly generous, as his handwritten notes specified that weekly allowances of three shillings, six pence for widows and one shilling, six pence for their children were to be discontinued after five years.[54] The most generous clause to survive Mr. Mowatt's edits stated that the committee could, at its discretion, provide up to five pounds to help a widow's son obtain an apprenticeship.[55] The provident society's rulebook outlined a number of conditions for widows' weekly allowances, including that the woman in question not be earning more than seven shillings per week, that she not be receiving allowances from other funds, that she produce for the committee a marriage certificate, that she not be insane or otherwise incapacitated, that she not remarry, that she not reside outside the country, that she not engage in immorality, that her children be legitimate, that she produce the proper documentation of her children's births, and that she testify in writing of her children's continued residence at her home.[56] These stipulations were remarkably baroque, even when compared with the moralizing conditions also imposed on male beneficiaries (e.g., the stipulation that sick pay would be revoked in the event that "it be discovered that [a member] has frequented a public house, or indulged in spirituous or other intoxicating liquors, or that he has occupied his time in gambling"[57]).

The elaborate scrutinizing of widows implied in this rulebook casts the provident society as a medium for a particular kind of cross-class collaboration between men—a collaboration that would assume and reproduce these men's authority over and responsibility to surveil widowed members of railway communities. We can see evidence for this sort of scrutiny-laden, patronizing relation to railway widows in the archives of a contemporaneous employee-run fund, the Railway Guards Universal Friendly Society, which was established in 1848.[58] Peter Kingsford highlights a particularly revealing passage from an 1851 report of this society, which is worth quoting here in full:

> In conclusion, it may be stated, that the object in adopting this plan was, because it was felt to be in *proportion to the means of the members*, although not to the *extent* of their *wishes*. The sum granted weekly is admitted to be small, but it is hoped that the *certainty* of receiving a certain sum weekly will prove a stimulus to exertion on the part of the widow, to make up the deficiency of such sum as may be found necessary to support her self and family. On the contrary, the knowledge that *no support* would be rendered except by the *uncertain* hand of CHARITY would doubtless frequently cause the poor widow to despair of ever maintaining her position in the world, or of providing food for her children and being overpowered by the gloomy prospect before her, sink under her troubles, and leave her children living monuments of a system of *thoughtlessness* and *improvidence* too often indulged in by the working classes, but which evil, this Society (being a humble portion of a vast and well directed system of provident and frugal principles, happily rapidly extending) is intended to remedy in a large class of men, daily increasing in number and importance.[59]

The passage offers a window onto the historical outlook and moral sensibilities of those managing this and other mid-century provident funds. The society is framed here as a node in a larger web of institutions, which together are imagined to be capable of reforming the habits of working-class populations. Along these lines, the fund's paltry payments to widows are conceived not as replacements for a late husband's lost income, but rather as spurs to self-activity. While this passage reads as a defensive response to benefit recipients' assertions of the inadequacy of their payments and acknowledges that higher payments would better reflect members' wishes, it nevertheless ultimately seeks affirmatively to justify the fund's ungenerous schedule of payments. In doing so, the passage leans on an emergent cultural framework for representing railway widows and other indirect victims of industry—a framework that construed these individuals less as innocent victims entitled to generous compensation and more as domestic subjects responsible for bearing up and managing their own affairs in the wake of loss. Whereas in radical cultural works like *The Ghost of John Bull*, accidents were treated as events that revealed the social allegiances of railway directors, in this new cultural dispensation, accidents were framed as events that put on display the domestic virtues of individual working-class subjects.

In November 1851—the same month that saw the publication of *Cranford*'s first installment—*Post Magazine* carried a story on the intrigue surrounding what was probably the final five-hundred-pound payment awarded by the *Railway Passengers Assurance Company* to a late railwayman's spouse. The story begins by noting that "an engine driver on the Edinburgh & Glasgow Railway ... was crushed so severely that he died. He was insured for five hundred pounds and had made a will leaving everything to his wife to whom he had not long been married."[60] The brother of the deceased, who worked on the same engine, apparently saw himself as entitled to a portion of the payout; he threatened his brother's widow, saying that he would claim that his sibling had been drunk at work if she did not promise to share with him some of the claim. She refused, and he ultimately carried out his threat. The story concludes: "The evidence was contradictory, but the widow was given the benefit of any doubt which existed and the claim was paid.... The false accuser, overwhelmed with shame and, let us hope, remorse, left the country and when the money was paid a week or two ago, the widow was accompanied by a stalwart friend of her late husband who, it appeared probable, would console her in the most effectual way by taking his place."[61]

Post Magazine here rewrites the story of a contested insurance claim as a morality tale, pitting an unscrupulous, and ultimately chastened, brother against an upstanding widow. Her refusal to be intimidated by a lie that would have impugned her late husband's moral character appears to help legitimize her inheritance—as does her association with her late husband's "stalwart friend," who is presumed to be preparing a marriage proposal. While there might be a hint of irony in this final line—perhaps the five hundred pounds helped focus the mind of this stalwart friend—the widow's orientation toward remarriage would seem to confirm her domestic virtue. Implied throughout this story though is the notion that a prospective five-hundred-pound payout would tend to introduce an undesirable volatility into working-class-family networks.

Other periodical stories of the time indicated how easily working-class women could appear undeserving of support in the wake of accidental injury. Take, for example, this parodic column about railway compensation published in an October 1850 edition of *Punch*. The column plays upon the mid-century grading of railway life, joking that:

> The *Railway Accident Assurance Company* will undertake to pay as much as £2,000 for the loss of a life and will give a "proportionate compensation" for any other injury; but we do not see how the price of the life will enable us to get at the value of a leg, an arm, or any other portion of the body.... There is one thing, however, that it would be utterly impossible to estimate by any rule, mathematical, philosophical or otherwise—we allude to a woman's tongue, which if it should happen to be lost in a railway accident might be a calamity utterly irreparable to the owner but a real blessing to all her friends and neighbors.[62]

The misogynistic joke around which this column is built renders in graphic fashion the rhetorical implication of the above-discussed 1851 *Railway Guards Friendly Society* report: namely, that women affected by railway accidents should bear their losses silently if they hope to appear deserving of support. We can see the same implication in the somewhat later, "Mrs. Shuttle Worsted," a Lancashire dialect tale written by J. T. Staton, in which a working-class woman trips on a bottle and injures herself; she declares brashly that she will sue the owner of the bottle for negligence but ultimately is made liable herself for breaking the bottle of milk. Her act of speaking on her own behalf in the street renders her ineligible for compensation, and even, in a reversal of the logic of the deodand, liable for the instrument of her injury.[63] The implication of these vignettes is stark: Women affected by accidents should silently bear their losses, lest they appear ineligible for sympathy or monetary support. And yet, the concluding joke of the *Punch* column implicitly recognizes the ideological quality of this imperative: The loss of a woman's tongue would be "a calamity utterly irreparable to the owner."

We can return now to Gaskell's *Cranford* in light of these mid-century journalistic works, all of which helped establish the imperative that working-class women affected by railway accidents bear up silently and suffer privately following their losses. The novel can be read as reiterating this imperative in its depiction of Miss Jessie's response to her father's death. Jessie processes her grief in a remarkably self-contained way, away from those who immediately gathered in the streets to share their shock. And, as in the *Post Magazine* story discussed above, her self-disciplined response to loss is framed by a marriage plot. News of Major Gordon's unanticipated arrival and intention to propose shocks Jessie out of a rare reverie of grief into which she and the narrator had fallen.[64] Then, at the moment of her engagement to Major Gordon, Jessie essentially disappears from the novel's plot. *Cranford* does not conclude, however, with Jessie's engagement. Rather, its subsequent installments focus on the quotidian lives of a number of the town's widows and spinsters, who pool their resources to support Miss Matty after she has lost her savings in a railway stock market crash. In this way, the novel pushes past the marriage plot, encouraging in its readers greater curiosity about the various possible life trajectories and domestic arrangements that could emerge in the wake of rail-related catastrophes.

While the novel's later chapters generally revolve around the single women of Cranford, an absent bachelor also casts his shadow across these pages, the story of his early life appearing in chapter 6. In "Poor Peter," Matty recounts the events that led to her brother's abrupt departure from the family home. She characterizes Peter as having been "a very gentlemanly boy in many things. He was like dear Captain Brown in always being ready to help any old person or a child. Still he did like joking and making fun; and he seemed to think the old ladies in Cranford would believe anything."[65] Matty further observes that Peter was adept at Latin, "an ornamental language; but not very useful, I think."[66] The incident that resulted in Peter's departure began with him donning his sister Deborah's clothing and tucking a pillow under her dress in order to give the impression that she was pregnant. Appearing on the scene, where a crowd had gathered, Peter's father "seized hold of poor Peter, and tore his clothes off his back—bonnet, shawl, gown, and all—and threw the pillow among the people over the railings: and then he was very, very angry indeed; and before all the people he lifted up his cane, and flogged Peter! 'My dear! that boy's trick, on that sunny day, when all seemed going straight and well, broke my mother's heart, and changed my father for life."[67]

This scene of violence reorganizes the fortunes of the entire Jenkyns family. In its immediate aftermath, Peter joins a ship's crew, which ultimately takes him to colonial India. Their mother dies within the year. And their father, who would be nursed by Deborah into his old age, bears a melancholic disposition for the remainder of his life, "the flogging ... always in his mind, as we all knew."[68] Their father's lingering regret seems to have softened him: He "was so humble,—so very gentle now. He would, perhaps, speak in his old way—laying down the law, as it were—and then, in a minute or two, he would come around and put his hand on our shoulders, and ask us in a low voice if he had said anything to hurt us?"[69] While this change in disposition offered some minor comfort in the face of his earlier act of violence, Peter's return to

Cranford and reunification with Matty in the novel's closing moments offered a more comprehensive narrative resolution for this traumatic event. Upon his return, the prospect that Peter might marry one of Matty's friends was raised, but he graciously declined. Instead, he helped patch up a quarrel between two of the women in Matty's circle, Mrs. Jamieson and Mrs. Hoggins. In the novel's concluding scene, Peter entered a party with the two of them on his arms and "fairly got them in conversation together. Major and Mrs [Jessie] Gordon helped at the good work with their perfect ignorance of any existing coolness between any of the inhabitants of Cranford. Ever since that day there has been the old friendly sociability in Cranford society . . ."[70] Peter thus helped facilitate the reconciliation of the community, even as he skirted the marriage plot that conventionally would have accompanied such a comic conclusion.

Elizabeth Gaskell's affecting account of the rupture and partial reconciliation of the Jenkyns family can be read as a literary elaboration of Arthur Helps's more abstract reflections on the ideal paternal manager.[71] As we have seen, Helps enjoined paternalistic managers to extend their sympathy even toward their subalterns' fancies and pursuits that they found difficult to understand or accept. To withhold such sympathy, which would prevent "an equal from becoming a friend, may easily make a superior into a despot. Indeed, I almost doubt whether the head of a family does not do more mischief if he is unsympathetic, than even if he were unjust." Tragically, the patriarch of the Jenkyns family appears to have learned this lesson too late, having initially performed the role of the despot toward his child—a child who, in the end, was unable to be "happy in his [father's] way." If Helps's passage elliptically gestured toward a certain open secret regarding sexual and gender nonconformity, Gaskell's literary treatment of the Jenkyns family effectively drew this subtext closer to the surface.

Cranford's final installment, which is organized around Peter and Matty's reunification, gives pride of place to an alternative domestic relation—between an unmarried breadwinning man and an independent female homemaker—a relation that was relatively common in early railway towns. The novel invites its readers to view with sympathy the character arcs of Matty and Peter. But with what mixture of sympathy and scrutiny, of liberality and despotism, might early railway managers have related to widow-run boarding houses and the relations nurtured therein? And more generally, how were dynamics of power negotiated between paternalistic managers, their unmarried railwaymen, and the heads of household who let rooms to these bachelors? In what follows, we will attend to these rather elusive questions by working through archival materials from the Great Western Railway Company, particularly those associated with the Swindon Mechanics Institution—an establishment that was located, both spatially and conceptually, at the heart of the paternalistic undertaking that was New Swindon.

THE MECHANICS INSTITUTION AND THE MAKING OF SEXUAL CULTURES IN NEW SWINDON

Hiring documents from the early 1840s indicate that candidates for employment with the Great Western were asked to bring two "testimonials of character" to their in-person examinations, the first from a previous employer and the second from a "housekeeper of undoubted respectability."[72] This latter stipulation suggests that—just as political citizenship was routed through respectable homeownership at this time—a young man's eligibility for employment as a railway policeman, porter, or switchman was contingent upon the apparent respectability of his domestic situation. But as these young men "entered the service," or "went over the fence"[73] that divided railway labor from other rural employments, they were typically compelled to move away from the family home. Arriving in a railway town like Swindon or Crewe, entry-level railwaymen were often not in a position immediately to marry and thus to form their own households. This structural problem was managed, above all, through boarding arrangements, wherein unmarried railwaymen let rooms from respectable heads of household, whether married men, widowers, or widows. Even as rail widows were made the objects of moralizing scrutiny at the mid-century, then, some of them were also taking on an important role in paternalistic housing arrangements. Up through the 1880s, railway managers increasingly relied on such women to provide entry-level employees with respectable places to live. For an individual widow, failing to maintain a respectable façade could quickly result in the loss of a rental arrangement or the loss of benefit fund payouts. But the presence of railway widows as a group in railway towns seems to have grown steadily over the course of the Victorian era. While, in 1861, roughly 10 percent of boarders in GWR company housing lived with widowed heads of households, by 1881, 25 percent of unmarried men lived with widows.[74]

We can begin to grasp the relational dynamics between managers, widowed housekeepers, and unmarried railwaymen by reading these relations through the conceptual pairing of direct and indirect rule—a pairing that we more typically use in analyzing colonial forms of governance. Railway managers tended to govern the various groups in their "parish"—to pick up on Seymour Clarke's metaphor—through a combination of direct and indirect agency. With respect to railway widows, managers at once directly controlled these women's access to housing, while also delegating to provident-fund boards the ongoing responsibility to scrutinize and maintain records concerning the domestic lives of such widows. But railway widows themselves also served as agents of indirect rule vis-à-vis their boarders, given that their authority as housekeepers was granted by the superintendent who lived down the road and that they could raise a concern with this superintendent's assistant about a boarder or could stop renting to a dissolute or deadbeat tenant. In other areas of railway governance, we see a similar structure of delegation, overlapping surveillance, and indirect management—for example, signalmen were to report on unsafe drivers, and drivers on firemen, and vice-versa, and all of these men could potentially be written up by inspectors or policemen, who themselves were observed by each other, and—in theory at least—this elaborate apparatus of mutual surveillance reliably resulted in relevant information flowing back to managers or superintendents.[75] In practice though, this apparatus could equally result in patterned silences and habits of mutual protection from managerial penalty. George Hawkins implicitly registered an anxiety about the limits of his vision in Circular 200, dubiously insisting to each of his employees: "Your conduct is being closely watched [and] you should remember that there is generally some silent observer of your actions in the train, valuing your services for what they are worth."[76] He and Seymour Clarke alike apparently were unsettled by the prospect that, across their small armies of rail servants, a true audit might uncover eye-service—that is, superficial performances of deference—all the way down. Ultimately, the archives of early railway life and labor would seem to indicate a reality somewhere between the extremes of a fully realized panopticism and a fully stocked arsenal of the weak. George Hawkins's blacklist was regularly filled out with the names of fined employees, but equally we can find references in workers' life writings and in trade union publications to railwaymen evading work and covering for each other. We can also find evidence for the forms of enjoyment railwaymen took during their working days and in their off-hours, including in and around mechanics institutions.

On 3 October 1854, GWR managers finalized a contractual agreement with the New Swindon Improvement Company (NSIC). Like the provident societies discussed above, the NSIC was established as a member-run organization, albeit one over which company managers continued to retain authority.[77] The NSIC's founding contract specified that this member-run organization was to rent from the GWR for one thousand years "a piece of ground in High Street New Swindon," on which they were to build and maintain a mechanics institution.[78] From at least the mid-1840s, some of the social and educational functions that this institution would provide its members had been carried out in designated areas of the locomotive workshops.[79] In addition to providing more adequate space for these classes and lectures, the newly constructed institution was to serve various other purposes as well. The 1854 contract specified that it was to contain "Lecture and Reading Rooms and Eating Room," as well as "Hot and Cold Baths to be used by the members of the Mechanics Institution . . . and by all other persons in the employment of the [GWR] at all reasonable times at moderate charges."[80] This was to be a center for education, socialization, and the care of the body.

An early ground plan for the Mechanics Institution indicates that a housekeeper's room sat just to the left of the front porch;[81] down a central corridor were doors to the dining room, council room, rest room, book room, cloak room, room of eight baths, and coffee room. At the end of this hall sat a larger reading room and library (see figure 1), beyond which were market stalls, arranged in a circle around a central fountain.[82] The Mechanics Institution underwent a major renovation in 1864, when the large upstairs theater was reconstructed, and when the baths—steam from which apparently had begun to damage the walls—were removed.[83] As the contractor specified in relation to the latter job: "I propose and agree to remove all the rubbish now in the large room lately used for public baths, to build necessary walls to carry joists and floor with proper ventilation traps, and to carry away all impure air."[84] The public baths in question had already effectively been supplanted by new Turkish baths, located just around the corner from the Mechanics Institution.

In 1860, the directors of the GWR had authorized a group of employees to build Turkish baths in the backyard of the unused barracks. Such improvised baths were then expanded in 1864 by GWR's Medical Fund, before being relocated in 1868 to a new purpose-built structure west of High Street, which contained two hot rooms, a shampooing room, and a cooling room with nine changing cubicles. These Turkish baths were built adjacent to thirty-two new slipper baths, which were lined up on either side of a single corridor.[85] This bathhouse complex was open to railwaymen every evening except Wednesday, when it was reserved for the

FIGURE 1. A photograph of the Swindon Mechanics Institution Library. In the foreground is a shelf containing books on the fine arts, indicating something about the range of subjects available to rail workers. TNA, RAIL 276/22. Swindon Mechanics Institution Library, n.d.

women of the town. The slipper baths west of High Street appear alongside other pools of water in Alfred Williams's *Life in a Railway Factory*, a collection of memories first published in 1915:

> Now and then, during the meal-hour, a hardy workman will strip himself and bathe in the big bosh used for cooling the furnace tools. In the evening, after a hard sweating at the fires, many of the young men will pay a visit to the baths in the town. Little Jim and his mates, who have no copper to squander upon the luxury of a dip under cover, betake themselves to the clay-pits in a neighbouring brick-field. There they dive down among the fishes and forget about the punishment they have suffered to-day, and which is certainly awaiting them on the morrow.[86]

Here, the baths appear as a popular after-work destination—a place where railwaymen could temporarily forget the injuries and exertions of the working day. The nominal fee charged at the door offers them a modicum of discretion, manifested in the two towels issued to visitors and in the curtains that could be drawn across the thresholds of individual bathing and cooling rooms. The baths built in Swindon over the 1860s were some of the first examples of Turkish baths in Britain. For comparison, the famous Jermyn Street Hammam—overseen by the diplomat David Urquhart—opened its doors in 1862. Four years before the establishment of this West End bathhouse, the New Swindon Improvement Company had invited Urquhart to give a lecture at the Mechanics Institution on the health benefits of Turkish baths. Urquhart's infant son died shortly before his scheduled talk, so Stuart Rolland took up the task in his stead. Considering the timing, we can assume that Rolland's talk at the Mechanics Institution may have given impetus to the group of railwaymen who secured permission in 1860 to put up a bathhouse behind the unused barracks.[87]

In October 1869, Anthony Trollope published a short story in *Saint Paul's Magazine* entitled "The Turkish Bath." The story—which helped establish the cultural associations that such baths would carry in Britain—opens with an encounter between two men in the Jermyn Street Hammam. The narrator, an editor at a London-based periodical, initially is impressed by his interlocutor's graceful movements, his not-too-loud voice, and his educated discourse: "That such a man should take so much trouble to approach us,—one who could quote Horace and talk about the 'to kalon,'—was an acknowledgment of our power."[88] This initial conversation is unmistakably flirtatious: "'There is nothing,' said he, 'to my mind so absurd as that two men should be seated together for an hour without venturing to open their mouths because they do not know each other. And what matter does it make whether a man has his breeches on or is without them?'"[89] But the mood takes a turn when this interlocutor, Mr. Molloy, importunately presses the narrator to read a manuscript he's drafted. The narrator relents, which sets in motion a sequence of unpleasant meetings in his office, wherein the editor breaks bad news to the writer about his manuscripts, while the latter attempts to pull the former's heartstrings with stories about a chronically ill wife and hungry children at home. At this point in the story, the reader—like the narrator—believes that Mr. Molloy initially deceived his interlocutor by performing as a "well-informed, well-to-do man of the world."[90] His refined speech, graceful manner, and spare tobacco—and, above all, his having paid three shillings, six pence to enter the Turkish baths—appear to have led the narrator astray. But when, in the concluding scene, the narrator visits the Molloy family home in Hoxton, he realizes that the aspiring writer's tattered gloves and stories of woe were actually the more deceptive signs, Molloy's living quarters being rather respectable, his children healthy, and his wife an effective household manager and day nurse at Saint Patrick's Hospital. In addition to her income, the family evidently received an annual one-hundred-pound pension from the father's relatives in Ireland. These details of the Molloy domestic economy seem to distinguish this family from their neighbors. The street they live on in Hoxton is characterized by the narrator as "[having] been erected solely with the view of accommodating decent people with small incomes. We at once priced the houses in our mind at ten and sixpence a week, and believed them to be inhabited by pianoforte-tuners, coach-builders, firemen, and public-office messengers. There was no squalor about the place, but it was melancholy, light-coloured and depressive."[91]

Hoxton appears here as a place where skilled artisans, railwaymen, and uniformed service workers live with their wives and children in single-family homes. Through the narrator's eyes, the place seems respectable yet painfully dull. This is a neighborhood, we are invited to imagine, where neither of the two personae Molloy fabricated likely would have lived. A gentleman bachelor probably would have inhabited a livelier West End neighborhood, nearer to cultural institutions, literary interlocutors, and the baths where he made his initial appearance. A destitute father, on the other hand, might have lived with his family in an overcrowded tenement, perhaps a bit closer to the docklands. For a story that turns on the slipperiness of class-based markers of identity, then, "The Turkish Bath" seems in this moment to reiterate a rather crude cultural geography. But then, of course, there's the anomaly of the Molloy family. The family's respectable standing has nothing to do with the father's employment status; rather, Mr. Molloy takes care of the children during the day, and apparently "there aint a young woman in all London that'd be better at handling 'em."[92] The family enjoys the financial underpinnings of respectability—and thus fits in well enough in their neighborhood—because of a combination of Mr. Molloy's pension and the steady employment and domestic governance of Mrs. Molloy, who acts "with that mixture in her face of practical kindness and severity in details which we often see in strong-minded women who are forced to take upon themselves the management and government of those around them."[93]

Through his treatment of the Molloy family then, Trollope invites the reader to recognize—just as the narrator undergoes the same dawning realization—that relational conventions don't necessarily reign behind the facades of respectable, working-class flats. In this way, Trollope's story aligns with the aims of this chapter, which seeks to foreground the presence of variegated, norm-stretching domestic and sexual relations in early railway districts. Social historians can sometimes sound like Trollope's narrator as he turned onto that "melancholy, light-coloured and depressive" street in Hoxton. We have a habit of implicitly universalizing what might have been culturally dominant domestic forms and of concluding based on a partial view that railwaymen and their ilk forged a respectable yet not terribly flashy or sophisticated culture.[94] That is to say, we have an inclination to assume that railway towns and other decent, "clean and orderly" working-class districts like Trollope's Hoxton existed at some remove—culturally as much as geographically—both from Jermyn Street and from Whitechapel Road.[95] As we have begun to see though, the world of New Swindon scrambled the cultural map implied by the juxtaposition of these three place-names. New Swindon's "single-family homes" were, like East End tenements, chronically overcrowded. The town featured Turkish baths, a reading room, and a theater—cultural institutions that, save for their affordability, were roughly analogous to West End destinations. Well-read bachelors and self-governing women alike could be spotted purchasing food in the covered market by the Mechanics Institution; and these two types of Swindon residents not uncommonly shared the same flats (if not the same fireplaces). All of which is to say: scenes reminiscent of both the opening *and* closing vignettes of Trollope's "The Turkish Bath" daily occurred in New Swindon. A well-read bachelor—akin to Trollope's first-person narrator, albeit of a different class background—might have encountered a similarly cultured man in the baths off High Street before returning home to the flat that he rented from a "strong-minded" and self-governing woman like Mrs. Molloy. Between these two encounters, he might have stopped off at the Mechanics Institution to take in a lecture or to rehearse a theatrical show. It is to this theater (see figure 2), which stretched across the second floor of the Mechanics Institution, that we now turn.

The Swindon Amateur Dramatic Society, whose members animated this second-floor theater, was one of a number of worker-run committees associated with the Mechanics Institution.[96] The theater club's rules—an undated copy of which has been preserved—indicate that the Dramatic Society was run along the lines of the various member-run societies we have considered above, including the New Swindon Improvement Company and the GNR Provident Society. Swindon's Amateur Dramatic Society was made up each year of twenty individuals who had self-selected from the broader membership of the Mechanics Institution. Three of

Imperfect Technologies of Moralization | 45

FIGURE 2. A photograph of the Swindon Mechanics Institution Theatre. The theater was situated on the second floor of the Mechanics Institution. A range of performances were staged there, including performances put on by the Swindon Amateur Dramatic Society. TNA, RAIL 276/22. Swindon Mechanics Institution Theatre, n.d.

these ordinary members were then chosen to serve on the society's governing committee. The two other members of the governing committee were selected from among the standing council of the Dramatic Society; one man from this latter group also was to serve as stage manager, and in this role was to select the plays for each season and to make casting decisions. Members who failed to attend regular rehearsals, who smoked on the premises, or who neglected to return their scripts after a show could be fined by their stage manager from between three and six pence. A more serious offense was refusing to "play the character cast for him," which, unless adequately justified, could result in a five-shilling fine.[97] Thus disciplined, the two-dozen members of the Swindon Amateur Dramatic Society regularly staged their own shows, while also acting in shows alongside established, London-based performers and troupes. These evening entertainments shared a performance calendar with classical music concerts, choral medleys, and educational lectures. Playbills and seasonal performance listings from throughout the 1870s remain extant, while spottier records going back to 1859 have also been preserved.[98]

On Wednesday, 23 April 1873, an event billed as a "grand dramatic performance" was held at the Mechanics Institution in order to raise money for the New Swindon park. This night of entertainment concluded with a "new and gorgeous burlesque extravaganza, entitled: Prince Amabel, or The Fairy Roses."[99] The show—which helps bring into focus some aspects of New Swindon's variegated sexual culture—was saturated with orientalist tropes, being organized around an opposition between an Italian and a Turkish ruler: the former, King Buonocore, who professed liberal ideals, and the latter, King Turko, who fully embodied Western stereotypes of the Eastern despot. King Turko was, as one of the musical interludes ironically noted, a "fine old-fashioned tyrant of the school legitimate. Who scorns the namby pamby rule of kings effeminate."[100] The titular Prince Amabel, Buonocore's heir, was performed by Miss Marion Taylor, a London-based burlesque star. The show—like many others performed at the Mechanics Institution[101]—featured extensive drag performance, while the script played throughout on the erotic and linguistically humorous possibilities of this setup, puns and double entendres being ubiquitous.

In terms of the plot, the show is organized around the star-crossed romance of Amabel and Violet, one of King Turko's three daughters. At two points in the performance, the tyrant is notably absent from his court, first when he wages a military campaign and second when he smells one of the fairies' magic roses, which renders him invisible. The king imagines that, being invisible, he will better be able to surveil his subjects, not realizing that invisibility also will make him effectively abdicate the throne. During the king's first disappearance, his subjects take advantage of their newfound freedom:

> My father's absence is a treat no doubt;
> Since he's been gone the court's one scene of jollity,
> Regardless of age, sex, condition, quality—
> Grave duchesses with skipping ropes are seen;
> While noble lords play leap-frog in the green.[102]

Later, when an invisible King Turko is taken to have abdicated, his subjects express a desire to be ruled by the liberal Prince Amabel. There is thus an unmistakably political valence in the burlesque's polarization of forms of kingship and in its playfulness around the conventions of gender and sexuality. Liberal governance, framed in opposition to an orientalist stereotype, is yoked here conceptually to a sexual egalitarianism and to a permissiveness around gender and sexual nonconformity.[103]

While not written particularly for a railway audience, *Prince Amabel* does contain some interesting railway references and generally speaks in striking ways to the dynamics of governance in early rail districts. At one point, King Turko's temper is blamed for the bad feelings of his subjects: "Caused by his temper, of all joys the loss; / Like Northern trains, all starting from King's Cross."[104] This comment, which turns on a cheap pun, resonates unexpectedly with the logic of railway paternalism. As George Hawkins's circulars about the Savings Bank and Seymour Clarke's memo on the provident fund have shown, paternalistic managers imagined that the "kindness" shown by directors would cycle down the chain of authority to workers all along the line, who would, in turn, reflect back to their superiors the same kindly sentiments. While physically absent, railway directors hoped that their paternal authority would motivate and be reflected in their subalterns. But, as we saw with Hawkins's anxiety-laden invocation of the "silent observer of your actions in the train," railway managers evidently were troubled by the limits of their vision and by the variable quality of their indirect governance.

While *Prince Amabel* effectively satirized aspects of railway paternalism, another drag show performed at the Swindon Mechanics Institution humorously repackaged the domestic relation that has held pride-of-place in this chapter—namely, the relation between the bachelor boarder and the self-governing woman in whose home he lived. On Wednesday, 27 January 1875, George Rose performed at Swindon a number of his "Mrs. Brown" monologues, including *Mrs. Brown on her Travels*.[105] Rose, acting under the pseudonym of Arthur Sketchley, impersonated in these monologues a lower-middle-class woman, whose voice and mannerisms he modeled loosely on Dickens's famous Mrs. Gamp. The character of Mrs. Brown was verbose, digressive, and assertive in her views.[106] She thus exhibited a way of being that, from 1851 or so, had effectively been proscribed for railway widows. The sort of brash, aggrieved public speech that characterized her monologues would have made such widows appear, within dominant cultural frames, less deserving candidates for support from company managers and provident society boards. Rose's humor therefore likely hit the audience at Swindon on an extra level. Audience members might have seen in his Mrs. Brown an amalgam of the widowed boarding housekeepers and the unmarried lodgers who cohabited in company-run flats surrounding the

Mechanics Institution. Proscribed speech flowed from the mouth of this hybrid character in an amusing stream.

Whether or not Arthur Sketchley's jokes landed in January 1875, comedic performances like his monologues seem to have made a strong impression on at least some of the residents of New Swindon. In his *Life*, Alfred Williams characterizes a group of younger railwaymen who, after work, "run and play or wrestle and struggle with each other on their way down the yard"; "carry a small mirror in their pockets, by the aid of which they comb and part their hair and study their physiognomies"; and, after washing and changing, "come back to the crowded parts of the town to see and be seen and be moved on by the policeman, returning late home to bed. In the morning they will often be sullen and short-tempered. This invariably wears off as the day advances, however, and they will soon be up to the usual games, singing popular songs and imitating the comic actors at the theatre, where they delight to go once or twice a week."[107] While elliptical in certain respects, the literary "physiognomy" Williams provides of this group of young men establishes a vital linkage between the shows staged on the second floor of the Mechanics Institution and the everyday life of New Swindon, indicating that the styles of song and bodily performance—including gender-unsettling performance—that characterized the late-Victorian stage regularly were replicated in the squares and workshops of this railway town.

Here and elsewhere in William's *Life*, we are presented with an account of nascent subcultural differentiation in Swindon. Williams describes how shared work roles or preferred evening entertainments separated railwaymen into cliques. The archives of the *Swindon Advertiser* suggest as well that marriage status served as a basis of subcultural differentiation in this railway town. In August 1877, for example, the paper reported on a cricket match "played . . . between eleven married and eleven single coach makers," which "resulted in an easy victory for the bachelors."[108] The *Swindon Advertiser* periodically reported on "bachelors' balls," which typically were held in local, privately rented venues.[109] Some number of railwaymen thus kept a distance from married life, sharing rooms and leisure activities with similarly unmarried residents. But such subcultural differentiation could only proceed up to a point, as Swindon's paternalistic social institutions and shared workplace culture ensured substantial social intercourse across subcultural and sectoral lines. Swindon's places of association beyond the worksite—the bathhouse, the theater, the library, the town center, the park, and the company flat—all were eminently respectable sites, bound up culturally with the project of working-class improvement. We could thus say that certain residents within railway towns adapted the moralizing institutions established by paternalistic managers, utilizing them in ways contrary to their original purposes. But this would be to imply a cramped and naïve managerial outlook—a paternalism stubbornly committed to making all employees find happiness in identical ways.

Whether we put more emphasis on managerial liberality or working-class subversion in explaining the emergence of variegated sexual and domestic cultures—cultures with enduring counterweights to the gravitational force of marriage—we should not lose sight of how the everyday micropolitics of railway towns were conditioned as well by large-scale social and historical shifts. Railway towns emerged in the midst of a volatile mid-century conjuncture, which concluded when a broad-based current of radicalism was broken up by a combination of Peel's reforms and the Duke of Wellington's cavalry. The conservative settlement that followed was characterized across industrial districts by a form of company paternalism shorn of its more generous elements (e.g., the deodands and bookselling sinecures of the 1840s) but nevertheless still implicitly attuned to the threat of popular backlash (hence, for example, managers' tendency to offer discretionary long-term tenancies to rail widows). Widows, especially those without children, could most easily make rent by letting their upper rooms to groups of bachelors, thus serving as respectable homemakers for unmarried railwaymen. Had railway widows continued to receive generous compensation payments after 1846, they perhaps would not have been as likely to take on this social role in railway communities. The mid-century transformations that helped make widow-run boarding houses fixtures of railway towns thus can be viewed as historical preconditions for the variegated sexual and domestic cultures that seem to have taken shape there.

The widow-bachelor domestic form not only put down roots within early railway towns but also found resonances in Victorian-era print culture, including in Gaskell's *Cranford*, Trollope's "The Turkish Bath," and in various minor narratives published in the *Swindon Advertiser* and other railway papers.[110] Such fictional narratives were actively scanned by the residents of rail districts, either in the reading rooms of Mechanics Institutions, or—managerial proscriptions notwithstanding—during time reclaimed from the working day. Likewise, theatrical performances such as *Prince Amabel, Mrs. Brown on Her Travels,* and *How Five Bachelors Kept House* were avidly consumed by audiences at Mechanics Institution theaters.[111] Literary, journalistic, and theatrical works thus did not simply run parallel to the emergent social worlds of railway labor; rather—as Alfred Williams indicates—these narrative materials helped facilitate self-making practices and processes of subcultural differentiation in early railway communities. Fictional writings and stage performances helped craft the sexual cultures that grew up in and around early railway towns. And insofar as we grasp some of the outlines of these sexual cultures, we are compelled to understand in new ways Victorian-era company paternalism and the respectable working-class communities that were composed in the shadow of this managerial form.

CHAPTER 2

Strains of Permissiveness, Fields of Force

Railway Paternalism in Colonial India after 1857

We will transition now to a discussion of railway labor in colonial India. Major railway lines in colonial India were built over the second half of the nineteenth century, and a burst of railway construction followed the uprising of 1857–8. Most workers involved in the building of railways were employed under subcontracting arrangements, just as, after lines had been built, many workers employed in locomotive workshops continued to be employed under subcontracting arrangements. Subcontracted Indian railway workers labored alongside formally employed white British and multiracial Anglo-Indian employees—groups permitted to live within segregated railway colonies. In what follows, we will consider the everyday lives of railway workers who lived in such segregated colonies. But we will begin with one such worker's experiences far away from his home in colonial India.

On 8 December 1906, Bertha Haynes (née Holder) sat down to write a letter to the secretary of state of India. Haynes, a carpenter's daughter living in the outskirts of London, asked her Whitehall interlocutor: "forgive me for taking the liberty I am taking in writing you."[1] Her letter concerned a man "who is at the present time working as an Engine Driver on the East Indian Railway," a certain W. J. Haynes. Evidently, the man had been on furlough in England the previous year, during which time he and Bertha had been married and had conceived a child. She was writing in search of "any information as to how [she could] obtain from this man . . . 'support' for [herself] and child."

Lest the secretary of state for India be inclined to doubt her claims of marriage and legitimate parentage, Bertha made sure to document her claims. She enclosed two letters addressed to her by the locomotive superintendent of the East Indian Railway (EIR). In the first, written 5 April 1906, T. R. Browne of the EIR reported on an interview he had with the driver in question: he "admits the paternity of the child about to be born" but "denies being legally married to you." The superintendent went on to inform Bertha that, while "Driver Haynes is a married man ... living in this country with his wife and children," he nevertheless claims to have "remitted to your address last month £8 and has undertaken to send you further remittances." Bertha responded by sending along to the locomotive superintendent's office in Jamalpur a certified copy of her and William James's entry in the register of marriages.[2] The superintendent, in his subsequent reply, suggested she pursue her claim for support "in the Courts at home," enclosing in return the document confirming their marriage. With the evidence contained in these two otherwise disappointing letters, Bertha established for the secretary of state for India that she and William James had indeed been legally married, that her husband had admitted paternity of the child, and that the child "about to be born" in April 1906 had without question been conceived after the couple's May 1905 marriage. Putting a fine point on their child's legitimacy, she noted: "W. J. Haynes married me—the writer—at St Johns Church Deptford on May 26th 1905, but since his return to India has left me & his child of *the* marriage 'destitute.'"

The "the" in the above sentence is one of two underlined words in Bertha's letter. The other appears in the initial description she offers for her distant husband: "I am writing you with reference to ... W. J. Haynes, who is a man of *colour* who came to this country on furlough." From graphological evidence, it seems that Bertha had to pause and think about how exactly to evoke her husband's race here, as the "a" in "a man of colour" is virtually unreadable under a pool of ink. Her seemingly definitive act of underlining perhaps belied a lingering uncertainty. But to what end did Bertha racialize William James in the eyes of Sir C. J. Lyall, the accomplished orientalist then serving as secretary of state for India? Did she mean in doing so to increase her leverage over her husband? To call forth pity for her multiracial child's potentially limited horizons in Britain? To frighten her addressee with the possibility of scandal? Or to forge, against the contrast of her husband's racialized body, a shared medium of whiteness with the Oxford-educated secretary of state? Whatever the case may be, her appeal failed. On 14 December 1906, Sir C. J. Lyall composed a reply to Bertha Haynes, informing her not only that "the matter to which you refer . . . is properly one for a Court of Law" but also that W. J. Haynes is "a servant of the East Indian Railway Company, and not of the Government of India." With this dubious distinction between company and government,[3] our Whitehall official attempted to close the book on the rather awkward matter raised by Mrs. Bertha Haynes.

Speaking pragmatically, Bertha Haynes's appeal must be judged a failure. She doesn't seem to have gotten her money. But for students of gender and the colonial archive, her endeavor's success in making its mark is surely equally salient. Bertha Haynes effectively set the gears of colonial officialdom in motion. Our superintendent was moved both to inquire into his multiracial Anglo-Indian driver's family life and to draft two replies to his correspondent from the home counties. Then, months later, our secretary of state opted to write an additional letter to Mrs. Haynes. In so doing, he added an enduring file to the copious records of the Public and Judicial Department. File 4145 offers a window onto two consequential years of Bertha and William James's lives, as seen through the eyes of the former. The file also allows for an imaginative remapping of historical materials and themes. That is to say, the remarkable record of Bertha Haynes's correspondence with colonial officialdom at the dawn of the twentieth century invites us to consider how intimate relations were forged along the infrastructures binding Britain and colonial India and to ask how translocal histories of domesticity, labor, and sexuality might recast our understanding of colonial railway governance up through the Great War.

To get at the multiple, overlapping historical contexts of Bertha Haynes's correspondence, we can begin by considering the two legal terms she places in single quotes. Haynes frames her letter to C. J. Lyall as a search for "support" from her distant husband, who has left her and the child "destitute." These technical terms draw us into the story of family-law reform in Victorian Britain—a story that forms a central thread in histories of modern liberalism, suffrage, and mass democracy. While the Elizabethan Poor Law tradition—refurbished in the New Poor Law of 1834—imposed family support obligations as a way to limit state payments, subsequent Victorian family law, under pressure from the Langham Place circle and others, established for women conditional rights to divorce, to retain custody of children, and to receive support from estranged husbands.[4] Bertha Haynes, writing on the eve of the first mass march for suffrage in Britain, not only showed a familiarity with this legal context, but also confidently asserted her rights under family law.

Strikingly though, she addressed herself not to a justice, but to a railway supervisor and to the secretary of state for India. While both men attempted to redirect Haynes to the domestic courts, their actions suggested they weren't entirely sure her appeals were misdirected. Their evident uncertainty, combined with Bertha's belief that she might make headway with her husband's employers, poses again for us questions of company paternalism, while also bringing into view some of the specific ways sexuality and domestic relations were governed in colonial contexts.

Feminist historians of labor and empire have shown how Victorian-era employers and colonial officials variously intervened in the intimate lives of their subordinates. Such interventions often took a paternalistic form, wherein managers sought to cultivate respectable family relations, in part by embedding select subalterns in company towns or segregated residential zones.[5] The railway colonies of the EIR were exemplary sites of this sort of managerial paternalism, serving as incubators for rational forms of recreation and respectable domestic relations. Distinctive structural conditions, however, shaped railway paternalism in colonial India, distinguishing this governing mode from its metropolitan counterpart. For one, railway districts often abutted military cantonments, meaning that the governance of upper subordinates on the railways often overlapped with the governance of soldiers. This was particularly consequential in the realm of sexuality, given that military officials maintained a sanctioned market for heteroerotic sex in and around cantonments.[6] Racially privileged railway workers were among those men who were permitted to engage in commercialized sex with registered sex workers. The city of Allahabad, where W. J. Haynes lived in 1906, contained three military cantonments, one of which sat alongside the local railway colony. Perhaps Superintendent Browne's interview with W. J. Haynes took place in the shadow of this military zone, where a market for heteroerotic sex had been maintained since at least the 1860s.[7] While scholars of sexuality in colonial contexts have interpreted the regulationist regime governing female sex workers as having been motivated by a fear of male homosexuality,[8] the history of sexual and domestic relations in railway districts puts some pressure on this view, as intimacies between men in railway colonies were relatively ubiquitous and were underwritten by company housing and recruitment policies. Another of the distinctive conditions that shaped railway paternalism in colonial India was the fact that higher-grade, racially privileged workers were recruited from the metropole. That many workers were recruited as single men from the metropole made it more difficult for managers to cultivate domestic married relationships and ultimately helped bring about a situation wherein domestic cohabitation between men within official bungalows was permitted by railway managers. As we have seen in chapter 1, bachelors often shared living space in company housing in the metropole, but they did so as boarders, not as heads of household. In colonial India, men were permitted to cohabit as heads of household, and there is some evidence that these domestic arrangements underwrote the formation of familial bonds among men. My inclination is to read such arrangements and bonds as evidence for the plasticity of domestic norms in colonial railway districts, rather than as evidence for the open flouting of such norms in the colonial context. In this vein, we can return to the exchange between Superintendent Brown and W. J. Haynes. That our superintendent felt obliged to respond substantively to Bertha's inquiry and that our driver was made to account for his familial and intimate life to his supervisor show how the maintenance of a semblance of domestic respectability was an obligation both for those managing and for those laboring along the railways of colonial India. Neither could insist upon a line of demarcation between domestic and workplace matters; nor could they explicitly cast aside domestic ideals. And yet, these two men's responses imply a flexible, if not cynical, approach to such ideals. Both initially seem confident in asserting the acceptability of a situation in which W. J. Haynes makes minimal arrangements to support a child born in London. Both also opt to bury information about William James and Bertha's marriage, lest this awkward detail unsettle the former's married life in Allahabad. On one level, these men were forging a patriarchal bond familiar from various times and places, together reiterating a fundamental disregard for the claims of women. But they were doing so in a particular historical and institutional context—a context that compelled them to speak the language of domestic responsibility during a labor-management meeting and that made our superintendent and secretary of state account for their actions to Bertha Haynes. In the chapter to follow, we will reconstruct aspects of this historical and institutional context by considering the various dynamics that gave shape to early railway paternalism in colonial India and by showing how some of those governed by this regime made lives together over the second half of the nineteenth century.

THE RAILWAY COLONY AS HETEROTOPIA

To ground an account of governance along colonial Indian railway networks, there are few better places to begin than in Jamalpur, where

T. R. Browne served as superintendent of the East Indian Railway's locomotive department. In 1862, D. W. Campbell, an agent of the EIR, decided to relocate the firm's locomotive workshops and offices from Howrah, a suburb of Calcutta, to Jamalpur, a small conurbation in eastern Bihar. As one of Browne's predecessors tells the story, Campbell decided to remove the department from the metropolis after: "He found three of his principal workshop foremen and two engine drivers enjoying themselves [at Wilson's Coffee Room] in a rather boisterous manner. They asked him to join them in having a peg. What he said in reply has never been recorded, but the men very quickly retired, and after that Mr. Campbell never rested until he had the workshops and Locomotive Offices removed from Howrah to Jamalpur."[9]

This origin story of the Jamalpur workshops suggests that a manager's desire to moralize his workforce drove the move away from Howrah. Another explanation from the same 1906 history of the EIR holds that "Jamalpur was adjacent to Monghyr, which had been known for years as the 'Birmingham of the East,' and it was conceived that a plentiful supply of skilled mechanics could always be drawn from that place."[10] By the turn of the twentieth century, the Jamalpur workshops were indeed drawing in massive numbers of mechanics: 3,122 men were employed in 1881, while 9,428 worked under T. R. Browne's supervision in 1906.[11] While higher-grade fitters and foremen were directly supervised by Browne, the bulk of workshop employees were supervised in an indirect way by Browne's "sergeants" in the plant. In addition to higher-grade workshop employees and clerks, our Supervisor also directly managed firemen, shunters, and drivers—men who were involved in moving locomotives from Howrah to Delhi.[12] Such traveling employees of the EIR were not especially concentrated in Jamalpur and were just as likely to reside near other major stations on the line, including in Allahabad and Howrah.[13] W. H. Haynes, for example, lived in Asansol in 1902 and in Allahabad from 1904 to 1908.[14] As the trajectories of Haynes and other EIR enginemen imply, Campbell's attempts to separate his subordinates from the temptations of urban life and to build in Jamalpur a self-contained, respectable railway colony could only partially be realized: the labor force demands of the company ensured that a certain porousness continued to characterize the railway communities of the EIR.[15]

Even so, the Jamalpur colony significantly structured the lives of its residents, who numbered in the hundreds, while also forming a model for segregated railway districts near other stations on the line. The colony was laid out as a linear grid along the eastern side of the tracks and was ringed on its other three sides by mountains. With its clear bounds, the railway zone effectively spatialized the racial divisions of labor characteristic of the EIR, isolating higher grade British and Anglo-Indian employees from their Bengali and Bihari coworkers, most of whom lived west of the tracks or in neighboring districts.[16] Housing was distributed in the colony on the basis of work role: foremen, fitters, and other skilled employees lived in bungalows, either with a coworker or with a spouse, while apprentices lived together in barracks.[17] In addition to housing, drainage, security, and grounds keeping, EIR managers maintained a number of segregated social institutions in the colony, including, by the turn of the century, a mechanics institute, a school, an infirmary, two churches, a swimming pool, a library, a shooting range, and sporting grounds. Jamalpur hosted the EIR Volunteer Rifles and its associated band, run by British and Anglo-Indian railwaymen, which regularly held drills and military parades on the fields east of the tracks.[18] The railway colony was thus something of a heterotopia: a fabricated society in miniature, notable for how it jumbled together institutions and practices that, in the wider world, typically would be kept apart.[19]

In 1888, Rudyard Kipling visited the Jamalpur colony as part of a journalistic tour of eastern India. His oft-cited portrait of the place exemplifies how this planned community was seen, at least by British observers with a credulous eye. Kipling characterized Jamalpur as the "Crewe of Eastern India," comparing the railway colony in Bihar to the leading company town of the London and North Western Railway in Cheshire. He was dazzled by the neat appearance of the Jamalpur colony: "It is laid out with military precision; to each house its just share of garden, its red-brick path, its growth of trees, and its neat wicket gate. Its general aspect, in spite of the Dutch formality, is that of an English village, such a thing as enterprising stage-managers put on the theatres at home.... From St. Mary's Church to the railway station ... everything has the air of having been cleaned up at ten that very morning and put under a glass case."[20]

The polished quality of the Jamalpur colony brings to mind for Kipling a theatrical stage-set or a museum display. But the colony was not, for that, lacking in life. Kipling portrays Jamalpur "alive with the tramping of tiffin-seeking feet," describes the din of the massive workshops, and stages a dramatic afternoon scene at the mechanics institute, wherein "the greater part of the flirtation of Jamalpur is carried out: here the dashing apprentice—the apprentices are the liveliest of all—learns that there are problems harder than any he studies at the night school, and that the heart of a maiden is more inscrutable than the mechanism of a locomotive."[21] In this passage, Kipling slips into the genre of theatrical précis, rendering life in the railway colony as an industrial romance. We are invited to imagine a play in which a youthful apprentice is put through his paces at work and in love before finding his way to one of those aforementioned cookie-cutter houses, with its just share of garden and neat wicket gate. For Kipling, the railway colony is evidently a place where successful coming of age journeys can be carried off. And in particular, it is a place where Anglo-Indian apprentices—many of whom would have lived in orphanages before having been adopted by the company—could grow into adulthood, ideally finding skilled employment, intimate companionship, and respectable domesticity as they go. In this way, the Jamalpur colony appears at once to be a place of moral remediation for a suspect population, and a place, set apart from the world at large, where successful transitions to adulthood could occur.[22] For Kipling's railway apprentices, the coming-of-age process occurred in a context bounded by institutions and techniques of moral reform—disciplinary apparatuses that could, at least in theory, give their early adulthoods proper shape and direction.

In the railway colony, the twinned processes of moral reform and coming of age were understood to be bound up with a prefabricated career trajectory. A young man's promotion from apprentice to fitter, or to some other skilled position on the railways, closely corresponded with his move from barracks to single-family home—a move that, for many, seems to have spurred a marriage proposal or an invitation to romantic cohabitation.[23] In Jamalpur, as in other railway districts of Britain and India, an employee's access to, and quality of housing improved as he ascended the ranks of the company. A particularly vivid, metropolitan illustration of this principle is provided by Springburn Hill, a railway district in Glasgow constructed by the Edinburgh and Glasgow Railway (EGR). As Frank McKenna notes: "The houses at the top of the hill were of a better standard and were for the top drivers, engineers and supervisors, while the lower blocks were for other drivers and lower grades. One entered through a warren of passageways, each giving access to what is known in Glasgow as a 'single end,' or one roomed-flat. They measured 12 ft by 8 ft and housed complete families."[24] Here, the verticality of the hill, combined with the "warren of passageways" carved into its slope, makes for a metaphorically rich return from work, whereupon the EGR railwayman is able either to reprise his successful career arc, or to see an image of potential future advancement. His vision of the career is materialized in and through a housing complex, implying a mutual co-constitution of domestic and work roles, of intimate and laboring lives. A similar implication can be drawn from Kipling's troubling précis, in which an apprentice's attempts to comprehend the "mechanism of a locomotive" are placed on the same plane as his efforts to understand the relatively inscrutable "heart of a maiden."

Up to now, we have adopted a credulous view of the railway colony, allowing Rudyard Kipling to guide us across its enclosed grounds, while charting out a normative life course for his lead apprentice. We've seen how this normative life course, undertaken within the bounds of the railway colony, could entail a near-seamless overlay of working and domestic lives, manifested in the tracing of a career arc, in the making of a heteroerotic romance, and in the broadening of a domestic circle. But as the case of W. J. Haynes reminds us, a rail worker's journey was not always so tidy: The different layers of domestic, sexual, and workplace experience did not always line up neatly. Perhaps most common were the cases of men promoted to skilled or supervisory positions on the railways who remained unmarried, either by choice or circumstance. In Jamalpur and other railway colonies, men in this situation typically found a co-worker with whom to live. The two then jointly maintained a domestic life, underwritten as a matter of course by the labors of domestic servants, typically consisting of a cook, sweeper, washer man, and gardener.[25] Already then, we can see how the parameters of domestic respectability were stretched in railway colonies, making for a situation wherein men of a certain employment status or grade could together maintain a sanctioned domestic life. While it is difficult to reconstruct the range of intimate bonds and domestic relations undertaken by such men—and surely there was wide variation in this regard—a remarkable scrapbook offers a textured portrait of such bonds as they were kept up by a group of British railwaymen in eastern India.

HENRY WINSHIP'S SCRAPBOOK

Henry Winship, an engineer with the East Indian Railway, kept a scrapbook as a record of his working life, which began in 1849 when he signed a contract with the newly formed rail enterprise and ended sometime in the 1880s.[26] When read closely—and necessarily somewhat speculatively—the scrapbook's three hundred pages seem to open onto a field of intimate relations, some with romantic overtones, that gave shape and color to Winship's railway career. As is typical of the scrapbooking form, such intimate bonds register through juxtapositions of word and image. A few dozen pages into the scrapbook we find a picture—sandwiched between two photographs of an estate near Monghyr—of four formally dressed white men, seated in a row behind a small white dog (figure 3a). Winship is positioned on the left, and over his head a handwritten label reads "Father."[27] Through this slight intervention with pencil, what might initially have seemed a mere gathering of coworkers takes on the appearance of a family portrait.[28] We are left wondering what sorts of affective ties bound these four men to each other and which domestic roles the three unlabeled figures might have inhabited. Two of the three men are featured on preceding spreads of the scrapbook, from which clues to the quality of their relations with Winship can be gleaned. One such spread features an oval-shaped portrait of M. Hall, surrounded by six rectangular newspaper clippings (figure 3b). Reading across these textual fragments, certain echoes sound forth. In one fragment, we find a commentary on oats' enduring powers of germination; in another, we read of "a machine to thrash 'wild oats.'" With this tired pun on masculine sexual experimentation, Winship evokes an erotic coming of age for his subject. Other clippings mention relational forms through which Hall's life might have been given shape and orientation: One fragment refers to receptions for royal brides at Dover Castle, while another calls for "a nurse maid to rock the cradle of the deep." This last phrase echoes the title of Emma Willard's 1831, "Rock'd in the Cradle of the Deep," a poem about sleep and/or death at sea, which was set to music in 1853. Willard's poem resonates in turn with the closing verse of Thomas Moore's "Nature," which Winship has clipped and pasted above Hall's head:

> There's nothing dark, below, above
> But in its gloom I trace thy love
> And meekly wait that moment when
> Thy touch shall turn all bright again.

Such is the field of resonance, distributed around the figure of dark depths, that perhaps offers a clue to the qualities of Winship and Hall's relationship—at least as this was perceived by Winship. Another clipping, pasted below Hall's portrait, draws this field of oceanic resonance away from intimate matters, evoking a utopian world of 2000 AD, which has been built following the tapping of warm water reserves thousands of feet below the earth's crust. Under the consequent "reign of chemistry,"

FIGURES 3A AND 3B. Pages from Henry Winship's Scrapbook. At the center of the left-hand page there is a family portrait. The right-hand page is an homage to M. Hall. British Library, Henry Robert Winship Collection, Photo 798 (29, 27): 1860s.

the earth "will be a vast pleasure garden, and the human race will live in peace and plenty." Such speculative flights of fancy are drawn to a close with a memento mori: "The year 2000 is so near, and yet it is so far off, since none of us can hope to see it dawn."

Before turning back to the previous page of Winship's scrapbook, which features a portrait of Thomas Stewart (who also appeared in the group photo), I want to jump ahead to a spread at the end of the book. Here we find an image of J. Campbell surrounded by rectangular clippings (figure 4b). In these clippings, we encounter again an erotic coming of age story juxtaposed with feminized domestic roles. While on M. Hall's page, mere passing references to the roles of wife and of nurse maid appear, on J. Campbell's, a domestic role is more clearly assigned. His portrait is captioned: "J. Campbell (our Chambermaid)." In keeping with this assignation, a white linen rests upon and spills over our photographic subject's lap. The page is invested with an erotic charge via the poem, "Wake, Buds," which features an extended floral metaphor:

> Break, little buds
> The glossy, silken coats ye wear
> That we may see your faces fair;
> Lay, sweets, your tender bosoms bare
> And fragrance all the laughing air. . . .
> Give, virgin flowers
> While swift do fly the summer weeks
> Your kisses to the bee that seeks;
> Show him your hearts, your tender cheeks
> And prize the love he truly speaks.

These verses of "Wake, Buds" can be read as prescribing an erotic coming of age. Given the gendered associations of blooming flowers, combined with the feminizing appellation of "our Chambermaid," I think we can plausibly cast Campbell into the role of the bud in this scenario. Assuming further that our scrapbooker understood himself to have acted the part of the bee, we can read this page as a memento for a past romance. That the relationship may have run its course by the time Winship pasted Campbell's photo into his scrapbook can be inferred from a number of the clippings, beginning with the closing lines of "Wake, Buds." Here we find a commentary on the virtues of allowing a lover to move on:

> So it is, flowers
> With us; that which we give away
> Of life or love or [illegible]
> Survives to bless another day;
> That which we keep doth soon decay.
> Heigh-ho, the winter of the year.

Elsewhere on the page, notes of remorse appear. "A Penitent's Hymn," ends with the plea, "By thy pardon set me free"; and "A Watchword," contains the passage:

> But there is nothing gained by tears
> *Work is the only cure.*
> Take heart, and lay your grief aside
> Be brave and fret no more."[29]

These passages suggest that, for Winship, railway work may have served as a form of penitence for fraught intimacies of the past, or simply as a salve for loss and unresolved longings.

As we have begun to see, Winship's scrapbook is suffused with a mournful air. References to railway accidents recur throughout, funereal scenes and sites feature prominently, and poetic allusions to life's expiration line the work. But the most direct and intimate engagement with death appears after J. Campbell's spread, on the final page of the scrapbook. Here, following spreads filled with programs for the Howrah Amateur Theatre, Winship sandwiched a funeral notice for Thomas Stewart between a print of Mary Queen of Scots and a small handwritten note informing our scrapbooker that "poor Tommy is dead" (figure 4a). On the printed funeral notice, Thomas Stewart is identified as a fitter for the EIR and is said to have passed away, aged twenty-nine, in February 1864. The handwritten note offers further details about the last hours of Tommy's life, recalling that "he was at Lindley's at half-past eleven at night singing."[30] The following day he fell ill, was taken to the Howrah General Hospital, and died of cholera: "This has thrown a gloom over us. I am not in a mood for writing further," writes Winship's correspondent.[31] The juxtaposition of these records of Stewart's death with a portrait of Mary Queen of Scots can be read in a number of ways. Winship may have been referencing, for those in the know, the slang term *Mary*, and he may have been playing on the lexical proximity between the surnames *Stewart* and *Stuart*. He may also have been commenting on Stewart's reputation. The epigraph printed beneath the portrait of Mary, drawn from Shakespeare's *Measure for Measure*, speaks of

... millions of false eyes
... stuck upon thee: volumes of report
Run with these false and most contrarious quests
Upon thy doings ...

From such lines, we might weave a story of damaging rumors that attached to the name of Thomas Stewart in the railway colonies of the EIR—an extrapolation that, as we will see, chimes with other materials in the scrapbook. And then, finally: Winship's juxtaposition of Mary's portrait with Tommy's funeral notice, like his designation of J. Campbell as "our chambermaid," playfully reworked the conventions of gender and status, rendering our poor railwayman as a queen.

The collection of materials on this late page of the scrapbook should be read in connection with the homage to Thomas Stewart that appears near Winship's family portrait. The page on which Tommy is featured looks like the others we have considered: an oval portrait in the center surrounded by eight rectangular clippings. The latter seem not to allude

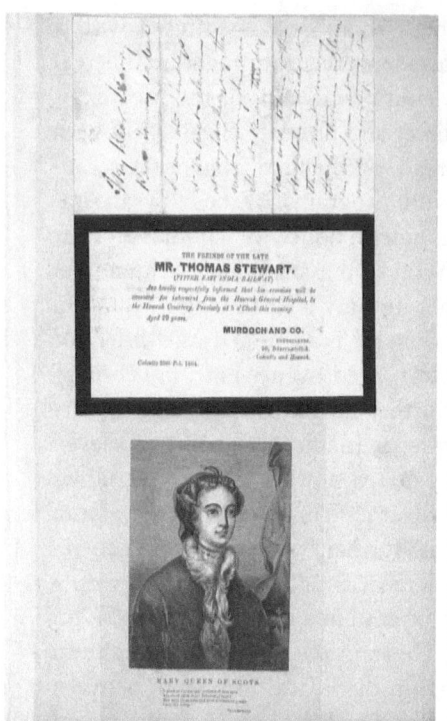 

FIGURES 4A AND 4B. Pages from Henry Winship's Scrapbook. On the left in the center is a funeral notice for Thomas Stewart; on the right, an homage to J. Campbell. British Library, Henry Robert Winship Collection, Photo 798 ("Thomas Stewart," 75): 1860s.

to an erotic coming of age. But, as we have come to expect, they do evoke a feminized domestic service role: "A Careful Little Maid," pasted next to Tommy's portrait, sketches the character of a fastidious maidservant, whose "slippers ne'er were known to squeak." Alternately, "all the prim and pretty ways of Little Prudence Maybe" are praised by parents as a model for their children and trashed by "girls whose games she does not share." This reference to girls who "[bandy] unkind opinions" recalls for us the epilogue adorning Mary's portrait and also resonates with an adjacent clipping's discussion of those who put on a brave face when "cutting, sharp, blighting words have been spoken, which send the hot indignant blood to the face and head.... They are the strong ones of the earth.... who know how to keep silence when it is a pain or grief to them." This passage's interest in the labors of discretion and dissimulation chimes with a number of other textual fragments on Tommy's page. The matter of dissimulation, of the play between being and appearance, is evoked in a clipping concerning the counterfeiting of money. This theme also registers in a quote from Seneca included in another clipping—"The way to gain a good reputation is to endeavour to be what you desire to appear"—and in a poem that opens with the following verse:

> Sea shell
> Murmurs swell
> To the roaring of the sea
> When the ear is laid to thee
> From thy walls
> A storm sprite calls
> With siren's voice to me.

The reference to the siren here reminds us that Tommy was said to have been singing at a friend's house on the eve of his death. Of course, the siren calls to mind a bit more than a musical hobby, evoking notions of feminine deception and the lashing of masculine desire as well. Wading as we are in this particular field of resonance, it is possible to imagine that we are seeing, in these literary fragments, a veiled allusion to late-night drag performances.[32]

This page on which Tommy is cast as a stoic siren, like the other pages of Winship's scrapbook we have considered, carries an especially powerful affective charge. These spreads seem to be imprinted with the intimate bonds kept up by Winship and his closest associates, offering a foggy window onto the familial and erotic relations that may have been maintained by this group of early EIR railwaymen. Reading closely, we can see how such relations appear to have been structured along the lines of an aristocratic household, with Winship occupying the role of patriarch, while his associates were arrayed into various upstairs or downstairs roles.[33] In contrast to these domestic spreads, most other pages of the scrapbook offer rather more affectively neutral portraits of the social institutions, technologies, and individuals that together made up the railway colonies of the EIR. We see photographs, for example, of churches, locomotives, barracks and bungalows—including the first bungalows built in the Jamalpur colony—as well as a literary institute, a volunteer band, and a group of engine drivers. Then there are pages that venture beyond the bounds of the railway colony and its segregated institutions, featuring ethnographic portraits of Bengali subjects, alternating with prints from further afield, the combination of which invests

66 | Strains of Permissiveness, Fields of Force

FIGURES 5A AND 5B. Pages from Henry Winship's Scrapbook. On the left at the bottom, there is an image of workers engaged in laying track in eastern Jharkhand. On the right, photos are captioned with "Our Palanquin Bearers" and "A mixed race." British Library, Henry Robert Winship Collection, Photo 798 (98, 99, 19, 20): 1860s.

the scrapbook with a decidedly orientalist cast.[34] Particularly unsettling are the images that traverse the line between ethnographic and quotidian, depicting Indian subjects involved in construction or service work in ways that collapse identity into role. Group portraits backgrounded by a domestic exterior include those of "our palanquin bearers," and the especially troubling "a mixed race," which features a group of young Indian men standing behind a seated European figure, whose gun rests on the wall behind (figure 5b).[35] A photo captioned "coolies of Rajmahal" features a posed group of more than a hundred people, all of whom were engaged around 1860 to lay track in eastern Jharkhand (figure 5a); while a photo captioned "our building operations," shows a group at work on a half-built railway colony.[36] Winship would have been involved in the direct and indirect management of such unfree labor forces.[37] Contractors and engineers like Winship oversaw bonded workforces and at times also forcibly compelled peasant cultivators to work on the construction of railways; these authorities not uncommonly used whipping as a means of discipline.[38]

While massifying images of Indian workers exist at some remove, formally and affectively, from the aforementioned domestic portraits, a clipping from an early page of the scrapbook offers a framework for reading these divergent materials together and gives us some indication of how Winship made sense of his involvement in the British imperial project. Below a photograph of St. Thomas's church in Howrah, we find a short reflection entitled, "The Worship of Wealth," which claims that "if you can fix some conception of a true human state of life.... You will know then how to build well enough; you will build with stone well, but with flesh better, temples not made with hands, but riveted with hearts, and that kind of marble, crimson-veined, is indeed eternal."[39] While the passage turns on a polarity between building "with stone" and "with flesh," the metaphorical play here blurs the distinction, offering us unsettling images of "crimson-veined marble" and hearts stretched into rivets. Taking this framing passage as an interpretive guide, Winship's scrapbook can be read not only as a record of the various building projects—intimate and infrastructural—that were overseen by its author but also as the medium through which the former fleshly constructions were made to endure. And just as the passage registers metaphorically the troubling, flesh-lacerating aspects of such building projects, Winship's scrapbook offers unsettling indications of the colonial violence that was he and his fellow engineers' stock in trade.

REBUILDING RAILWAY LABOR IN THE 1860S

Winship's family circle apparently came together in the context of a railway construction boom in the early 1860s. We know that Winship's family portraits must have been taken before 1864, as this was the year of Thomas Stewart's death. And we will recall that the family portrait proper, upon which Winship inscribed the label "Father," was pasted between two images of an estate in Monghyr. Other intimate portraits of Winship's associates were similarly juxtaposed with building sites in Monghyr and Jamalpur, on which intensive construction work was taking place between 1859 and 1862.[40] In line with this circumstantial evidence, the scrapbook's title page offers the date of 15 May 1862. Locating the emergence of Winship's family circle in this post-1857 moment of largescale construction allows us to frame the scrapbook more precisely in relation to the history of railway governance in colonial India. Winship's chosen family appears to have been forged during a key transitional period for colonial governance in India—a period during which British officials put particular emphasis on the strategic significance of the railways. In the wake of mass insurgencies in 1857–8, officials saw the expansion of rail networks across the subcontinent as a key strategic priority. Such networks promised to provide an efficient means of communication and transport, especially for the army, while larger rail stations were envisioned as defensible sites to which officials and soldiers could retreat in the face of unrest. In the 1858 Parliamentary Committee on Colonisation, moreover, representatives imagined rail lines as the means by which deputized white settlers based in hill stations could descend rapidly on rebellious zones below.[41] Such were the strategic fantasies that attached to post-1857 projects of infrastructure development. But these projects were not merely the brainchildren of reaction: Significant portions of rail construction had been planned before 1857 and could finally be pursued following the suppression of insurgency in northern and central India.[42] Such preexisting plans were then augmented insofar as the government of India opted in 1858 to extend guarantees on interest payments that had been written into the original 1849 contract between the EIR and the East India Company.[43] In this conducive political and economic context, engineers and laborers working for the EIR were able relatively quickly to build a trunk line from Howrah to Allahabad and to link this line, albeit with a bit of a hitch, to a pair of trunk lines running toward Bombay and Delhi respectively. The trunk line from Howrah to Allahabad was the undertaking on which our scrapbooker was occupied in the early 1860s.

During these years of large-scale rail construction, various governing bodies in colonial India, including the agents of the EIR, experimented with new approaches both to the management of their upper subordinates and to the regulation of Indian populations. Such experiments were motivated in part by anxieties over the health, respectability, and loyalty of European subordinates, who now were more numerous, dispersed across a wider arc of territory, and invested with novel strategic import. Railway, military, religious, and other authorities registered concern in the early 1860s about relatively high rates of venereal disease among British and Anglo-Indian subalterns and, more generally, about manifestations of roughness, including especially public drunkenness, from members of these groups.[44] While such concerns were widely shared, the approaches that governing bodies took to addressing them were not always identical. The early 1860s thus were defined by experimentation, by the adaptation of models originating elsewhere, and by inter-agency negotiation. What emerged from this ferment was a complex amalgam of techniques of governance combining various approaches to the management of upper subordinate employees and entailing new forms of regulation against Indian communities.

From the early 1860s, agents of the EIR pursued a range of paternalistic interventions, most of which drew upon models provided by British company towns, including Swindon, Derby, and Crewe.[45] Such paternalistic interventions, realized most fully in the Jamalpur colony, included the maintenance of bungalows for higher-grade employees and the establishment of sites of "rational recreation" and of moral reform, such as mechanics institutes, swimming baths, churches, and sporting grounds. In addition to these measures designed to improve the health and domestic respectability of upper subordinates, the EIR established a pension fund in 1868 in an effort to reward steady, long-term service to the company.[46]

Representatives of the colonial state were, to varying degrees, involved in the provision of these institutions of moral reform and rational recreation. As holders of the capital balance for the EIR, state officials could either put such funds to work on a given paternalistic project, suggest that EIR agents pay for the project out of company revenues, or require that a project be funded privately.[47] Over the 1860s, railway agents and government officials carried on a tense exchange over the question of how the provision of clergymen in railway districts should be funded—an exchange that perhaps shows how variable officials' assessments were as to the value of this particular intervention. In 1863, agents of the EIR asked the government to release funds for a pastor at Bamangachi, a town along the recently constructed line from Howrah to Allahabad. Their appeal expressed hope that a clergyman would "diminish those vices to which men of the class of Railway subordinates are prone ... reduce the ratio of sickness and mortality" and promote "habits of temperance and frugality and other virtues conducive to their temporal welfare."[48] While expressing a shared commitment to these aims, the government encouraged the company to pay for the pastor out of their own revenues. The government's proposal prompted a fraught exchange between EIR agents and their British-based shareholders. The latter objected—on pseudo-legal grounds—to the government's proposal that the EIR divert revenues to clergymen's salaries, citing the example of metropolitan railway boards. Because these boards were effectively barred by precedent as joint stock companies from spending funds in ways that were not anticipated by their acts of incorporation, company shareholders were in the habit of privately raising money for the provision of religious instruction in railway districts.[49] While such precedents did not similarly bind colonial railway managers, EIR agents, hemmed in both by the government of India and their shareholders, nevertheless undertook this sort of private fundraising effort.

At the same time as their colleagues at the Public Works Department were refusing to release capital funds for the provision of religious instruction in railway districts, representatives of the colonial state were formalizing a regulatory regime to govern commercial exchanges of sex in and around military zones. In 1864, the government passed the first cantonment act (Act 22), drawing military districts under the contagious diseases (CD) regime. This regime entailed systems of regulation, coercive examination, and potential incarceration in lock hospitals for women suspected of engaging in sex work who lived near the cantonments of colonial India.[50] In Allahabad, where railway works abutted military districts, the establishment of the CD regime coincided with a wave of prosecutions against *hijras*—suggesting that state officials desired to draw a boundary around officially sanctioned sex workers on the basis not only of health but also of birth-assigned gender.[51] These techniques of repression and regulation carved out a market for relatively "safe," heteroerotic sex—a market oriented in particular toward British soldiers. While the CD regime was built with soldiers in mind, the market for sexual exchanges it helped establish was also available to upper subordinates on the Indian railways. Indian women subjected to the regulationist regime were enjoined to engage in commercialized sex only with "European" men[52]—a category of consumer that, judging by their cameo appearances in reports on the workings of the CD regime, evidently included higher-grade railwaymen.[53] The governance of railwaymen thus entailed more than simply the moralization of a strategic, industrial workforce. Rather, from the early 1860s, governing bodies implicitly made concessions to higher-grade rail workers in the sphere of sexuality, lacing paternalistic projects with hierarchizing strains of permissiveness.[54]

The criminalization of hijras in the 1860s would seem to suggest, however, that colonial officials' permissiveness had its limits, and that they would draw the line at homoerotic expressions of sexuality. In her gloss on Philippa Levine's work, Anjali Arondekar underlines this notion, arguing that the CD regime was animated by colonial officials' "constant haunting fear of homosexuality, the presence of which would undermine the manly adventure of conquest."[55] As Arondekar has shown, the colonial state developed a practice of quietly relocating British soldiers and officers back to the metropole in the event that their intimacies with other men caused troubles for officials.[56] But if we shift our attention from the military cantonment to the railway colony, we are perhaps compelled to formulate a revised understanding of how, after 1857, sexual politics were caught up in the maintenance of empire. As Winship's scrapbook suggests, intimacies between men were not simply spectral matters within early railway districts. Erotic and familial bonds between railwaymen did not trouble from the margins a colonial regime committed to respectable domesticity or to manly adventure. Rather, these intimacies helped constitute the post-1857 colonial order and its domestic apparatuses. In Jamalpur, single men with an employment status that enabled them to occupy an official bungalow were encouraged to room with one another. Together, they comanaged homes that put Kipling in mind of an idealized English village.

Bachelor cohabitation in railway colonies followed directly from managers' methods of distributing housing tenancies but was also indirectly enabled by their approach to the recruitment of metropolitan railwaymen. Notwithstanding partial efforts to fund the relocation costs for rail workers' wives, over the second half of the nineteenth century, colonial railway agents adopted an approach to the recruitment of British workers that prioritized the hiring of single men. This prioritization of unmarried recruits ensured the reproduction of a substantial gender imbalance in railway colonies up through the turn of the century; it also made for a situation wherein those who had remained unmarried longer than was typical for men of their class would be uniquely qualified for jobs on the Indian railways. While tracking the career arcs of such labor migrants, I was particularly struck by the employment records of two unmarried men, aged thirty-one and twenty-four, who signed contracts with the Great Indian Peninsular Railway (GIPR) on the same day in December 1881. In the months leading up to their January departure for Bombay, where they both intended to take up posts as firemen, Charles Illman and James Field shared a residence in Brighton. Illman, who appears to have returned to this beach town following his term of employment with the GIPR, died in 1926, willing his possessions, valued at 190 pounds, to "Frank Williams railway guard and George Miller

Wood merchant."[57] Charles Illman was able to travel with his roommate to Bombay and more broadly to craft a life oriented around lasting bonds with other working-class men in two locales in part because rail managers prioritized the hiring of older, unmarried labor migrants from the metropole.

In the archives of the Public Works Department, which oversaw the railways of colonial India, we find a well-worn justification for this recruitment policy—namely, that British men who wished to abandon family responsibilities were especially inclined to take jobs on the Indian railways. In 1890, a consulting engineer responsible for selecting British labor migrants explained in a report why he preferred unmarried applicants: "As to age, we want, if possible, unmarried men, and working men, as a rule, marry very early. I never willingly take a married man. It means too often ruin to both man and wife. I have also, I may mention, known a married man to go to India as a way of deserting his family."[58] By 1912 on the Indian State Railways, this approach to recruitment had been officially encoded as policy: "Candidates must be British subjects of about 24 years of age, and should be unmarried."[59] There are a few different ways to interpret this policy. First, from a financial point of view, recruiting unmarried men was advantageous for railway bureaucrats. Doing so allowed companies to avoid paying money for a family's relocation or for an initial family allotment—a payment that some managers worried would be squandered in the event that the railwayman quit, was dismissed, or became incapacitated shortly after his hire.[60] Second, as noted by our consulting engineer, married men who aspired to carry on long-distance relationships with spouses in Britain seem regularly to have found this an impossible and painful undertaking. Whether due to the consequent demoralization such employees exhibited or to the complications that a subaltern's estrangement at times brought to railway bureaucrats—a complication highlighted by the case of Bertha Haynes—managers seem to have aspired to avoid hiring men who would attempt to carry on such long-distance relationships.[61]

The papers of George Cole, an engine driver based in Howrah during the early 1860s, illustrate rather dramatically how such long-distance relationships could quickly unravel. Upon arriving in Howrah, Cole initially kept up a brisk exchange of letters with his wife Lucy, as well as with siblings, extended family members, and former coworkers in and around Stratford. The letters between husband and wife were fraught and volatile; George's writings oscillated between effusive and accusatory—it seems that he quickly came to suspect Lucy of having slept with a boarder she had taken on—while Lucy's missives balanced updates about the children, requests for remittances, reports on neighbors, and declarations of fidelity. To Lucy, and to family members who wrote on her behalf, including upon her eviction, our engine driver insisted that he did not have surplus funds, though invoices from local alcohol distributors would seem to suggest otherwise. In addition to such invoices, George kept a collection of newspaper clippings, including one advising husbands to share only kind words with their wives and another reporting on the trial of a British man who had attacked a boarder upon returning from work abroad, apparently out of suspicion that the boarder and his wife had been romantically involved. These clippings register something of the ambivalence that defined George's relation to Lucy—a relation that lacks any archival traces beyond the first months of George's life on the subcontinent.[62]

From cases such as this one, railway officials seem to have converged on the view that their upper subordinates' long-distance marriages were not uncommonly short-lived. Some also seem to have concluded that not a few married railwaymen took jobs in India with the conscious intention of escaping family relations and obligations. Reading symptomatically this line of argument, I think we can see a certain disavowal at work vis-à-vis the recruitment of unmarried men. On its face, the claim about family abandonment evokes the figure of the deadbeat father—a figure with a rich genealogy in post-Elizabethan Britain, who in his various guises was evoked incessantly down the centuries, most notably in the "enforced narratives" told to justices of the peace by women seeking poor relief.[63] As Carolyn Steedman notes, "[For justices to] extract the name of a putative father and charge him with maintenance, or to return an expectant mother to her true place of settlement offered a clear saving against local rates."[64] The extraction of the name of the father was thus performed to save money but was framed as a moral undertaking. There is an echo of this cynical operation in our consulting engineer's claim that he prioritized hiring unmarried men out of a desire to prevent would-be deadbeat fathers from escaping their family obligations. His putative concern for domestic responsibility covered over a more basic financial motive. But there was another, more striking, disavowal at work here. A recruitment policy that ultimately helped draw unmarried men into domestic relations with one another was justified in the name of domestic morality. The consulting engineer thus assumed a moral posture in relation to a policy that itself put pressure on domestic norms.

In this chapter, we have attended above all to the specific confluence of techniques of governance that allowed some upper subordinates to forge domestic relations with one another along the railways of colonial India. The housing and recruitment policies that we have considered, along with the patterns of everyday life that grew up around the official bungalows of early railway colonies, helped stretch domestic norms in these exemplary colonial heterotopias. By emphasizing how sanctioned intimacies between men contributed to the stretching of domestic norms in early railway colonies, my research builds on Sharon Marcus's account of the plasticity of marriage in the Victorian era. As Marcus has shown, marriages between women were widely acknowledged in nineteenth-century Britain and were lionized by marriage reformers in the years immediately following the 1857 Matrimonial Causes Act. Such marriages promised the mutation of norms, rather than their subversion or collapse.[65] This chapter offers further evidence for the plasticity of domestic norms—and even perhaps of marriage—in the Victorian era, contextualizing this plasticity in relation to the practicalities of colonial governance and labor management.

Zooming out a bit from this consideration of how policies of recruitment and housing helped facilitate the distension of domestic norms in railway colonies, we can conclude by registering one of the grim ironies from this era of colonial governance. Over the early 1860s, as we have seen, significant railway construction work was taking place across the North-Western Provinces (NWP), stretching from Benares in the southeast past Allahabad and then to Delhi in the northwest. During this time, as Jessica Hinchy recently has shown, the NWP was in the throes of a moral panic concerning the public presence of, and domestic relations maintained by, hijras. The speculative notion that most provoked fear, and that circulated in the vernacular press, was that hijras might coerce young boys to join their houses, surgically remove their testes, and sell them to buyers across the subcontinent. Provincial authorities, acting in the name of local communities, carried out a series of prosecutions against members of this gender-variant group over the 1860s; then, in 1871, these authorities formalized discriminatory regulations and modes of surveillance under part 2 of the Criminal Tribes Act (CTA). Through this act, hijras were barred from soliciting sex or from wearing women's clothing in public places, colonial officials were authorized to remove young boys from hijra households, and hijras were prevented from willing property to heirs of their choosing. These forms of state repression were orchestrated by officials in Allahabad—the city where the EIR trunk line forked. As we have already noted, the attacks on hijras' houses in the 1860s dovetailed with the formalization of the CD regime in and around military districts, including around those cantonments carved out of Allahabad's urban fabric. J. F. Stephen, the colonial official who drafted the CTA, asserted that hijras "carried on a system of unnatural prostitution" and "solicited employment by public exhibitions of singing and dancing often dressed as women."[66] Stephen's quote clarifies how the repression of hijra communities was entangled with colonial efforts to establish and to police the boundaries of a sanctioned market for "natural" and "safe" sex work, maintained especially for the benefit of soldiers but accessible as well to upper subordinates of the railways. Moreover, at the same time as hijras' houses were coming under the scrutiny of NWP officials, rail managers from Howrah to Delhi were formalizing arrangements that enabled upper subordinates of European descent to make homes with each other. As Winship's scrapbook attests, at least some such households appear to have been maintained by intimate couples and to have hosted drag performances into the wee hours of the night. There was thus a stark bifurcation in how colonial officials related to what were genealogically distinct, but formally parallel, sorts of gender and sexual variance. In the shadow of imperial infrastructures, the color line split the sexual sphere: White queens could shelter under the protective cover of domestic respectability, while hijras faced attacks on their homes by agents of the colonial state.

PART TWO

Making Railway Unionism between Britain and Colonial India, 1870s–1880s

CHAPTER 3

Paternal Figures

*The Politics of Race and Gender
in Early Railway Unionism*

In the early 1870s, groups of higher-grade railway workers built craft unions. In the metropole, the first of these unions, the Amalgamated Society of Railway Servants (ASRS), was formally open to all grades of railway workers but in practice was dominated by guards and by other workers who had advanced beyond entry-level roles. In colonial India, a sister chapter of the ASRS was formed in 1874. Membership in this union was restricted to those who were permitted to live within railway colonies—that is, to white British and multiracial Anglo-Indian workers. The ASRS in India organized in defense of the color bar, demanding that Indian railway workers not be promoted to the roles of driver and guard. In what follows, we will consider the history of early railway craft unionism in Britain and colonial India, contextualizing craft unionist projects in relation to preexisting managerial practices and to wider cultural discourses of labor. We will see how craft unionists adapted paternalistic managerial technologies in building benefit funds; how, in the name of morality, craft unionists surveilled railway widows who were receiving payments from such funds; and how unionists drew upon and helped advance cultural discourses of labor that imbued higher-grade, public-facing workers with an aura of paternal responsibility. In other words, we will be considering from various angles the politics of race and gender in early railway unionism.

In relation to the wider arc of *Respectability on the Line*, this can be thought of as a transitional chapter. The first two chapters of the book showed how paternalistic managerial technologies shaped domestic lives and sexual cultures within railway districts. While social historical in orientation, these chapters also incorporate cultural historical analysis, demonstrating how alternative domestic arrangements, familial bonds, and erotic attachments registered in cultural materials consumed or produced by railway workers. The chapter to follow carries forward this cultural historical thread, showing how unionists reiterated normative discourses of gender and family in promoting projects of unionization. The chapter also continues to trace the influence of paternalistic managerial practices, in this case showing how company-sponsored provident funds served as models for the funds established by early railway unionists. In subsequent chapters, we will carry the story of railway unionism forward into the early twentieth century, keeping at the center of the picture questions of race and gender. Let's begin then with a vignette that illustrates how early, public-facing railway workers came to be imbued with the aura of paternal responsibility—a vignette that can help frame our discussion of the politics of race and gender in early railway unionism.

On 2 July 1916, William Temple, the future Archbishop of Canterbury, composed a letter to Ellen Langdon, his former nursemaid and longtime housekeeper. Dispensing with the usual pleasantries, Temple's letter to his "dearest Nana" began in media res: "Yes; it is just as horrid as anything can be."[1] The horror to which he referred was her retirement from domestic service. Ellen had worked for the Temple family since William's birth in 1881. At the time, William's father Frederick was serving as Bishop of Exeter, while Ellen's father Roger was stationmaster at Silverton, two stops east of Exeter on the Great Western's trunk line. In the Spring of 1886, after Ellen had moved with her employers to Fulham Palace, the Langdons hosted the Temples at their company-owned home in Silverton.[2] While Ellen would continue serving the Temples until the time of the Great War, she was able in the months following her mother's 1908 death to bring a book to publication, editing and supplementing her late father's memoirs under the title, *The Life of Roger Langdon* (1909).

This remarkable book's preface was written by Henry Lambert, a gentleman whose father was the general manager of the Great Western Railway (GWR) and who, like the Temples, had visited the Langdon family home in the late 1880s. Henry Lambert writes that his father's "attention had been called to the personality and attainments of the Silverton station-master." He continues, "and as I was at that time doing a little journalism in odd moments it was suggested that I should run down and write something for the *Great Western Magazine*, which I was very pleased to do."³ Twenty years after this journalistic trip to Devon, Henry Lambert again was asked to write about Roger Langdon—this time, by Ellen.⁴ In his 1909 preface, Henry wrote warmly of the hospitality he had received during that first visit to the Langdon family home:

> At that little wayside station just on the London side of Exeter I therefore found myself one summer afternoon. The village of Silverton, distant two miles from the station, was not visible, and the principal features in the immediate vicinity were the station-master's house, with the front garden between it and the station, and in the front garden a circular iron building with a cone-shaped revolving roof, which, I found, was an observatory sheltering a telescope for celestial observation. The tall, slightly stooping, white-bearded old station-master at once arrested attention. A dignified, patriarchal type of man, with a kindly, pleasant and simple manner, he was evidently much averse to all forms of affectation and cant. I was quickly made welcome and introduced to his wife and well-ordered home.⁵

Lambert's scene-setting remarks here introduce us to Roger Langdon's three most salient roles: respectable family man, self-taught astronomer, and GWR stationmaster. These three roles each were lived in the immediate vicinity of the Silverton station and thus within the limits of company property. The spatial pileup of Langdon's domestic, leisure, and work roles was responsible for perhaps the worst family tragedy suffered by the Langdons. As Ellen recalled in her supplementary contributions to *The Life of Roger Langdon*: "My eldest brother was killed [in 1869] by an accident at the station. This was a terrible blow to both my parents, and the trouble turned father's auburn hair as white as snow."⁶ The station appears here as the scene of a domestic catastrophe that leaves lasting marks on Roger's body. Later, Ellen recounts how another tragedy at the station similarly affected Roger and Ann Langdon's intimate lives: "Father rushed out to warn [a passenger who was on the line], but it was too late, for the engine was upon her, and she was instantly killed. The shock was very great to both of my parents and they could not sleep for weeks."⁷ In this passage, the reader's attention is pulled from the station to Roger and Ann's bedroom. We see how an accidental injury was experienced by both members of the couple as a shocking personal loss. Ellen's supplementary contributions thus portray Roger as a caring father figure in overlapping domestic and work roles, demonstrating that these roles were ultimately inseparable, at least in terms of how they were affectively lived. Through these vignettes, Ellen writes her father into the role of the paternal railwayman.

In what follows, we will consider how certain groups of rail workers in Britain and colonial India came to appear—in the context of their work roles—as paternal figures. The association of railway labor with paternal obligation was especially pronounced in the print culture of early railway unionism, which took shape between colony and metropole during the 1870s. But this association was not originally forged by craft unionists. Rather, the cultural association of railway labor with paternal regard appears in fictional texts and company publications from the 1840s through the 1860s, including in works authored by the children of railway managers and employees. Henry Lambert—the GWR general manager's son—drew upon this literary tradition when he portrayed the Silverton stationmaster as "a dignified, patriarchal type of man, with a kindly, pleasant and simple manner," who "introduced [me] to his wife and well-ordered home."[8] And Ellen, in editing and supplementing her father's memoirs with vignettes that showed the linkages between her parents' intimate lives and Roger's work responsibilities, similarly entered into this literary stream. But neither the association of railway labor with the paternal role nor the creative acts undertaken by the children of railwaymen in forging this association were simply literary matters. The intergenerational alchemy by which children fabricated paternal identities for rail workers also took place on shop floors. In Swindon and Crewe, the daughters of railway workers were employed in textile factories that daily churned out the liveries issued to public-facing employees.[9] In the Victorian era, these uniforms served as badges of a specifically paternal sort of respectability.

Uniforms were curious, fungible things. A guard's jacket, while carrying its own distinctive scuff marks, was meant to be seen as exchangeable with the jackets of all other guards—that is to say, the uniform indexed a bureaucratic role. This role was at once abstract and gendered; it could be occupied, theoretically at least, by any man. In addition to imprinting a gendered work role upon its wearer, the uniform also served visually to indicate that the bearer of this role had been delegated a certain authority. The guard moved from train to station with an authority that derived, ultimately, from his board of governors. Considering the paternalistic idiom of early railway management, we might say that a thin patina of delegated paternal authority graced our guard's livery. We can thus begin to see how the cultural association of railway labor with paternal obligation was overdetermined. This association had, by the 1870s, become a literary topos, or commonplace, implicitly registering both rail workers' responsibility for maintaining the well-being of passengers and the structure of delegation that linked railwaymen to their paternalistic managers. This literary topos was reinforced by a broader cultural discourse on the uniformed working class and by the particular gender divisions of labor that had emerged in railway districts, wherein "daughters" manufactured the uniforms of "fathers." Finally, the association of railway labor with paternal responsibility picked up on the fact that higher-grade railwaymen typically, though not universally, were themselves husbands and fathers, heads of households, and after 1867, electors. In debates surrounding the Second Reform Act, the men set to be enfranchised were sometimes referred to as of the "George Stephenson class";[10] railwaymen were coming to exemplify a new sort of respectable, working-class masculinity. The *paternal railwayman*, as cultural artifact, was thus akin to a sedimentary stone. Layers of social experience and meaning had been pressed together to form what at least appeared to be a robust cultural category. But, as we have seen in previous chapters, this layering of different levels of social experience sometimes had ironic consequences. In this case, rather than making fatherhood relatively unavoidable for railwaymen, the overdetermined association of railway labor with paternal regard, combined with the proliferation of stories about individual rail workers' family lives, could give cover to those employees who opted to remain bachelors. Because the bureaucratic role he occupied was imbued with a paternal aura, an individual railwayman could be seen as a respectable father-figure regardless of whether he himself was married or had children. He might be unmarried and renting a room from a widowed boarding housekeeper or living with a coworker, but still he could appear in public as an exemplary paternal subject. Within railway contexts then, paternal status came to be partially unmoored from family situation.

This unmooring of status and situation did not simply offer a protective shield to unmarried railwaymen. That something of a paternal status could be secured independent of fatherhood and that this status was associated with the work role and its fungible vestments also facilitated the emergence of new patriarchal projects in railway districts, including among early craft unionists. The fungibility of paternity—the relative availability of this status to all who wore the uniform—was an enabling fiction for unionists who wished to stake a claim as the proper protectors of their fatally injured coworkers' wives and children. Union leaders—whether themselves married men or not—cast themselves as guardians of widows and children, implying that fatherly responsibility was a mobile thing within railway communities. They tended to frame their paternalistic initiatives in the language of self-help—a term that functioned as a shorthand for working-class mutual aid but that also carried other associations, including those linked to individual self-improvement and to masculine breadwinning. In 1880, the general secretary of the *Amalgamated Society of Railway Servants* (ASRS) opposed self-help to charity in arguing for the union's newly established orphans fund and against the union's continued involvement with the Derby orphanage, which had been supported since 1874 by a combination of members' dues, company sponsorship, and gentlemanly patronage: "There is ample scope for both institutions. The difference between them is that ours leans on self-help for its main support, Derby on charity. Ours diffuses the help in the children's home, helping each one alike; Derby bestows all its help on one child, separating it from the family. The help from our fund reaches every family of orphans of members who subscribe; that of Derby reaches only one of the family elected by favor."[11]

Here, allusions to late-Georgian and early Victorian working-class history help give force to the polarization of self-help and charity. That the orphanage *separates* a child from his or her mother makes this form of charity appear similar to the despised workhouse system of the 1830s and 1840s. As Anna Clark has shown, the *Poor Law Amendment Act* of 1834 was justified with reference to the supposed domestic immorality of the working classes and was excoriated in radical writings for how it pushed families into workhouses where they were separated by gender. The notion that politics should operate in the service of domestic morality was thus a shared presupposition of what were otherwise antagonistic social forces. This underlying cultural consensus drew the bulk of working-class organizers toward a more fulsome embrace of domestic ideology and the breadwinner ideal around the mid-century.[12] The 1870s and 1880s witnessed a further turn of the screw in terms of the sexual politics of working-class organizers—a turn that followed in the wake of a few decades of company paternalism. In chapter 1, we considered how, from the 1840s, metropolitan railway managers promoted a host of social institutions, including provident funds, that were organized along mutualist lines. While such provident funds ultimately were controlled by managers and other gentlemanly patrons, they were maintained on a day-to-day basis by higher-grade railwaymen, who assumed responsibility for surveilling and distributing benefits to injured coworkers, widows, and other claimants. As Simon Cordery has shown, early rail unionists drew upon experiences with mutualist organizations in establishing union-run benefit funds, often importing directly the regulations of provident funds into the rulebooks of their self-help institutions.[13] Whereas Anna Clark's working-class organizers had, in advancing the breadwinner ideal, spoken in the name of individual fathers who aspired to assume responsibility for their wives and children, the craft unionists of the 1870s and 1880s spoke as individual fathers but also as representatives of a distributed or collectivized paternal agency, thus claiming a broader sort of social responsibility. Rail unionists pitched themselves as akin to paternalistic managers—they too looked out for the welfare of the traveling public and provided aid and comfort to railway families in times of need—but with the crucial difference that the union's support for railway families purportedly could come absent any whiff of charity, with its customary degradations and uncertain hand. As the 1880 ASRS report observed, the union's orphan fund "diffuses the help in the children's home, helping each one alike. . . . The help from our fund reaches every family of orphans of members who subscribe; that of Derby reaches only one of the family elected by favor." Here, an implicit contrast between egalitarian versus hierarchizing practices is deployed to help strengthen the case for the ASRS's Orphan Fund—a fund that, rhetoric notwithstanding, bore striking similarities to those that had been established by railway managers from the mid-century.

Early rail unionists thus promised a sort of mutual aid that would flow equally to the families of all members and that would bolster rather than erode their fellow workers' sense of dignity and collective agency. But from the beginning, conflicts emerged within craft unionist settings—including between benefits claimants and union boards and between different factions of unionists—over the practicalities of self-help. And while a shared print culture linked higher-grade workers in Britain and colonial India, these geographically dispersed groups of railwaymen did not always understand the tasks of self-help in identical ways, nor did they frame their responsibilities as paternal agents in equivalent terms. Craft unionists on the subcontinent composed a more explicitly racialized discourse of paternal responsibility—a discourse reciprocally bound up with the everyday forms of segregation and labor hierarchization that characterized the colonial Indian railways and their residential districts. In 1874, a group of British labor migrants established a short-lived sister chapter of the ASRS, promoting benefit funds and campaigning to codify the exclusion of Indian men from higher-grade roles. This white supremacist craft union disbanded in 1878, before being founded again on a somewhat less exclusionary basis in 1897.[14] The 1870s thus were a watershed for railway labor in Britain and colonial India, but the organs of collective action that emerged over this decade borrowed in more than superficial ways from the paternalistic technologies, gender discourses of labor, and racializing logics of governance that had ordered labor forces from the mid-century. Early rail unionists thus adapted paternalistic techniques of governance and politicized existing domestic cultures of railway labor; in doing so, they helped set the terms for the political conflicts that would roil railway communities through the turn of the century.

MAKING RAILWAY UNIONISM IN BRITAIN

On 24 June 1872, in the midst of strike wave in the metropole, the first railway trade union in Britain was formed. More than sixty delegates from around the country had traveled to the capital in order officially to establish the Amalgamated Society of Railway Servants (ASRS).[15] A month later, strikes would break out at a number of stations in North London, contributing to a summer of work stoppages in the capital spearheaded by builders and other craft unionists.[16] The successful formation of the ASRS in the volatile summer of 1872 followed upon organizing efforts that had begun in 1865—the year of the Reform League's founding.[17] The enfranchisement two years later of "registered and respectable" workingmen, along with the protections extended to unions following the Royal Commission on Trade Unions (1867–9), gave a fillip to rail unionization efforts, not least as these reforms incentivized politicians to patronize railway workers. While no national politicians had supported the unsuccessful unionization efforts of 1865–7, at least four members of Parliament supported the formation of the ASRS in 1872.[18] Of particular significance in this respect was the backing of Michael Thomas Bass, Liberal MP for the railway town of Derby. In addition to sponsoring the ASRS in 1872, Mr. Bass had over the previous two years disbursed funds to Charles Bassett-Vincent, a former Railway Clearing House clerk and current trade unionist who used the money both to help establish the *Railway Service Gazette*—a weekly newspaper that ran through the 1870s—and to carry out an inquiry into the high rates of accidents and injuries along the lines. In the course of his inquiry, Bassett-Vincent was able to meet with workers around England and to help build networks critical to the formation of the ASRS.[19]

While the post-1867 political conjuncture was thus conducive to the establishment of the ASRS,[20] economic conditions also crucially propelled this early phase of rail unionism. In the early 1870s, industry- and system-wide dynamics enabled railway firms to realize significant profits, while also generating staggeringly high rates of accidents.[21] As Philip Bagwell has argued, the profits taken in by railway firms from 1868 to 1872 seem to have made managers less committed to the sorts of coordinated repression that had enabled them to defeat unionization drives in 1865–7. In 1871–2, by contrast, railway boards agreed to settle wage disputes with workers on a company-by-company basis. The relative profitability of the railway system up through 1872 rested on highly exploitative and unsafe conditions of work—conditions that gave an urgency to collective organization. As R. J. Irving has shown, managers competed for passengers in these years by offering faster and more frequent trains—a sharp "speedup" of railway operations that exacerbated longer-term trends.[22] The period from 1856 to 1889 was marked by a dramatic increase in the ratio of train trips to the overall mileage of the rail system. Over this time, the number of journeys multiplied by 6; tonnage of freight by 4.5; number of miles travelled by passengers by 4.75; length of the railway system, however, by only 2.5.[23] Accident reports from the period of 1867 through 1876 suggest that the increasing concentration of trains on the lines exacerbated other unsafe conditions of operation—including especially the persistence of rudimentary brake technology and the slow adoption of the safer "block system" of signaling[24]—making for one of the most dangerous periods in the history of the British railways.[25]

In addition to raising the number of accidents on the lines, the more intensive running of trains also fostered injurious conditions in railway sheds and repair workshops. This causal relationship was foregrounded in a February 1872 *Railway Service Gazette* story:

> The inquest that was held at the end of last week on the body of Rooks, the unfortunate engine-fitter who was crushed to death between two engines at Camden, gave occasion for certain remarks on the part of Dr. Lankester, the coroner, that just now apply with peculiar force to the disturbed state of the relations between railway servants and the various companies. First, as to the enormous waste of human life in the particular district over which the gentleman in question officially presides. It was stated by him that thirty railway servants were killed on the London and North Western line every year, and he not unnaturally wished to be informed if such wholesale slaughter was altogether unavoidable. The answer to this was that so many engines entered the shed in the course of the day that the men employed therein "became careless." It is questionable, however, if this is a perfectly impartial statement. May it not be that "so many engines entering the shed," all to be attended by a not over abundant number of hands, is the cause of an amount of desperate haste that may well pass as "recklessness"?[26]

This concluding rhetorical question succinctly registers the injurious effects of a system-wide speedup on employees engaged in the maintenance and repair of locomotives. The report quoted here was published in the same year as the ASRS's establishment and only months before a strike of railway porters employed by the London and North Western Railway (LNWR).

The strike began innocently enough. In the spring of 1872, a group of London-based porters petitioned the LNWR board of directors for a wage increase. While their petition was granted by the directors, the supervisor on the spot, Mr. Greenish, refused to disburse bonuses except to workers he perceived as especially loyal. Around the same time, Greenish fired a number of employees suspected of involvement in union organizing (including those attempting to coordinate an independent benefit fund), an act that echoed his earlier mass firings of those involved in bringing a wage-oriented memorial.[27] In response, London-based porters brought a memorial calling for the reinstatement of fired workers and for the removal of Greenish. When the Board refused to consider the latter demand and when Greenish opted to punish Broad Street porters by withholding their wages, workers engaged in a spontaneous strike, calling out to each other with the slogan: "No pay, no work!"[28]

The unauthorized strike that was thus initiated on 26 July 1872 set in motion a series of confrontations, both internal to the ASRS as well as between workers and representatives of the LNWR and the British state. The first such confrontation, between workers and a line of police, occurred on the afternoon of the 26th. As word of the strike spread from one goods depot to the next, servants from various stations gathered at Broad Street and then marched northwest through Islington and on to the Chalk Farm goods depot, the gates of which, "were found closed and a line of policemen drawn across. Speeches were delivered from the top of a cab.... After the speeches the men and their wives, in groups, discussed their grievances. They entertained no doubt whatever that they would ultimately be joined by the men at all the depots, that railway *employes* throughout the kingdom would support them, and that the directors will soon come to terms. The women here and there, it is true, talked about the dearness of provisions, but the men were perfectly sanguine and light-hearted as to the result."[29] In addition to providing a sense of the gender diversity of the crowd at Chalk Farm, this passage conveys the enthusiasm the Broad Street strike provoked amongst workers stationed along the London portion of the LNWR line. The enthusiasm of 26 July, which seems to have varied somewhat along lines of gender, was an effect of workers' optimistic view that sympathy strikes at other stations, depots, and workshops would shortly follow.[30] As it happened, workers at only one other station—Poplar—joined the strike in solidarity with Broad Street porters, despite promises of sympathy from porters stationed at Camden Town station and from workers in other sectors. Had such solidarity been forthcoming, business in London would have nearly been ground to a halt, as the Broad Street strike occurred at the same time as a major strike of builders and other skilled craft unionists in the city.[31]

While the railway strike's restriction to porters at only two stations ultimately sealed its fate, this relatively limited strike action nevertheless imposed significant costs on the company. As the *Railway Service Gazette* noted, the company "lost some thousands of pounds, owing to goods of a perishable nature being thrown on their hands, because they could not deliver the same promptly. Tons of dead meat and fish had to be carted away to Willesden ... and there buried."[32] In addition, while the company ultimately was able successfully to draw strike breakers from other cities, an early attempt at hiring workers in London to cross the picket lines apparently backfired on managers, as those hired proceeded to ransack the goods station: "The daily papers on Monday contained statements to the effect that old hands had played this havoc; but such reports were utterly untrue. The men on strike are far too manly and too sensible to do such things as these."[33] In his postmortem on the strike, published a mere week after this report, ASRS president Dr. Baxter Langley took the disavowal we see here one step further, denying not only that "manly and sensible" railwaymen had engaged in looting but even that the looting of the station had ever taken place. Langley further outlined a new policy on strikes, which barred local chapters from taking collective action unilaterally, and insisted that the Broad Street strike had been discredited largely because of "intemperate expressions [that], we are sorry to say, escaped some of the speakers at public meetings."[34] Langley's intervention helped shift the practice of the ASRS away from confrontational strikes and toward what early historians of the union referred to as its "friendly society" orientation.[35]

A key manifestation of this friendly society orientation appeared in the form of an orphan fund, which was established by the ASRS in 1880. Before this fund was established, however, the union pursued an alternative approach to addressing the crisis of social reproduction faced by railway widows. In 1874, the union helped establish an orphanage in the railway town of Derby. While we might intuitively think of orphanages as places where children without parents or other legal guardians are housed, in Victorian contexts, orphanages were not infrequently homes for children whose fathers had died or left the territory but whose mothers had not. The Railway Servants' Orphanage housed both parentless children and those whose mothers were still alive. Thus, until the ASRS Orphan Fund was established in 1880, railway widows could only receive something like support from the union insofar as they were caring for young children and successfully applied to have one or more of their children admitted to the orphanage in Derby.

Like the ASRS itself, the orphanage received much of its initial impetus from the efforts of Charles Bassett-Vincent, who subsequently came to be marginalized in relation to the operation of the institution. In his memoir, Bassett-Vincent passes over in relative silence his efforts to establish and maintain the orphanage, noting simply: "It was at the above meeting I had the opportunity of formulating the scheme I had long in view—the establishing of an orphanage, and it met with approval. But I wish to observe that the description of the building up of it is of such historic interest during the first six years of its growth as to form the subject of a special book, a book that I, would like to have published under the auspices of the 'Amalgamated' and a portion of the profits from the sale of the work devoted to the Orphan Fund."[36] Aside from this passing reference to an unrealized intention to publish, the only stories about the formation of the orphanage that are included in Bassett-Vincent's *Authentic History* were supplied in an "appendage" to the 1963 version, which was composed by his granddaughter, Mrs. C. E. S. Hallam. There, she recalled that her mother helped care for the first five children admitted to the orphanage and that, when the original building was being redecorated for a different purpose years later, "scribble was still there under the layers of old wallpaper which were being stripped off, reminiscent of the Orphans who were cared for there."[37]

Polarizing debates over the Railway Servants' Orphanage erupted amongst ASRS members only a few years after the formation of the institution in Derby. A significant question in such debates concerned the role of the union in the institution's founding. While the impetus for the orphanage had been provided by those, such as Charles Bassett-Vincent, who were directly or indirectly involved in the ASRS, from its earliest moment the orphanage relied as well upon charitable support and coordination from beyond the union's ranks. The coordinating committee, based in Derby, was composed of both unionists and independent philanthropists, and donations for the orphanage were collected both at and beyond local union halls. Despite this breadth of support, unionists initially understood the founding of the orphanage to constitute both a charitable effort and an act of self-help. From the 1874 ASRS annual report: "The members became active canvassers, and by the end of the year the establishment of an Orphanage for the destitute little ones of killed railway servants was an accomplished fact. Rarely has any charitable effort been so signally successful, and whoever may hereafter control what is hoped will be a national institution, the credit of having originated the Orphanage, and placing it in a fair way towards successful completion, will remain with the Society, and will be a lasting testimony to that principle of self-help which forms the very basis of our union."[38]

In the final years of the 1870s, this notion of self-help would be mobilized by those arguing that the orphanage was not fit for purpose and that an alternative initiative would better support railway widows and their children. We will recall that the 1880 ASRS general secretary's report polarized the newly established orphan fund against the orphanage on the grounds that the former was based on the principle of self-help, while the latter had come to rely merely on the uncertain promise of charity.[39] General Secretary Evans's 1880 report additionally echoed rank-and-file unionists' criticisms of corrupt practices at the Derby orphanage, and challenged directly the class and gender discourses undergirding this charitable institution:[40] "I know it is sometimes urged that mothers are careless of their children, and that if they were given the money it would be improperly applied. This, I believe, would be the exception. In the majority of cases the mother's love for her children would be a guarantee of a careful use of the money for their benefit. Such an argument as I have mentioned is a reflection on the women who are today the wives of railwaymen."[41] As this passage makes clear, debates in the ASRS about the proper care of orphans turned in part upon competing conceptions of working-class motherhood. While General Secretary Evans certainly expressed a more "positive" view of working-class women as mothers than those who would advocate that, for their own benefit, children should be removed from their families of origin, his position nevertheless presumed a moralizing, paternalistic relation to railway widows. This paternalistic relation would be codified in the bylaws of the ASRS Orphan Fund, which was established in 1880.

In the years immediately preceding the establishment of the orphan fund, some unionists advocated that railway widows, regardless of whether they were caring for young children, should also be supported by members' dues. In the 5 September 1879 edition of the *Railway Service*

Gazette, Mr. Cordwell, the Manchester branch representative, argued for the establishment of a "Railway Servants' Widows' and Orphans' Fund," which would help ensure that "our widows and our orphans [were] blessed and cared for."[42] Then, during the delegates meeting at which the orphan fund was established, those representing the Spa Road and Cambridge branches proposed "that the benefits of the Fund be extended to widows, and be termed a 'Widow and Orphan Fund.'" The Cambridge representative then proposed that "for the present scale of benefits substitute 'One shilling per week for each child under 14 years of age,' and insert 'Each widow shall receive from the fund the sum of five shillings per week.'"[43] These proposals would fail, however, as the union ultimately established a fund for orphans but refused any guarantees of support for women without young children. This bar would be given force in the 1881 Resolution #1572, which stated "that the word 'family' used in the Orphan Fund Rules shall mean one or more children."[44] In addition to clarifying the bar on payments to women without children, the bylaws associated with the orphan fund made explicit the paternalistic and scrutiny-laden stance of the union toward women receiving funds for the care of their children.[45] These bylaws suggest that unionists understood the ASRS to be something of a surrogate father for children of fatally injured co-unionists—an institutional body toward whom railway widows were expected to remain faithful, lest they lose access to the surrogate wage of orphan fund payments. A reference to widows "guilty of immorality" in bylaw xx.9 demonstrates the degree to which the mid-century moralization of railway widows—effected in part by company-established contributory funds—was carried forward into early unionist projects, while bylaw xx.7 shows the imagined transactional function of the orphan fund vis-à-vis women's reproductive labor. Unionists evidently saw themselves as paying widows to maintain their children's "cleanliness, clothing, schooling, and general treatment."[46]

Some indication of the fraught quality of this transactional and paternalistic relation between the ASRS and individual railway widows can be gleaned from the minutes of executive committee meetings, wherein individual cases related to the orphan fund were considered. Initially, we can note cases in which the executive committee denied, on various grounds, widows' applications for support, as, for example, a July 1880 reply: "the committee regret the position of Mrs Broughton, of New Holland, but have no funds from which to assist her."[47] Or the response to the "claim preferred [sic] on behalf of Mrs. Mills, of Bury," which "could not be considered, as her children are grown up."[48] Or again: "On the motion of Middlesbro' and Child's Hill, it was unanimously Resolved—That we cannot entertain the application of the St. Helen's Branch for aid on behalf of the imbecile child of the late J. Taylor, owing to its being over the age provided for by rule."[49] Despite their mere reproduction of bureaucratic platitudes, these moments in the minutes offer trace evidence of gender antagonisms in the railway sector, with women and supportive branch representatives asserting through their applications a sense that the parameters established for the orphan fund should not apply to their particular cases, that these parameters are faulty, or perhaps even that women attached through relations of dependency to the railway industry should generally be entitled to support, regardless of whether they are caring for young children.

Beyond such moments in which the executive committee curtly refused support to applicants who attempted to push the limits of the orphan fund, the minutes of executive committee meetings from the late 1880s also give some indication of how unionists exercised discretion in their enforcement of bylaws pertaining to widows' "immorality." In 1887, the committee passed a resolution introduced by Abergavenny and Leeds representatives, "That the payments to the family of the late T. Wright, of Middlesbro', which have been stopped on account of the widow's misconduct, be resumed, and that the branch be requested to appoint a guardian to look after the children's welfare."[50] Along similar lines, in 1887, "On the motion of Birmingham No. 2 and Leicester, it was Resolved—That the allowance to the orphans of the late W. E. Cave of Cambridge, be resumed, and that the Branch Secretary be requested to act as guardian to the children, and see that they are in no way neglected."[51] These resolutions seem to imply that particular union representatives had in fact withheld payments following their assessments of neglect or misconduct but also that, upon request by local representatives, the executive committee had chosen to reinitiate the payments and at the same time to formalize tighter lines of surveillance. Such resolutions suggest that early rail unionists took seriously their commitment to surveilling and disciplining railway widows—but also that they reserved the right to act with discretion in relation to individual cases. In this way, they borrowed more than simply bureaucratic bylaws from their paternalistic managers. They took on as well paternalistic ways of being, acting as responsible and sometimes magnanimous decisionmakers committed to the moral welfare of railway widows and to the care of their late coworkers' "orphaned" children. As we will see in the following section, unionist adaptations of paternalistic technologies and ways of being dovetailed with the representations of such men disseminated through a broader Victorian-era print culture, which tended to frame railway workers as paternal figures in relation to travelling members of the public. Just as rail unionists borrowed paternalistic ways of being from their managers in administering benefit funds, public-facing railwaymen appeared in a range of Victorian-era cultural works to carry a delegated paternal authority—an authority that derived, ultimately, from their board of directors.

THE PATERNAL RAILWAYMAN IN VICTORIAN PRINT CULTURE

Mid-century novels were some of the first cultural works to depict railway employees as paternal figures vis-à-vis their passengers. Initially, we can consider Charles Dickens's *Dombey and Son*, a novel published in serial form between 1846 and 1848.[52] At a certain point in the novel, the paternal protagonist, Paul Dombey, takes a ride on the train. Dombey's six-year-old son has recently died, and Paul's ride on the train—a bumpy, helter-skelter affair—metaphorically depicts the disordered state of his mind.[53] As he is boarding the train before this journey, Paul has a brief conversation with Toodle, the locomotive driver, who asks for material support in caring for his own son, Biler. Biler has apparently "gone on the wrong track." Toodle thus comes across as a caring father, making a bid for support from Paul on the basis of their shared concern for the fates of their sons. Of course, the reader knows that this bid probably lands like a knife blow, as Paul has just lost the son to whom he had hoped to bequeath ownership of his shipping business. The reader comes away from this scene with a sense of the missed connection between these men, separated not only by the gulf of class but also by the scale of their sadness.

Dickens's *Dombey and Son* was published at a time when public confidence in the railway industry had been shaken. In 1846, a speculative bubble in railway stocks burst, setting off a general financial panic. Meanwhile, stories of gruesome railway accidents regularly appeared in national news articles. In this context, Parliament took steps to regulate the railway industry, balancing the interests of railway owners with those of the riding public, while contravening the interests of those who worked the lines.[54] Railway owners argued at the time that their profitability was threatened by the revival of the *deodand*—a medieval legal doctrine that radical coroners had reworked from 1838 in order to impose significant costs on companies for the accidental deaths of workers and passengers. The deodand was duly abolished in 1846. In its place, Parliament codified a legal right of compensation for passengers and their heirs; subsequent court cases clarified that this right of compensation did not extend to workers, even when they were not at fault for an accident.[55] The missed connection between Toodle and Paul in Dickens's novel can thus perhaps be read as a comment on the contemporaneous delinking of the legal status of passengers and workers. For workers like Toodle, the reforms of 1846 meant that generous financial compensation from owners like Paul was no longer forthcoming. As we have seen, this legal transformation set in motion a series of cultural or discursive shifts that significantly altered working class life. For one, the management of accidental injury came to appear as a matter of individual domestic virtue for working-class women and men. Women were held responsible for bearing up and piecing together a respectable life for themselves and their children following their husbands' workplace deaths, while men were held responsible for providing for their families, even in the event of their own accidental injury or death. They were enjoined to do so by putting a portion of their wages into savings banks, life insurance plans, or benefit funds—mechanisms for pooling risk that defined a nascent culture of working-class improvement.

Elizabeth Gaskell's novel *Cranford*, considered in chapter 1, reiterated and commented upon the moralization of railway workers and widows after 1846. The first installment of Gaskell's novel was published in the December 1851 edition of Dickens's *Household Words*.[56] This installment depicts a rail worker's lapse of concentration at work, the avoidable but nevertheless courageous paternal sacrifice that follows, and finally the devastating aftereffects of this event on his family and community. The spread of shock is finally interrupted when his daughter bears up valiantly in order more effectively to nurse her sister. Jesse's display of resilience and domestic virtue offers an exemplary model of working-class responsibility in the face of accident and injury. The novel thus treats the industrial accident as an occasion for the revelation of working-class individuals' domestic virtues and relative self-possession—a framing of the accident that aligns with the contemporaneous legal responsibilization of railway workers and widows and with the ascendancy of moral improvement amongst working class communities.

Another mid-century novel that invokes the domestic consequences of a rail worker's injury is Ellen Wood's 1864 *Oswald Cray*, an example of the sensation fiction increasingly popular at this time. The novel depicts the immediate aftermath of a violent derailment. Bigg, a railway stoker scalded in the crash is initially passed over for care by Mark Davenal, one of the doctors sent to the scene. When confronted about his oversight by Dr. Oswald Cray, Mark insists: "He's only a fireman.... No one expects these rough fellows to be sensitive to pain." The doctors' exchange follows immediately upon Bigg's expression of concern for his family: "It might be my death-blow sir. And what's to become o' my wife and little uns? Who'll work for 'em?"[57] Mark's callous comment following Bigg's appeal echoed contemporaneous medical research, which held that rail workers were relatively impervious to shock.[58]

This vision of rail workers' roughness and insensitivity to pain coexisted awkwardly with the imperative that they exhibit sensitivity to their passengers' physical and emotional well-being. A worker could face criminal prosecution and incarceration if his negligence was found to have contributed to a passenger's accidental injury. Moreover, as an early manual for the Great Northern Railway insisted, guards and other public-facing workers were responsible not only for maintaining passengers' bodily integrity, but also for calming annoyed or anxious passengers' nerves.[59] The law and company policy thus imposed an elaborate burden of care on railway workers. The conceptual tension between their obligation to care and their portrayal as rough, insensitive fellows was managed in part through the depiction of the rail worker's regard for his passengers as a familial sort of care. According to contemporaneous biological research, familial regard was a matter of automatic response, requiring no particular skill or exertion. John Carter's 1855 physiological studies found that an automatic "riveting" of attention occurred when a family member's life was threatened, and that workers obliged to maintain an unbroken focus on the job exhibited a similarly automatic attentiveness.[60] Of course, when rail workers wrote directly of their experiences of labor, they generally emphasized how exhausting it was to remain constantly alert to possible dangers on the job.[61] Despite such testimony, railway labor continued through the nineteenth century to be reduced in writing to a matter of automatic attention or paternal regard.

The 1867 short story "Snowed Up" reiterates this discursive reduction of railway labor. The story opens with Arthur, the son of a railway director, catching one of his father's trains back to London after the holidays. Arthur is welcomed by the train's guard, "our old servant Bob," who shortly thereafter is entrusted with the care of Polly, a young woman heading home to Hexton. The journey is interrupted by a snowstorm, and Bob initially occupies himself with "assuring the excited crowd at the station that somehow from somewhere a mythical 'pilot' would come to their rescue." In other words, he first takes on the emotional labor of calming anxious passengers' nerves. Upon returning to the train, Arthur reminds the guard of Polly, which provokes Bob to "clap his hand to his head, as though a sudden sense of care and responsibility had perplexed him." Bob's regard for Polly materializes here as a sudden shock, unmediated by conscious reflection. The two men then locate Polly, who announces that she would like to brave the elements and walk the remaining three miles to her family home. Bob, of course, cannot accompany her on this journey, but, in a remarkable passage, the guard vouches for the younger Arthur. He insists: "If you trust Master Arthur, you trust Bob Martin; and if you trust Bob Martin, you trusts Master Arthur's father, the very best master ever servant had in all Northshire; by whose favor ... said Bob holds his present responsible situation, miss.'" Arthur observes, "This long speech seemed to satisfy, as it certainly somewhat amazed, the young lady; so trusting in the good faith of the guard, passenger, and passenger's father, thus incorporated in my person, she began to prepare herself for the walk." Bob's speech "incorporates" the father's simultaneously *paternal* and *executive* trustworthiness into the body of his son. The economy of trust thus instituted not only authorizes the son but also configures the railway company as a harmonious system in which the benevolent paternalism shown by the director toward his subordinates is echoed in the paternal care shown by servants toward passengers.

Up to now, we have considered a series of literary sources in which the figure of the paternal rail worker appears. We have seen how the association of railway labor with paternal regard meshed with various imperatives of governance and accumulation at the mid-century. The paternal rail worker appeared in texts that cast working-class subjects as morally responsible for preventing and managing the effects of accidental injury, in texts that portrayed workers as insensitive to pain or that downplayed the cognitive capacities required of such workers, and in texts that extolled the benevolent paternalism of railway managers. But members of working-class railway communities also adapted this trope to their own ends. When those involved in railway labor portrayed the care they showed toward passengers as a paternal sort of regard, they often did so in order to emphasize the emotional toll, or impossible burdens of responsibility, imposed by railway labor.

One source that emerges from working-class railway communities is the aforementioned *Life of Roger Langdon*. Roger Langdon worked from the 1860s through the 1880s as a stationmaster in Silverton, a small town in Devon. During this time, Langdon also pursued an amateur passion for astronomy. The book that recounts his life includes a preface by Henry Lambert, who was the son of the general manager of the GWR; the memoirs of Roger himself; reprints of Roger's astronomical writings; and supplementary writings by Ellen Langdon, the stationmaster's daughter. *The Life* suggests that Langdon related to his passengers in ways that paralleled the care he showed for his children. As noted above, this parallel comes into focus through Ellen's supplementary remarks, which describe the shock her parents experienced at the accidental deaths of her brother and of a passenger at the Silverton station. The narrative implies that Roger Langdon's stargazing enabled him indirectly to process these shocking losses. The association between grief and stargazing is established early in the memoir, when Roger recalls how, upon the childhood death of his sister, he began looking for her face in the night sky. After his eldest son is killed at the station in 1869, Roger pours himself into the construction of a more powerful telescope, which he subsequently uses to follow the transit of Venus. *The Life* reprints verbatim the daily observations Roger made of this celestial event: "On May 1, 1871 ... Her shape was that of the moon when a little more than half full. distinctly saw a dull, cloudy-looking mark along her bright limb, curving round parallel to it, and extending nearly across the disc, each end terminating in a point; joining this at the eastern extremity was another and darker mark of a club shape, its small end joining the point of the mark previously described. I watched these marks for half an hour...."[62]

Langdon's daily notes, including this one, render Venus as an uncanny surface. A similarly unsettling portrayal of a celestial body appears as well in Langdon's imaginative epistle, "A Letter from the Man on the Moon," originally published in the *Exe Valley Magazine*:

> [Y]ou may safely consider the whole mass of the moon to be a huge, exhausted, burnt-out cindar.... [H]ere in the moon we have no such thing as an atmosphere: we therefore have neither clouds nor rain, nor frost nor snow; and in the words of the poet—
>
> *Here are no storms, no noise,*
> *But silence and eternal sleep.*
> *All here is as quiet and silent as the grave.*[63]

The quotation is drawn from Shakespeare's *Titus Andronicus*, a play that engages thematically with the question of a father's responsibility for the deaths of his children. The quotation enables Langdon to draw an association between the stillness of the moon and the silence of the grave—an associative chain that suggests Langdon's contemplation of celestial bodies may have offered him an indirect means for processing his intimate losses, including those for which he may have felt responsible.

The theme of failed paternal responsibility cuts across other, contemporaneous rail workers' writings. The anonymous author of an 1873 pamphlet, for example, attempts to generate outrage about workers' long hours by invoking their paternal role, describing a fellow-servant who had not seen his children for months on end except when the kids were asleep, observing that "the poet sings of Britannia, that 'her home is on the deep.' There can be no mistake as to where this man's home was—on the *chemin de fer*."[64] A similar move is made in the 1889 melodramatic novel entitled, *Railway Life behind the Curtain*, which depicts an engine driver sacrificing himself to save his passengers. The novel implies that, while this worker dramatically failed in his paternal responsibility toward his wife and child—who themselves subsequently perish in a fit of shock—he perhaps fulfilled this responsibility in another, parallel, sphere, by giving up his life for the sake of his passengers.[65] The family tragedy is witnessed by the novel's narrator, a single man who made a habit of boarding with the ill-fated railway family.

In contrast to this trade unionist novel and to the other workers' writings we've considered, which emphasized the impossible burdens of care imposed on railway workers, an 1889 short story published in the *Railway Service Gazette* entitled "Kitty's Sketches" invokes the trope of the paternal railway worker in a way meant to provoke critical self-reflection amongst workers. The story, written by Emma Finniswood, describes how a guard took care of the recently orphaned Kitty:[66] "The guard was so sorry for me and so good," Kitty recounts. "He told me lots of things, all about his wife and children. He said he had got a little Kitty of his own."[67] Here, the guard cares for the orphaned passenger by invoking his domestic attachments, drawing a connection between Kitty and his daughter. The railway worker thus brings on board his domestic identities, assuming a paternal role in relation to his vulnerable passenger. This idealized worker who cares for Kitty by invoking his domestic relations serves as a foil for a series of negative portraits of railway workers. In the story, Sophie recounts her experiences with a number of railwaymen, reserving her most strident criticisms for a stationmaster named "Doubleface of Goneby," who made Sophie "'creep,' as we say of our involuntary shrinkings from evil things." This creepy worker "fawned and cringed" over Sophie in a way that set her "very teeth on edge."[68] Here, the text invokes the threat of sexual violence, calling attention to the experiences of women travelers faced with predatory workers and fellow passengers. "Kitty's Sketches" thus makes explicit a threat that remained merely subtextual within the story "Snowed Up." There, Bob's speech, which invested Arthur with a kernel of paternal responsibility, was said to have reassured Polly that she would be safe traveling with the young man. In a similar rhetorical move, "Kitty's Sketches" contrasts an idealized paternal worker with a threatening worker. But Finniswood's story is notable as well for how it establishes this contrast by deploying an orientalist trope: "'Bless the man! How his back must ache!' cried her somewhat abrupt ladyship one afternoon, when Mr. Doubleface had bowed and smirked like a gutta-percha Mandarin for five consecutive minutes at the door of the Hauteville carriage." Here, sexual violence is imaginatively distanced from British masculinity, as Doubleface's creepiness comes into focus as a stereotype of East Asian masculinity. Anti-Asian tropes such as we read here were not uncommon in the *Railway Service Gazette*, which in an 1878 editorial endorsed Chinese exclusion acts in the US, justifying them in part on the racist grounds that Chinese workers were purportedly skilled at imitation and thus untrustworthy.[69] In the section to follow, we will see how the *Railway Service Gazette* served as a medium for the circulation of white supremacist perspectives and thus contributed to the making of what Jonathan Hyslop has characterized as a cross-imperial project of *white laborism*.[70] By publishing letters from British labor migrants employed in colonial territories, the *Gazette* hosted arguments in favor of the hardening of racially exclusionary labor regimes—arguments that bolstered practical campaigns waged to this effect by the ASRS in India and by other newly formed white laborist associations of transit workers.

THE ASRS IN INDIA AND THE RACIALIZATION OF PATERNAL RESPONSIBILITY

On 16 May 1879, the *Railway Service Gazette* published a letter on behalf of the Battersea branch secretary of the ASRS. The letter had been written by "J. W.," a former South London railwayman who had emigrated to Osaka for work on the recently constructed Imperial Japanese Government Railways. In his report from abroad, J. W. described recent negotiations he had led on behalf of his fellow labor migrants, explaining that he had gained the trust and "hearty thanks" of his mates when he refused to cover for a certain supervisor who had been training Japanese men as firemen and drivers. When asked by this supervisor to obscure a locomotive's late arrival to Kyoto, J. W. refused, noting: "I have been anxiously waiting for the opportunity of putting a stop to their driving." In "consequence" of his refusal, the drivers and firemen of Japanese descent who had been working this and other trains "were reduced to cleaners." Our writer went on to summarize the petitions he had subsequently composed for his fellow expatriates, including on matters of hours and overtime pay, dubiously implying that their demands had become possible following the establishment of a racial bar against the promotion of Japanese men to the roles of driver and fireman. Finally he wound down his commentary, first by asking the Battersea secretary to send him a few copies of the *Railway Service Gazette* and then by warning British railwaymen only to take positions overseas when these were accompanied by a written labor contract: "I consider it a scandalous shame that they should get men to come out here without singing [sic] an agreement in England, if they do they will do just as they like with them when they get them here."[71]

J. W.'s insistence that readers of the *Railway Service Gazette* should avoid taking a job overseas in the absence of a formal agreement likely would have seemed sensible to such men, given that written agreements had become a standard feature of employment on some of the more prominent railways in colonial territories. For British labor migrants entering into employment with the East Indian Railway, for example, the signing of such labor agreements was, by the 1870s, a well-established practice. Railwaymen bound for Howrah typically signed agreements in London following their written correspondence with a recruitment agent. In September 1861, Thomas Robertson, a platelayer based in the northern town of Wakefield, received a letter from Mr. Rendel, a Westminster-based recruiter for the East Indian Railway Company. The letter informed Thomas that Mr. Rendel could offer him a four-year appointment as platelayer for the EIR at a rate of four pounds per week.[72] The appointment, to which Thomas had applied in July, was "dependent on [his] passing the medical examination of the company physician in London." The letter continued, "Therefore if you accept the above terms, it will be advisable for you to consult your own doctor as to your suitability for the climate of India, so as to run as little risk as possible of rejection in London."[73] Shortly thereafter, Thomas received a follow-up appointment letter from the East Indian Railway House, based in the City of London, which indicated that he was to be on the steamer leaving Southampton on 4 October and that he should "attend to these offices a few days before that time to sign [his] agreement." These two extant letters, which Thomas Robertson received from the EIR recruiter and then from the company's London-based secretary, illustrate that the hiring of metropolitan railway workers was typically carried out in a relatively impersonal manner. A recruiter would place advertisements in national periodicals and an interested railwayman would write to the recruiter's office; the former would then fill out an application form, and finally—upon receiving confirmation of his appointment—this budding footplateman of empire would set off for London to sign an employment agreement. Prior to his arrival on the subcontinent, then, a British labor migrant's interactions with company officials and recruiters were almost entirely mediated by written documents. While the written agreements these railwaymen signed would become more elaborate in the sixty years between 1860 and 1920, the mechanics of their recruitment would remain remarkably static.

To illustrate this continuity, we can consider how British railwaymen were recruited to colonial India in the wake of the Great War. In 1919, as a result of wartime dislocations, the managers of various Indian railways confronted significant labor shortages. In attempting to fill their higher-grade, supervisory roles—especially various foreman roles in locomotive and carriage workshops—such managers looked to the metropole. Under the auspices of the Railway Department, a number of railway agents coordinated to again employ a Mr. Rendel of Westminster, who was working in partnership with two other recruiters. These three recruiters—Messrs. Rendel, Palmer, and Triton—placed a listing that advertised more than a dozen foreman jobs in the following British periodicals: "Times; People; Engineering; Daily Chronicle; The Engineer; Manchester Guardian; Railway Gazette; Birmingham Daily Post."[74] Their advertisement instructed interested railwaymen to include the following information in their initial letter: "age, whether married (if so, what family) or single, and full particulars of career, with dates and names of firms by whom employed to present time." As we have seen in previous chapters, the information requested here implied both an imbrication of workplace and familial roles, as well as governing technologies that transected domestic and work spheres. A railwayman's employment history—the arc of his career—when considered in conjunction with his current family situation, apparently offered prospective employers enough of an outline of the man to help them determine his employability. For the workshop foremen hired in 1919, the recruiters' request for the "full particulars of career" made a certain amount of sense, given that men working in, or interested in being promoted to, the role of foreman necessarily already would have advanced beyond entry-level roles in metropolitan workshops. For many metropolitan workers who took jobs on colonial Indian railways between 1860 and 1920, however, the move to the subcontinent was precisely what enabled them to get promoted out of entry-level roles or to move smoothly along a career track that may have been blocked up in the metropole.

In his quantitative study of early railway careers on the Great Western Railway in Britain, Mike Savage found that, in the 1850s, promotion from locomotive cleaner to driver generally took a decade (mean: 11 years; median: 7.5 years; n: 8). Between the 1850s and 1910s, this measure of time doubled to two decades (mean: 20.9 years; median: 21 years; n: 38), rising more-or-less steadily over this sixty-year period.[75] In contrast, I have found that for British locomotive cleaners who signed contracts with the EIR or with the Great Indian Peninsular Railway, advancement to driver appears to have remained a mere decade-long affair up into the twentieth century. Labor migrants with only entry-level experience in Britain were able to sign four-year contracts to serve as firemen with the EIR or GIPR. These contracts, hundreds of which are extant, detailed terms of service, dates of embarkation, wage rates, obligatory benefit funds, and options for remitting money to family members "back home."[76] Between the 1870s and 1900s, those who signed such contracts generally had worked previously on the railways in Britain for only a few years (mean: 3.5 years; median: 4 years; n: 11). At the conclusion of their four-year contracts as firemen, such workers had the opportunity to ascend to the rank of driver, making for significantly accelerated career trajectories vis-à-vis their coworkers in the metropole.[77]

The accelerated pace of promotion for British labor migrants was an effect, in large part, of racial divisions of labor on colonial Indian railways. Up through the interwar period, Indian workers found it difficult, if not impossible, to advance to driver, passenger guard, foreman, or other higher-grade roles, a bar to advancement that, in turn, opened up for British labor migrants enviable career tracks.[78] In his 1934 memoir, John Mitchell, a traffic supervisor on the Bengal-Nagpur railway, notes that, "the Conductor Guards on the Bengal-Nagpur mail trains were usually Englishmen; on the freight and coal trains the guards were Anglo-Indians or Indians."[79] As this quote suggests, racial employment barriers were neither absolute nor inflexible: Superintendents of various departments were empowered to exercise discretion in determining where exactly to place the racial bar to advancement, and this bar generally inched up the career ladder over time. Regardless of where a given bar was set, however, patterns of promotion on colonial Indian railways—like payscales, housing arrangements, and state investments in employees' social reproduction—systematically privileged workers of European descent.[80] As we have seen, this racially hierarchizing labor regime was overdetermined. In part, it followed from colonial administrators' perceptions that railways were key infrastructures of imperial power and that employees of European descent were more reliable agents of repression. This view was encoded in the cliché, repeated by British colonial officials and labor migrants alike, that Indian railway workers generally lacked the responsibility and masculine character traits required to respond effectively to emergencies on the lines—traits presumed to be exhibited by workers of European descent.[81] In line with their purportedly responsible nature, British labor migrants—including engine drivers, station masters, and passenger guards—were deputized by the colonial state, armed, and encouraged to participate in volunteering regiments. By essentially reserving higher-grade roles for workers of European descent, deputizing them, and subsidizing their social reproduction in segregated railway colonies, colonial administrators aimed to cultivate and maintain a loyal force of imperial repression, capable of acting to restore a violent colonial order in moments both of social unrest and of technological breakdown.[82]

While racial hierarchies of employment thus were imposed from above, they were also bolstered through the practices of British labor migrants themselves. In 1871, EIR managers floated a proposal to train greater numbers of Indian men as shunters, drivers, and guards in order to reduce the company's labor costs.[83] To defend their privileged labor market position, a group of British railwaymen organized against the proposal, remaking existing benefit societies into a white laborist trade union, the Amalgamated Society of Railway Servants of India (ASRSI). This initial 1870s iteration of ASRSI was riven by leadership disputes and financial troubles, and the union ultimately fell apart in 1878, having only incompletely realized its exclusionary agenda.[84] Before we consider in more detail the rhetoric and practices of ASRSI organizers between 1874 and 1878, it is worth explaining the EIR proposal against which they were reacting. EIR managers' partially successful plan to adjust the racial bar to promotion in their locomotive and traffic departments emerged from a process of accounting and deliberation initiated by the Public Works Department. In 1870, the PWD solicited quantitative information from the various railway agents of colonial India. In particular, they were curious

TABLE 1. "EUROPEAN AND EAST INDIAN" MEN EMPLOYED BY EIR DEPARTMENTS

	Locomotive	Carriage	Traffic
1870[a]	819	128	518
1888[b]	558	132	599

[a] IOR/L/PWD/3/72, "Mayo et al, Letter to the Duke of Argyll, Secretary of State for India, dated 6th January 1871." Data from 30 September 1870.
[b] EIRC, *EIR Alphabetical List of Europeans and East Indians in the Company's Service* (EIRC Press, Calcutta, 31 December 1888).

about the overall number of "Europeans and East Indians" employed in the different departments of the rail companies under their jurisdiction. (For these numbers, see table 1.) They were also interested in determining how many of these railwaymen were "dismissed for some fault" annually and, within this group, how many had originally been "engaged in England." Given the significant labor cost discrepancies between the three groups implicitly differentiated through this inquiry—namely, 1) British labor migrants, 2) British or Anglo-Indian men hired on the subcontinent, and 3) Indian men whose colonial status as "natives" rendered them ineligible for residence in railway colonies—the Public Works Department's accounting here seems to have been motivated by a desire to determine how labor cost savings might "responsibly" be pursued. What they found, among other things, was that the EIR locomotive department, which employed 819 "Europeans and East Indians," far outstripped in this metric any other railway departments under the PWD's jurisdiction.[85] The colonial state's process of accounting and implicit comparison thus seems to have made visible the anomaly of the EIR locomotive department, and in this way to have spurred EIR managers' 1871 proposal to train more Indian men as shunters, drivers, and guards (the latter group, to be clear, would have been employed in the traffic department). By comparing the results of this 1870 audit with EIR employment lists from 1888, we can see that, while the proposal to employ more Indian men as guards seems to have been stymied, some progress along these lines ultimately was made in the locomotive department.[86]

This quantitative accounting helps illustrate the uneven effects of ASRSI's campaigns in defense of racial hierarchy along the lines. ASRSI organizers tended to argue for the maintenance of white supremacist labor regimes by advancing a racialized rhetoric of paternal responsibility—a rhetoric that seems to have made more headway in relation to the public-facing roles of guard and stationmaster, while making less headway for the roles of driver and shunter, involving as they did technical operations carried out in relative isolation on the footplate.[87]

In an 1879 *Fortnightly Review* article on trade unionism in India, William Trant issued a postmortem of sorts on the short-lived ASRSI. Trant, a British trade unionist who recently had spent time with Bombay-based labor organizers, was especially critical of ASRSI's white laborist orientation. The organizers of the union, he observed:

> imagine that it is a monstrous injustice that a dark skin should be allowed to compete, and perhaps rival, the pale-faced race.... Eurasians, half-castes, country-born people, and "poor whites," as a certain class are called, were already employed in considerable numbers, and the Society considered these would be an acquisition to the society, especially as it is sometimes difficult to draw the line of nationality; and especially, too, as they have not that antipathy to a community from which many of them have taken their wives. There was, therefore, no objection to those whom, to avoid using names that are not pleasant to them, they called "Christian," and admitted them within their ranks; but no Parsee, Hindoo, or Mahomedan could join their union.[88]

This passage from Trant's postmortem suggests that ASRSI leaders formulated their racially exclusionary membership policies in large part on the basis of existing divisions of labor, patterns of residential segregation, and dynamics of family formation along the lines. While Trant not implausibly frames the union's religious bar to membership as a matter of euphemistic disavowal—to say "Christian" is "to avoid using names that are not pleasant to them"[89]—we can perhaps elucidate a bit further the social significance of the union's religious basis for membership. Christian churches were fixtures of segregated railway colonies. These institutions, which usually were company approved though not directly company funded, played an integral role in the prefabricated coming-of-age journeys described in chapter 2. We will recall that, when an apprentice was promoted to a higher-grade role, he could choose either to make a marriage proposal or to cohabit with a coworker. If he opted for the former path, he and his fiancée typically would be married at one of the rail colony's churches, before moving together into their new company bungalow. Marriage rituals thus helped mark the life transitions British and Anglo-Indian railwaymen undertook in overlapping workplace and domestic spheres. By tying union membership to Christian identity then, ASRSI organizers evoked prospective members' affectively freighted transitions to adulthood, implying that the union would defend railwaymen's interests not only as workers but also as husbands, fathers, and leaseholders in railway colonies. In line with this interpretation, ASRSI leaders made the case for the union by invoking in sometimes hyperbolic ways racialized notions of paternal responsibility.

The union's secretary and most prominent spokesperson was an Allahabad-based engine-driver named F. T. Atkins. Prior to sharing quotations from some of Atkins's more inflammatory circulars, William Trant recounted how this engine-driver rose to prominence by leading an 1874 campaign among fellow locomotive department employees against wage cuts and the lengthening of the working day.[90] To help coordinate and formalize the campaign, Atkins and his fellow organizers founded ASRSI.[91] Later that year, the nascent union broadened its geographical base when an association of Bombay-based railwaymen joined up in the midst of their own dispute with GIPR managers. Then, in order to bolster the financial standing of the union, Atkins endeavored to incorporate two existing benefit societies—the East Indian Society and a branch of the Locomotive Steam Enginemen and Fireman's Society—whose capital accounts were funneled into ASRSI's newly formed benefit funds. Trant believed that these cobbled together benefit funds rested on shaky foundations, as "no actuary was consulted, and the tables of fees, &c, were compiled by the rudest rule of thumb, chiefly from comparison with other tables referring to totally different circumstances. . . . [T]he Society did not live long enough to be appreciably affected by this basis of ultimate insolvency."[92] As ASRSI began to fracture in the late-1870s and as its secretary's leadership position increasingly came under pressure, Atkins took to composing hyperbolic circulars, including a strike appeal to his fellow residents of railway colonies pitched in a grim rhetoric of paternal obligation:

> Are you prepared . . . to look forward with almost absolute certainty to the knowledge, that when you are gone to your long rest, these little links that rivet all your affection in that centre home will lose all that buoyancy of spirits, that little sparking eye will lose its brilliancy, those little limbs will lose their roundness, that cheerful smiling face will become sad—and that shrunken little form, those pinched and sharp features, the result of want, gaunt want and poverty, will constitute a deep but lasting reproach against you. Oh fathers, look on your little ones, and in your mind's eye conjure up the truthful picture I have drawn.[93]

Here, Atkins deploys the figure of the impoverished child to make vivid for his readers a bleak historical outlook—an outlook that we could characterize as the pessimism of the racially privileged. Through the circular, Atkins attempts to activate in his presumed-to-be-paternal readers a fear that, absent collective action, the racially hierarchizing labor regimes that underwrite their cloistered middle-class existences ultimately would evaporate. An anonymous editorial published around the same time in the *Indian Railway Service Gazette* offers a similarly fearful vision, this time attempting to rouse anxious, racially privileged fathers by invoking both their familial and laboring responsibilities:

> What, does he mean to say, the very men on whose attention, diligence, and foresight the lives of thousands depend, that they are inattentive? The response is: Yes! Perhaps not to their duty; but to their interests, the present and future welfare of their families and children. But are not railway men generally kind fathers and attentive to their children's welfare? Yes, but unfortunately, only to a certain extent. Nearly every railway man will acknowledge the force of unity, but how few will endeavor to practice it? Every one complains of the dark prospect the future presents; but how few attempt to remedy it?[94]

Here again, the reader's presumed experience of fatherhood is evoked in order to draw a bridge not only between the present and the future but also between discrepant levels of historical experience. Railwaymen's quotidian experiences of work and family life were imaginatively linked through such invocations to broader historical and political vistas. Our anonymous editorialist hoped to convince his readers that a more muscular practice of paternal responsibility in the present could potentially clear up their purportedly gloomy political futures. Of course, this linkage between present action and future effect could only ever be a matter of fictional projection. But such was the grotesque fiction of white laborism—a project that worked to activate the anxieties of racially privileged railwaymen and to propel them "as fathers" into collective action in defense of racially hierarchizing regimes of labor in colonial India. While white laborism would persist well into the twentieth century, we can close the chapter by noting that Atkins's circulars and anonymously written editorials seem to have been viewed by most of his readers as unhinged rantings rather than as compelling calls to arms. ASRSI collapsed under the weight of its various contradictions in 1878. In the chapters to follow, we will see how other organs of collective action, some oriented toward more emancipatory futures, ultimately would win adherents in the years to follow. While the ASRSI was eventually refounded in 1897 and maintained a white laborist basis into the first years of the twentieth century by excluding "menials" from membership,[95] collective organizations of Indian signal operators were also built around the turn of the century and, through advocacy and strike action, began to chip away at the racially hierarchizing labor regimes of colonial India.

PART THREE

Mass Movements and the Making of Social Liberalism, 1890s–1910s

CHAPTER 4

Laboring behind the Curtain

Industrial Unionism and Social Liberal Governance in Britain

On 8 May 1913, W. J. R. Squance composed a letter to the British Board of Trade. Writing on behalf of engine drivers and firemen employed at the locomotive depot in Llanelly, Squance challenged the exclusion of these footplatemen from the government's conciliation scheme, which provided a mechanism for resolving disputes between labor and management. According to the terms of this scheme, railwaymen "concerned in the manipulation of traffic" had recourse to a conciliation board, but employees not so concerned—like those at the depot who drove freight from the docks to the main line—fell outside the board's jurisdiction. "Other grades now enjoy an eight-hour day by virtue of the movements performed while on duty," Squance noted, "while we, who are directly responsible for the possibility of these movements are debarred from enjoying this condition of service."[1] A similar letter of protest was written the previous year by Charles Humphries and Leonard Horne on behalf of Swindon-based shunters, who also did not have access to a conciliation board as they fell outside the so-called conciliation grades. Humphries and Horne's 1912 letter illuminates how Swindon's shunters understood their role vis-à-vis drivers of passenger trains: "We are all under one Superintendent, and one Foreman in the running department and paid at the Engine Shed, and supplied with uniform, book of rules and appendices and sign for all circulars, and allowed annual leave similar to the traffic Dept and are subject to the periodical eyesight test. We contend we are all engaged in the manipulation of the traffic, having therefore a desire to come under the conciliation scheme."² We, too, are members of the uniformed working class, our letter writers insist; we, too, are subject to the work discipline of those much-lauded guards and drivers of passenger trains. On the one hand, these letters were written with reference to the specific terms governing railway conciliation boards. But then, these terms, which spoke of men "concerned in the manipulation of traffic," echoed longstanding hierarchies within the industry—hierarchies that had also informed early railway trade unionism.

In the previous chapter, we considered the cultural construct of the paternal railwayman. This figure, less brittle in Britain than in colonial India, was associated with uniformed, respectable, and *public-facing* roles on the railway. Emma Finniswood's caring passenger guard, Ellen Langdon's paternal stationmaster, and J. Leahcimrac's self-sacrificial driver exemplified the type. Broadly speaking, higher-grade, public-facing railwaymen—the sorts who could appear as father-figures vis-à-vis passengers and who first would be classed as conciliation grade employees—had founded the Amalgamated Society of Railway Servants in the 1870s. In the union's early propaganda, workers' purportedly shared interests with the traveling public, and paternal regard for the public featured prominently. But given that the social base of railway unionism broadened around the turn of the century as lower-grade employees and those who labored "behind the curtain" joined trade unions, the terms by which unionists appealed for recognition and redress necessarily evolved. As the letters above suggest though, this evolution did not involve the displacement of guards and drivers from their elevated role in unionist discourse. Rather, as the curtain was drawn back, these exemplary, public-facing paternal railwaymen came to be surrounded by a wider chorus of railway laborers.³ The enduring prominence of the paternal railwayman in unionist discourse mattered politically, as did unionists' increasing focus on those behind the curtain. As we will see, the complex combination of these at once rhetorical and organizing tendencies helped orient the politics of railway labor during the volatile and transformative two-and-a-half decades from 1889 through 1914.

Beginning in 1889, industrial unionism began to remake previously established forms of craft unionism in the railway sector. The General Railway Workers' Union (GRWU) was formed in 1889, prompting the ASRS to recruit more actively among lower-grade line and workshop employees—recruitment drives often associated with "all-grades movements." As company-operated internal labor markets slowed down around the turn of the century—meaning that engine cleaners and porters, for example, had more dubious prospects of being promoted—railwaymen of various grades embraced industrial militancy. In 1900, a cross-section of workers on the Taff Vale Railway in South Wales struck for higher wages and union recognition, winning none of their demands. During this short-lived strike, the company sued the ASRS for damages and won, first in court and then in a decision by the House of Lords. The Taff Vale decision, which marked a nadir of post-1867 labor rights in Britain, spurred the growth in membership of the Labour Representation Committee, which in turn helped prepare the ground for the 1906 parliamentary breakthrough for Labour. The era of social liberalism that followed saw a significant restructuring of labor relations on the railways, as labor-management conciliation boards were established by the Board of Trade in 1907. These boards at once facilitated the organization of new layers of rail workers, as implied by some of the sources we've already considered, while at the same time spurring challenges from below by syndicalist militants who saw participation in the boards as tantamount to class collaboration. Both the national railway strike of 1911, which featured mass pickets and other tactics characteristic of syndicalist militancy, and the establishment in the same year of the National Insurance Act gave impetus to industrial unionism in the railway sector. In 1913, three unions—the ASRS, the GRWU, and the United Pointsmen and Signalmen's Society—combined to establish the National Union of Railwaymen, a more properly industrial union representing British railway workers of various grades. In what follows, we will traverse this history, attending to the ways that social, political, and cultural transformations combined to help recompose railway labor in the years leading up to the Great War.

ALL-GRADES UNIONISM AND THE GENDERING OF RAILWAY LABOR

In 1889, J. Leahcimrac authored a semifictional work about railway life and labor, entitled *John Ingram: Or, Railway Life behind the Curtain*.[4] In the previous chapter, we considered the tragic climax of this book, wherein an engine driver's self-sacrificial act was followed by the deaths of his wife and young child. In what follows, we will consider *John Ingram* in a more rounded way, showing how this trade unionist text mapped railway life and labor, while also highlighting some of the tensions of the text—tensions that reflect and anticipate the competing impulses of "all-grades" unionism. The tragic loss of life that forms the book's dramatic crux was witnessed by John Ingram, the eponymous protagonist of the book. Ingram was boarding with the engine driver's family at the time, so he was present when the driver's lifeless body was brought back to his company-owned flat. This was the third occasion in the book when Ingram lived as a boarder; the first two were during his apprenticeship to become a signalman. In this earlier section, the book's omniscient narrator described the signalman's role in the following terms:

> What with attending to signals, and marking in a book the time that each train and engine passes his cabin, he has scarcely a minute that he can call his own. No meal hours for him; his food has just to be gulped down while he works; and his mind is always on the tension in fear of mistakes, for the pulling of a wrong handle, or the giving of a wrong signal, may cause a catastrophe, horrible even to contemplate. And yet there he is, day after day; and as the passengers, perhaps, give him a casual glance as they go careering past, very few, if any, ever think that their lives and limbs are in his hand. No. Sometimes he is looked on as if he was some needless ornament set up, or some uncouth watch, more to be laughed at than honoured. But these are the men who should be respected. Take the word of one who knows, and give those men who guide the traffic of the railway all due regard. These are they who make railway travelling so safe and punctual.[5]

Here the narrative voice breaks, revealing a certain familiarity with railway labor that, while implicit throughout *John Ingram*, is not elsewhere so baldly claimed. Moreover, this passage thematizes a structural aspect of the narrative—namely, its interest in traversing the line between public-facing and relatively invisible railway labors. The signalman is, in a sense, halfway behind the curtain, subject to little more than a "casual glance" by most members of the traveling public. How such imagined travelers are said to see the signalman is significant as well. Rather than respected like a father figure, the signalman purportedly is seen as an "ornament" or "uncouth watch"—more akin to a rough gargoyle than to a carefully wrought statue of Joseph. And yet, the signalman holds the lives of passengers in his hands and bears the weight of this responsibility in his mind. He should thus be seen as respectable and caring to the same degree as a passenger guard or driver.

In his 1980, *The Railway Workers*, Frank McKenna devotes a section to early signalmen, highlighting some of the imputed traits and cultural associations that attached to those who occupied this role. He notes that "the signalman was a creature apart." They were characterized by a fastidiousness on duty. They developed an intricate, "special language of bell codes which eliminated evesdroppers." They maintained a dictum: "If you are unmarried when you take over a box, chances are you will never marry."⁶ In other words, within the railway world, the role of signalman was associated with a certain buttoned-up bachelorhood. Given this association, *John Ingram*'s sympathetic treatment of signalmen can begin to be read for the ways it pushed against otherwise hierarchizing gender discourses of railway labor. Rather than serving as a marginal character to be half-disregarded if not made a figure of fun, the signalman appears in the narrative as an exemplary, caring railwayman, and—perhaps more importantly—as the vehicle for critical knowledge about the railway system. Ingram himself began his career as a signalman before taking a brief reprieve from the service. He then reentered the service as a booking clerk, before being promoted to stationmaster—a role into which "so much work of various grades [had been] amalgamated."⁷ For nearly the entire narrative, Ingram was a bachelor, bouncing around between different boarding arrangements, including at one point boarding with a widow. This mobility, which, as we saw in chapter 1, was characteristic of the experience of early railway bachelors, allowed Ingram—and, by extension, the reader—to view in intimate detail various scenes of railway labor and domestic life. Bachelorhood thus was integrally related to the form of the narrative—a narrative that enabled an elaborate cognitive mapping of the railway system. *John Ingram*'s map outlined the common subjection of railwaymen to the arbitrary authority of managers and to dangerous working conditions in the shadow of deadly infrastructures, orienting the reader toward social democratic and trade unionist politics.

While Ingram moved across much of the narrative as a bachelor, *John Ingram* advanced throughout a marriage plot. The text describes a romance between John and Annie that finally resulted in their marriage during the narrative's closing scenes. Annie is introduced following the death of her mother, to which Annie responds by valiantly bearing up and supporting her siblings—a characterization akin to that of Miss Jessie in Gaskell's *Cranford*. One of the scenes that offered a preview of their married life occurred during John's period of service as a booking clerk. While Annie was occupied with other work, John took care of her younger brother Willie, even though technically John was on the clock at the time. A rival in the service threatened to report him and then later contrived to have him fired, before himself being badly injured in a railway accident. That John cared in a paternal way for Willie and that his detractors in the service were prevented by accident—a kind of deus ex machina—from testifying against him solidifies John's moral standing and foreshadows his status as husband and father. Even though for much of the narrative John moves as a bachelor, he is imbued throughout with the aura of the paternal railwayman. We can thus begin to see how *John Ingram* anticipates some of the tensions of all-grades unionism. Even as the book focuses throughout on the lives of bachelor railwaymen who labor at least partially "behind the curtain," the narrative *orientation* of Ingram's life is toward marriage and toward the higher-grade, public-facing role of station master. In this sense, the book continues to center the figure of the paternal railwayman even as it pushes beyond the bounds of this figure, bringing onto stage a wide array of railway workers, including lower-grade workers and those whose lives cut across the edges of the domestic norm. Something of this double movement would animate the politics of all-grades unionism in the decades following the 1889 publication of *John Ingram*.

That same year, 1889, was the year of the famous London dockworkers' strike, which signaled the turn to industrial or "new" unionism in Britain. During the years that followed, unionists increasingly worked to organize all employees within a given industry, including those in marginal or entry level roles. On the railways, new unionism emerged first through the establishment in 1889 of the General Railway Workers' Union (GRWU) and then through a reorientation—under the pressure presented by this general union—of existing craft unions, above all the ASRS. As Philip Bagwell notes, the GRWU initially found centers of strength among porters and workshop employees—groups that had been relatively underorganized by the ASRS. The first edition of the GRWU's journal, *The Railway Express*, published in October 1890, described mass meetings in workshop towns, including a meeting in Swindon headed by noted social democratic agitator, John Burns.[8] Burns shared a platform with leaders from the GRWU and the ASRS, demonstrating that these two unions were jockeying for support among at least partially overlapping memberships. The GRWU had some advantages in recruiting among entry-level employees. In 1889, the ASRS Congress had contemplated a more affordable, three-pence-per-week membership level but ultimately decided against this change. That same year the GRWU formed, offering union membership at this same, more affordable level. GRWU leaders further sought to differentiate their union from the ASRS by putting members' dues solely into a strike fund rather than into union-operated benefit funds as well.[9] While thus eschewing benefit funds, GRWU leaders nevertheless framed their organizing in terms of the breadwinner ideal and the protection of railway families.[10] Reciprocally, ASRS leaders refashioned themselves at this time as fighting unionists rather than primarily as operators of benefit funds—a rhetorical shift partially belied by the fact that their Orphans' Fund expanded over the early 1890s more quickly than it had over the 1880s.[11]

During the strike wave of 1890, ASRS and GRWU leaders worked to demonstrate their support for industrial action when and where workers moved toward militancy.[12] Centers of union organizing and strike activity at the time included Ireland, Scotland, South Wales, and the Northeast of England. In some of these locales, striking workers compelled directors to negotiate with representatives of the ASRS and the GRWU, while in others, directors were able to deflect demands for reform to upper managers, who set terms of employment on a grade-by-grade basis. During an 1890 strike in Scotland, the directors of the Caledonian successfully evicted a number of railway families from company-owned housing, even in the face of mass action to prevent the evictions.[13] This strike in Scotland was one of the less successful from this 1890 strike wave, in part due to the relatively limited participation of most grades of railwaymen. As Bagwell notes, "the strike was virtually confined to the goods guards, drivers, firemen, signalmen and examiners."[14] Even in some of the more militant regions of Britain then, the dawn of "new" unionism did not immediately break through the grade-based limits of craft unionism.

Between 1890 and 1906, there were three periods of particularly intense organizing on the part of railway unionists—periods when "movements" of particular grades were subsumed into all-grades movements. These periods of activity occurred in 1890, 1897, and 1906. Unlike the Associated Society of Locomotive Engineers and Firemen (ASLEF), founded in 1880; the United Pointsmen and Signalmen's Society, founded in 1880; and the Railway Clerks Association (RCA), founded in 1897, the ASRS and GRWU aspired to represent workers of all grades. As we have seen though, especially in the case of the larger and more prominent ASRS, this aspiration did not for some time align with the reality on the ground, and campaigns not infrequently were waged only on behalf of better-organized, higher-grade employees.[15] But particularly in the context of all-grades movements, unionists endeavored to organize workshop employees, permanent-way employees, porters, cleaners, and other "lower grade" workers, many of whom labored "behind the curtain." The 1906 "all grades" movement was particularly successful in mobilizing a wide cross section of employees toward coordinated action and culminated in a broad-based strike threat in 1907. At a mass rally in Sheffield to build for the strike, Edward Carpenter spoke to over three thousand railway workers at the invitation of C. T. Cramp, a railway unionist.[16] The union's demands included recognition, as well as national wage rates and limitations on working hours, to be applied, albeit in scaled ways, to workers across all the grades.[17] As the Fabian researchers, G. D. H. Cole and R. Page Arnot argued in 1917, "The 'all grades' movement of 1906–7 was the beginning of the revival of the ASRS."[18] On the eve of the threatened 1907 mass strike, Lloyd George's Board of Trade intervened more forcefully in the industry than it had during previous periods of militancy, establishing national conciliation boards for higher grade railway employees. These conciliation boards significantly altered the dynamics of labor-management relations along the lines, interposing the state into the relations between workers and those who governed railway enterprises.

THE SOCIAL LIBERAL TURN

To properly understand the emergence of railway conciliation boards, it will be necessary to consider in a wider frame the post-1906 period of social liberal governance in Britain. In the 1906 general election, Labour and the Liberals coordinated to avoid running candidates against each other. This coordination helped Labour to gain 29 seats, while the Liberals won 397, enough to form a government. One of the first acts of Campbell-Bannerman's government was the Trades Disputes Act of 1906. This act effectively overturned the restrictive labor rights regime set out by the 1901 Taff Vale decision, which had allowed company owners to sue unions for economic damages when union members went on strike. Perhaps more than any other single cause, the Taff Vale decision inspired working-class organizers to participate in the Labour Representation Committee (LRC)—a grouping, formed in 1900, that included representatives of the Independent Labour Party (ILP), the Social Democratic Federation (SDF), and trade unions. Organizers justifiably saw the passage of a bill through Parliament as the most plausible route to overturning the effective ban on strikes imposed by the Taff Vale decision. But even before Taff Vale, railway unionists in particular had been protagonists in the formation of the Labour Representation Committee. Frank Bealey and Henry Pelling note that "the ASRS was indeed, of all the unions of any size, by far the most enthusiastic for independent labour politics."[19] This enthusiasm was overdetermined. First, as Bealey and Pelling note, questions of railway governance had become relatively common matters of parliamentary concern, so the prospect of avoiding the parliamentary sphere altogether seemed relatively untenable. Second, the union had not yet won recognition from railway directors—a state of affairs that led some unionists to seek Board of Trade intervention during industrial disputes. While the fate of railway labor thus was substantially tied to the actions of state officials, the internal structure of the ASRS facilitated political independence, as rank-and-file workers composed the executive committee. In 1899 this leadership body, made up of workers inclined toward social democratic perspectives, insisted that the Liberal secretary of the union, Richard Bell, run for office as an independent in the railway town of Derby.[20] Independent labor politics thus emerged from rank-and-file agitation as much as, if not more than, from external socialist organization and leadership.

In 1906, the Labour Representation Committee ran on a manifesto that laced matters of social reform together with some of the issues dividing Liberals from Conservatives, including free trade and indentured labor in South Africa—an issue fought out on anti-Asian terms.[21] While Bealey and Pelling, prominent mid-century historians of Labour, strongly argued against the centrality of social issues to the 1906 election—a plausible enough argument—they were perhaps less convincing in arguing against organized workers' commitment to these issues.[22] The 1906 LRC manifesto included some of the following statements: "The aged poor are neglected"; "The slums remain"; "Underfed children are still neglected"; "Protection, as experience shows, is no remedy for poverty and unemployment. It serves to keep you from dealing with the land, housing, old age, and other social problems!"[23] Pelling argues against organized workers' support for social reform by highlighting their deep and abiding commitment to self-help and their general distrust of the state.[24] But we should not mistake workers' desire to distribute their own wages or to administer their own funds with an aversion to social reform as such. As the history of the ASRS demonstrates, self-help was understood at least from the 1870s as entailing unionists' paternalistic responsibility for ameliorating widows' and orphans' poverty. Rail unionists had framed benefit funds at once as self-help initiatives and as means for protecting and maintaining those in the community who had been separated from the male wage. They thus anticipated the gendered logic of social benefit programs. Furthermore, rail unionists had long campaigned to revise the laws concerning compensation for accidental injury, suggesting that state reform to help ameliorate widows' destitution was not seen as inconsistent with self-administered means for addressing such poverty.

While we can thus see the turn to social liberal governance after 1906 partly as an effect of Labour's breakthrough in the general election, this does not mean that social reform's concrete manifestations followed closely Labour's blueprints.[25] Rather, cross-cutting political interests combined in giving shape to the social reform initiatives of the prewar period. This period of reform featured the establishment of state-regulated schemes for old age pensions, unemployment insurance, and health insurance coverage, as well as state-administered labor-management conciliation boards. The latter were motivated by state officials' and business owners' shared interest in averting strikes within essential industries, including on the railways. And the National Insurance Act of 1911 was motivated in part by state officials' and military officers' eugenic concerns for the health of the national body and of the soldiery in particular—collective bodies conceived of as state resources in the context of interimperialist rivalries. Such were some of the wider contexts and histories that shaped the emergence of social liberal governance in Britain. But certain immediate crises also focused the mind of state officials. The 1907 strike threat on the railways, for example, helped convince Lloyd George of the need for labor-management conciliation boards. Company directors, for their part, agreed to the conciliation scheme as a means to deflect demands for union recognition. At the same time as they were contemplating signing on to the conciliation scheme, rail managers were issuing threats against workers who might have been contemplating striking. The GWR general manager issued a circular in October 1907 insisting that those "who may waver in their allegiance to the Company should, in their own interests and in those of their families, deliberate long and seriously before taking a step which would irrevocably sever their connection with a service which affords regular employment."[26] In the making of railway conciliation boards, the companies held the upper hand: The parameters of the 1907 scheme were drawn up by the general manager of the Great Central Railway, and workers' representatives were given very little time to decide whether to sign off on the scheme.[27] There was thus a certain continuity between the 1907 railway conciliation boards and the many labor-management committees—often organized by general managers—into which railway workers had been drawn from the 1840s. The one salient difference here was that disputes on issues of wages and hours which did not yield resolution through the conciliation mechanism were to be referred to an independent arbitrator. While fulltime union officials were not permitted to sit on the conciliation boards, they were permitted to represent workers' interests in front of this arbitrator. Moreover, in early elections to the conciliation boards, rank-and-file unionists—especially those affiliated with the ASRS—won the vast majority of seats. As Bagwell notes, for all of their faults, the conciliation boards "provided a valuable training ground for the local leadership of the ASRS to advocate the union's policy. Many non-unionists were drawn into the life of the union through what they saw of the work of ASRS members on the Conciliation Boards."[28]

Archival holdings from the Ministry of Trade would suggest that most workers preferred to be represented on the conciliation boards than to remain outside their purview. While workers' memorials on issues of wages and hours first were to be sent to company directors or managers and only subsequently could they be taken up by conciliation boards, memorials pertaining to the operation of the boards themselves immediately could be directed to the Board of Trade. Many of these latter memorials, as we have begun to see, were sent by representatives of workers who did not yet have access to conciliation boards. Over time, these memorials helped broaden the bounds of the conciliation grades, and the memorials themselves were mechanisms of labor organizing. But a handful of memorials directed to the Board of Trade ran in the opposite direction, asking how groups of workers might opt out of the conciliation mechanism and its binding settlements. In 1908, for example, R. Pullen wrote a letter on behalf of a group of enginemen employed by the London, Brighton and South Coast Railway (LB&SCR). Pullen posed the question of how, if a majority of workers in a given grade did not want to bring a grievance to arbitration, they could prevent a minority of workers in the same grade from moving forward to arbitration. He implied that such a situation was taking place on the LB&SCR conciliation board and that in protest he and a pair of other enginemen had resigned their positions as representatives to this board. Presumably this group formed a minority of workers' representatives on the board but saw themselves as sharing a perspective with the majority of those enginemen they represented.[29] While Pullen's letter posed a question about *how* workers should be represented on conciliation boards rather than *whether* workers should be engaged in such a scheme, his act of resignation and memorial to the Board of Trade offer evidence of a fundamental disillusionment with the conciliation mechanism.[30] Further evidence for such disillusionment can be found in the rise of syndicalist sentiments among railwaymen during the period from 1907 to 1911. An important figure in railway syndicalism at this time was Charles Watkins, a signalman based in Sheffield, who, in 1911, published an article in *The Syndicalist Railwayman* entitled "Conciliation or Emancipation, Which?" The article, subsequently published as a pamphlet, called on workers to embrace an industrial unionism oriented toward workers' self-management rather than toward the state mediated amelioration of conditions in the railway industry.[31] In 1911, as a result of a national railway strike, the conciliation boards were set on a new foundation: A means for increasing ASRS representation across the various boards was set in place, and a number of other reforms to the conciliation mechanism were made.[32] State officials sought to draw workers back into this mechanism for fostering labor peace at a time when critical masses of workers were embracing mass strike action, often against the instruction of trade union leaderships.[33]

THE 1911 RAILWAY STRIKE

The national railway strike of 1911 took place in the context of a wider industrial strike wave. In 1910, miners in South Wales had waged militant strikes, and in June of 1911, dockworkers undertook effective strikes in Liverpool and across other port cities. Dockworkers' strikes drew in railway workers, who increasingly refused to transport "hot goods" from the waterfront. Such sympathetic strike action around the ports was one component of a broader upswelling of strike activity on the railways of Britain and Ireland during the summer of 1911. When such strike activity reached a critical mass in August, union officials kicked into gear. On 15 August, executives of four major railway unions issued an ultimatum that company representatives meet within twenty-four hours to negotiate a settlement. The Board of Trade then convened railway executives and at the same time asked union leaders about their demands. Above all, labor leaders insisted that railway firms recognize established railway unions for the purposes of collective bargaining. Company officials struck an intransigent pose, while state officials merely offered a Royal Commission to review the conciliation scheme, prompting union leaders to call a national strike on 17 August.[34] During these same negotiations on the eve of the railway strike, state officials promised company directors that police and military forces would be made available in the event that strikers effectively blockaded rail infrastructures.[35]

The fact that the genesis of the national railway strike of 1911 was to be found in sympathetic strike action from below gives ballast to

James Cronin's argument that "the fundamental strategic innovation of 1910–14 was the 'sympathetic strike.' Known before but seldom utilised, it revealed and served the new desire to counter employers' strength with broad working-class unity, as concretised, for example, in the Triple Alliance. . . ."[36] During the railway strike itself, sympathetic action was particularly pronounced in mining centers, where workers shut down collieries in solidarity with striking rail workers. Strike participation in the railway industry itself was somewhat uneven; in certain regions rail traffic was all but stopped on the 18th, but in others service was simply reduced. Companies worked in various ways to induce employees to continue working, while also attempting to redeploy clerks and other office workers to more active roles in the operation of the lines.[37]

In addition to sympathetic strike action, a key feature of the 1911 strike on the railways was the use of mass pickets at railway crossings, depots, and other strategic sites. The mass picket, like the sympathetic strike, manifested the desire to "counter employers' strength with broad working-class unity." Mass pickets along the lines were composed not simply of railway workers but of broader working-class constituencies as well. The turn to mass pickets during the summer of 1911 helped workers overcome certain limits to the realization of their structural power, especially when faced with police and military intervention. Outside of major urban junctions and workshop towns, rail workers were relatively dispersed, with anywhere from a couple dozen to a few hundred workers based near any given station. Their numbers were not necessarily sufficient to prevent police forces from clearing the lines in the event of a blockade. Barring effective blockades of particular sites along the lines, rail unionists had to rely on the near-universal solidarity of, in particular, engine drivers, firemen, and signalmen. While the former had long maintained an ambiguous relation to all-grades unionism, many of the latter were deeply invested in responsibly maintaining their posts—a responsibility that some clung to in 1911 even in the face of assertive pickets.[38] Mass pickets, which drew in members of the working class who lived near rail crossings, enabled more effective shutdowns of particular spans of track, even in the event that some drivers, signalmen, or others in the industry continued working or in the event that strikebreakers were deployed to operate trains or signalboxes. In this way, associations at the local level between rail unionists of all grades and working-class groups outside the industry helped workers overcome challenges to the realization of their structural power.[39]

In Llanelli, for example, a town in South Wales known for the manufacture of tin products, a broad cross-section of the town's working class blocked the central railway crossing to help enforce the strike. While there were 500 or so rail workers stationed in the region, the pickets at the station ranged from 1,500 to 5,000 people.[40] When locomotives approached, picketers stayed on the lines and called for drivers to brake, encouraged them to leave their engines, and then put out the engine fires. After days of confrontations between police and picketers at the Llanelli rail crossing, soldiers who had been deployed to the town conducted a bayonet charge against the picket, whose members retreated to the top of an embankment that jutted up against workers' houses. Strikers threw rocks at passing trains and at soldiers below, who responded by firing shots into the crowd, killing two people. Shortly after the shooting, crowds looted and burned the approximately one hundred railway carriages in the area, while also looting warehouses owned by the local notable held to be responsible for calling in the military. The identities of the two picketers who were killed are a testament to the cross-sectoral quality of the mass picket: John John was a mill-worker employed at Morewood Tinplate Works, and Leonard Worsell was a Londoner with tuberculosis who had been sent to convalesce in a South Wales sanitarium.[41]

While the Llanelli mass picket thus drew in all grades of railwaymen and a wide cross-section of the town's working-class community, the picket was led by an established railway unionist named John Bevan. Bevan was a signalman from South Wales with experience in formal organizations, including in the ASRS and as a worker's representative to the Great Western Railway's Provident, Widows and Orphans, and Pensions Societies.[42] Bevan's rhetoric during the strike and his writings from the late nineteenth century show him to have been invested in the "protection" of railway widows and orphans. At one point during the strike, passengers asked for their train to be let through, saying they sympathized with the railwaymen's demands. "They were told," according to the *Llanelly Guardian*, "that sentiments would not feed the workers' wives and children..." John Bevan then said: "If there are women and children in need of a bed, we will find free accommodation in our own houses."[43] In 1895, Bevan wrote a poem about Reverend John Davies, which contained the following lines:

> He'll fight for liberty,
> We always find him ready
> To do whate'er he can

To help the wives and children
Of the poor hard-working man.⁴⁴

Bevan's career thus illustrates well the aforementioned organizing and rhetorical tension that shaped railway unionist contexts around the turn of the century. In his advocacy, we can hear notes of the politics of respectability associated with mutualism and craft unionism, wherein higher-grade railwaymen assumed a paternal responsibility for the well-being of railway widows and orphans. But on the ground in Llanelli, forms of solidaristic action were pulling against such respectable, paternalistic frameworks: The widows and orphans of whom Bevan spoke were just as likely as respectable railwaymen to have joined the looting in Llanelli on Saturday 19 August.

In addition to the use of mass pickets and sympathetic strike action, another notable dimension of the 1910–12 strike wave was the central role played by police and military forces in shaping class antagonism. The deployment of soldiers, who in some cases shot and killed strikers, not only sparked local riots but also became an important matter of working-class agitation and national political contention.⁴⁵ In September 1911, five thousand workers in London held a funeral procession to mourn the two picketers killed in Llanelli. They carried a banner that read: "In loving memory and in kind sympathy for our comrades in Llanelly and Liverpool killed in the interests of capitalism. Workers remember Trafalgar Square 1887, Mitchelstone 1887, Featherstone 1893, Belfast 1907, and now Llanelly 1911." The same banner was unfurled the following week in Llanelli for a mass procession and rally, at which Ben Tillett spoke.⁴⁶ The banner offered a chronicle of class violence, linking the recent shootings in Llanelli to state assaults on, among others, tenant organizers in the south of Ireland, striking miners in Yorkshire, and anti-Coercion demonstrators in London. Not only did the banner discursively articulate dispersed acts of protest and repression; it also passed across the hands of those in both London and South Wales, making for a shared fabric of protest between these sites. Such was one of the rituals that helped bind together different sectors of workers in the transformative prewar years—a period that saw the emergence of the National Union of Railwaymen (NUR) in 1913 and the forging of a triple alliance between dockworkers, railway employees, and miners in 1914. The story of how industrial unionism came to the railways, however, is not simply a story of solidaristic action from below. The breakthrough for industrial unionism in 1913 also followed from the difficulties railway unionists had in administering insurance funds associated with the 1911 National Insurance Act (NIA). In other words, industrial unionism followed from the social liberal dispensation not simply in a negative way, through a process of workers' disillusionment (e.g., with the 1907 conciliation boards), but also through positive or "productive" relations of power, as the 1911 NIA burdened railway unions with responsibilities they could not easily fulfill on their own.

NATIONAL INSURANCE AND THE NUR

In his comprehensive history of the making of the NUR, Philip Bagwell presents the 1911 strike as the event that almost singlehandedly enabled the merging of three railway unions into the more properly industrial NUR. On the ground, as he shows, workers from various unions together held pickets in August 1911, while at the highest levels of the union bureaucracy, leaders acted in concert during negotiations with the state and with company representatives. These experiences and the relationships they had helped solidify formed the basis for moving forward months later toward industrial amalgamation. Union leaders had been meeting periodically for more than a decade to try and work out the means for merging into one big union, but until the winter of 1911–12, these conferences had either ended in acrimony or had led to plans membership was lukewarm about. In the winter of 1911–12 though, union executives from the ASRS, GRWU, and UPSS embraced a plan for amalgamation. ASLEF executives, who had forwarded an alternative plan for federation, notably stood aside from these negotiations. Then, in May of 1912, GRWU members overwhelmingly voted in favor of merging into a new National Union of Railwaymen. The vote among ASRS members ran into June but ultimately resulted in a successful ballot, wherein two-thirds of members expressed support for industrial amalgamation. On 10 February 1913, executives reconvened and four days later founded the NUR.[47]

While the national strike of 1911 can reasonably be seen as the immediate cause of union amalgamation, the disruptive effects on railway unions of the 1911 National Insurance Act also played a role in fostering a spirit of cooperation among union executives. The NIA, which allowed unions to operate "approved societies," put significant strain on the bureaucratic capacities of railway trade unions, creating a practical incentive toward combination. In 1908, as part of a wider turn toward social liberal governance, the Board of Trade began to consider the possibility of reforming on a national basis programs of unemployment and health insurance. The Trades Union Congress, worried that a national insurance scheme would undermine existing unions by rendering superfluous union benefit funds, sent a delegation to Germany to determine how state-run social insurance had affected trade unions there. The TUC report concluded that state insurance "has in no way exercised an injurious effect upon the trade unions of that country."[48] TUC support for what would become the National Insurance Act was contingent upon unions' capacity to become approved societies under the Act. Friendly societies were, from early days, also set to become approved societies. Much debate around the act concerned the question of whether private insurance companies, such as Prudential, would also have the capacity to become approved societies; ultimately, these companies were permitted to administer approved insurance policies.[49] As George Alcock recounts in his *Fifty Years of Trade Unionism*, one of the frustrations trade unionists had with the bill that ultimately passed in 1911 was that it gave "railway companies and other employers, as well as capitalistic insurance companies (whether of the 'Friendly' type or otherwise) power to set up a society."[50] Alcock lamented the number of railway workers who opted for these capitalistic enterprises, whether because of more effective advertising or on the basis of their slightly more favorable terms. The rush by approved societies to sign up new members occurred in the summer of 1912,[51] right around the same time that union members were voting on whether or not to amalgamate and months before union executives had to take up and approve internally the details of their emergent amalgamation scheme. While Alcock would have preferred that, in the summer of 1912, rail workers had put "trade union over all," the story he told of the aftermath of this rush to sign up members suggests that the ASRS had more railway workers sign up for their approved society than they could properly handle.

As Alcock noted, the setting up of an approved society under the NIA "involved a new sphere of work."[52] Processing membership cards for the insurance society required an amount of clerical labor beyond the capacity of those employed full-time by the ASRS. Faced with this challenge of undercapacity, the general secretary of the ASRS hired fifteen out-of-work railwaymen from London branches to process the cards, paying them at the union's lower, part-time rate, even though they were working overtime. This new cadre of clerical workers, well-versed in unionist principles, insisted that they be paid at the full-time rate. In building their small campaign, they met with the full-time clerical staff of the ASRS, who apparently expressed a commitment to act in solidarity with their newly hired coworkers. The general secretary of the ASRS, for his part, went to some length to gather evidence that the men he had hired to process cards were working well behind the normal pace of clerical labor. As Alcock notes, "Mr Williams made tests of time and work with regard to the cards.... He asked two of his clerks to work fairly for an hour on these cards." And he inquired at "other places" to try and find a benchmark for his employees' labor. Deputations between the workers and the union's executive committee did not resolve the matter, prompting the precariously employed clerical workers to picket the union's headquarters at Unity House. The union's executive committee insisted that if those picketing failed to express regret for their actions then the union not only would fire them but would also revoke their membership. Two of the men apologized; twelve asked for more time to submit their defense and were summarily excluded from membership in the union. The executive then summoned the permanent clerical staff for a hearing "with a view to ascertaining their connection or connivance with this matter." The men were duly reprimanded.[53]

The ASRS thus faced a labor relations crisis at the moment they tried rapidly to expand, on a temporary basis, their clerical labor force. The general secretary's decision to hire out-of-work members at part-time wages resulted in a situation unsatisfying both for union officials, who wanted a faster pace of production, and for clerical workers themselves, who saw the emergence of a two-tier system of clerical work within the office. This episode, which apparently had a lasting adverse effect on General Secretary Williams's health, seems to have framed the issue of clerical labor within the union for some time to come, as Alcock's official history of the union, written in 1922, devotes significant space to telling the story of this internal crisis of discipline. In 1913, the first year of the NUR's existence, a similarly acute demand for clerical labor arose but was met in a more harmonious manner. The formation of the NUR galvanized new strata of railway workers to join the union. As Bagwell notes, while in April 1913, nearly two thousand membership application forms were received weekly, by October of the same year more than four thousand application forms were received each week. The newly founded NUR required more clerical staff to process these forms; this time around, however, the hiring of additional staff took place without incident.[54] The same General Secretary Williams who had assumed responsibility for the day-to-day operations of the NUR seems to have avoided some of his previous mistakes in this arena.

In addition to the position of general secretary, the NUR generally drew heavily upon the administrative and institutional resources of the previous ASRS. The union was housed at Unity House, the former ASRS headquarters. The late secretaries of the GRWU and of the UPSS became assistant secretaries of the NUR, while Williams served as general secretary and J. H. Thomas, also of the ASRS, served as a third assistant secretary. While pains were taken to present the establishment of the NUR as something other than the submerging of two unions under a third, in practice the old ASRS held a hegemonic role in this new organization. In part, this position of power followed from the larger membership of the ASRS. But the ASRS also held disproportionately more institutional and administrative capacity than either the GRWU or the UPSS, due in part to the former's longstanding operation of benefit funds. This mattered especially in the context established by the National Insurance Act, which rewarded organizations capable of operating an approved society. For the GRWU in particular, the NIA came as a shock to the system. We will recall that the GRWU had distinguished itself from the ASRS by not putting members' dues into benefit funds, but instead pouring nearly all of the members' dues into strike funds. The union thus had a relatively thin bureaucratic layer and little experience in managing member benefits. The stark transformation wrought by the NIA can be discerned in the annual rulebooks of the GRWU. In July 1912, the GRWU held a special delegates meeting to reconstruct their official rules and bylaws. The rulebook adopted at this meeting contained two parts; the first included modified versions of long-established articles pertaining to the day-to-day operations of the union, and the second included "Rules relating to the business of the Society under the National Insurance Act." This latter section included thirty-two articles, detailing the various benefits that accrued to members of the approved society.[55] This second part seems to bear no organic relation to the rules contained in the first part; the NIA-related articles neither supersede nor modify anything that has come before. In the summer of 1912, the union was entering onto wholly uncharted territory. Then, just over six months later, the union dissolved into the NUR, which would be operated in large part by ex-ASRS officers and clerical staff.

In the history of British railway labor, the long year of 1912 was highly eventful, stretching from the national strike in the fall of 1911 to the founding of the NUR in the winter of 1913. In the months between these well-marked bookends, railway trade unionists were engaged in intensive deliberations designed to bring about a "fusion of forces," even as they were also scrambling to establish and recruit members to approved societies under the NIA. This latter undertaking pressed union administrative capacities to their limits and previewed the administrative challenges that would follow amalgamation, as thousands of railway workers moved to join the NUR. In light of the longer-range histories we've been considering in this chapter and across the book more broadly, we can register some of the ambiguities of this decisive year. On the one hand, the establishment of the NUR entailed the creation of a more properly industrial railway union—a union in which workers of all grades might be represented on a national basis. Notwithstanding the persistence of the ASLEF, the establishment of the NUR thus helped overcome grade-based craft unionism in the industry. A much wider cross-section of employees entered into formal trade union organizations. Amalgamation was also woven together with trade unionists' expanded involvement in managing social insurance—a project historically associated with the craft unionism of the early ASRS. The intervention of a social reform–oriented state thus enabled the advancement of what were in some ways competing tendencies within early railway unionism. We see in 1912 a broadening of the base of unionism to bring in more of those who labored behind the curtain, and we also see a solidification of the relation between trade unionism and a paternalistic orientation involving the protection and care of railway community members. Moreover, while syndicalist currents helped advance the project of industrial amalgamation, as this transformation occurred, railway trade unions came to be more extensively bureaucratic institutions and more imbricated with state institutions. These observations help to frame the meaning of industrial unionism along the lines, complicating many of the polarized accounts of the "turn" to this form of unionism in the volatile prewar years. The breakthrough for industrial unionism in Britain was coterminous with the continuation, or reconfiguration, of institutional and cultural forms cultivated through early craft unionist projects—projects that, for their part, borrowed liberally from company-sponsored mutualist institutions.

We can further parse out the cultural dimensions of this two-sided transformation in 1912, beginning with the name of the new industrial union founded the following year. In the unions' "fusion of forces" deliberations during the summer of 1912–13, delegates discussed the problem of how to name the new union they were bringing into being. Delegates wanted to avoid the impression that one of the three unions had absorbed the others. So, when the head of the UPSS observed that "railwaymen" might be an unhelpfully gendered term, his union having begun to organize with women workers, the other delegates pointed out that alternatives—the National Union of Railway Workers, for example—might give the impression of the GWRU having absorbed the other unions. The male delegates agreed, noting that soon enough in any case "railwaymen" would be interpreted to be inclusive of women.[56] There is of course a historical irony in the fact that the masculine gendering of railway labor came to the fore with the naming of the NUR on the eve of the War, when the gender composition of the railway workforce would radically, if somewhat temporarily, change.[57] The forms of masculinity advanced in railway unionist discourse were varied, at once truculent and paternalistic, masculinist and open to nonheteronormative manifestations. The changing class composition of railway unions or the infusion of unionism with more radical currents—whether in 1889, 1906, or 1911—brought to the fore the experiences of unmarried railwaymen and heightened antagonisms between labor and management—but not in ways that ultimately displaced from center stage the paternal railwayman.

CHAPTER 5

Conveying Grievances in the Vernacular

Nationalist-Aligned Unionism and Social Liberal Reform in Colonial India

In colonial India, as in metropolitan Britain, labor struggles intensified in the first years of the twentieth century. A wave of strikes took place between 1905 and 1907. These strikes built on years of labor organizing in the sector. In colonial India, labor organizing at the turn of the century was relatively bifurcated, with white laborist projects running alongside nationalist-aligned labor movements. Whereas in chapter 3 we considered the early history of white laborism in colonial India, in what follows we will attend above all to the history of nationalist-aligned labor struggles. A watershed moment for nationalist-aligned labor struggles occurred in 1899, when Indian signal operators employed by the Great Indian Peninsular Railway organized a strike that was supported by important figures in the national movement.

This chapter offers a somewhat novel account of early nationalist-aligned railway labor struggles, emphasizing the pragmatic reasons workers turned to nationalist editors to help them mediate grievances and coordinate strikes. Because of the way discriminatory managerial projects configured the working and living experiences of Indian railway workers, many found pragmatic alliances with nationalist leaders appealing. When practices of management changed in 1911 with the generalization of certain social benefits, groups of Indian railway workers began to seek out alliances not only with nationalist editors but also with organizers affiliated with the refounded ASRS in India and Burma. In what follows, we will track the history of nationalist-aligned labor struggles from 1899 through the Great War, showing some of the continuities in the relationships maintained between workers and nationalist editors across this span of time, while also showing that important shifts both in organizing practices and in labor management relations occurred between 1911 and 1913, the same period that witnessed the emergence of the NUR in metropolitan Britain. We will begin with a vignette that helps illustrate how workplace grievances could draw certain employees toward alliances with the national movement.

In July 1907, K. S. Sanghani, a former assistant engineer with the Public Works Department (PWD), composed a letter to the secretary of state for India. Sanghani petitioned the Right Honorable John Morley for some relief from the decades-long limbo he had suffered and that he continued to endure. In 1892, Sanghani effectively had been dismissed from his post for challenging certain unlawful actions taken by his supervising engineer. His petitions for reinstatement had been met with evasive responses, leading this "late assistant engineer" to experience a frustrating uncertainty as to his employment status with the PWD. Not having received a definitive dismissal, Sanghani had been left "holding [a] curious and unprofitable post for the [previous] 15 years." The colonial state's refusal either to adjudicate his case or to communicate directly with him had been radicalizing. As he wrote in a 1908 memorial: "The present policy of those in power is to support their inferiors even by transgressing the main principles of Law of the country and the result will be, if it is not already, a chaos and persecution of the public. And such a state exists everywhere at present. Messrs Tilak, Pranjpe and such other publicists are only the outcomes of such a policy of Government."[1]

Bal Gandahar Tilak, a militant nationalist and political prisoner at the time of Sanghani's writing, had served as editor of two papers, *The Mahratta*, an English language journal, and *Kesari*, a Marathi paper. The causal relationship Sanghani outlines here between the colonial state's refusal to take up memorials challenging supervisors' abuses of power and the emergence of a politicized vernacular press will serve as an orienting historical argument for this chapter. Among those whose employment was overseen by the Public Works Department—from assistant engineers to entry-level workshop employees—the inability effectively to petition higher-ups formed a persistent matter of concern. Turning both to vernacular and to English-language papers to publicize grievances likewise formed a persistent oppositional tactic. The *means* workers devised to convey and politicize grievances in the face of company and state obduracy shaped the *ends* toward which these workers struggled: Workers' reliance on the vernacular press to publicize grievances drew at least some of them into close working relations with leaders of the national movement. The story of how Indian railway workers interfaced with nationalist editors in the first decade of the twentieth century can help frame, if not explain, some rail workers' decisions during the 1905–7 and 1919–22 strike waves to seek out nationalist leaders as representatives—decisions that imbricated their workplace struggles with national political projects and that involved a certain delegation of agency across lines of class.[2]

Rail workers interfaced with nationalist editors and leaders in part due to the structural constraints they faced in their working lives. Indian railway workers' general exclusion from company-sponsored institutions of social reproduction, combined with well-established supervisory arrangements along the lines, created a situation wherein the majority of railway workers in colonial India effectively lacked any means of petitioning or otherwise engaging with upper managers around their conditions of life and labor. In the workshops, sergeants had wide leeway in disciplining their supervisees, while the majority of workshop employees had little recourse in the event that they were unfairly dismissed or were subjected to corporal punishment. This contrasted with British and Anglo-Indian railway workers, who tended to be directly managed by superintendents in matters of promotion and discipline and who interfaced with these and other authorities within segregated railway colonies. While higher-grade, British and Anglo-Indian railwaymen experienced what could be termed "paternalistic" forms of governance, they generally were not drawn into the forms of "mutualist" comanagement that also defined railway labor relations in the metropole.[3] The East Indian Railway Company's provident fund, for example, stipulated that its executive committee was to be composed of "five principal Officers of the Company," to be appointed by the agent, as well as one member of the provident institution (i.e., a railway employee), appointed at the discretion of the executive committee.[4] Whereas most company-sponsored funds in Britain were effectively managed by groups of employee representatives, the EIR provident institution was governed more directly by upper managers, who imagined the executive committee as a place where a single employee representative might be trained in managerial responsibilities. Even for racially privileged workers, then, a less liberal dispensation shaped their working lives.

The longstanding absence of mutualist forms of comanagement in colonial India affected how company and colonial state authorities responded to workers' unrest. Following a strike wave in 1905–7, which included, at its tail-end, mobilizations by higher-grade British and Anglo-Indian guards and drivers, conciliation boards were briefly established under the auspices of the Railway Board. These conciliation boards, which soon fell into disuse, were designed as racially exclusionary vehicles for the workplace enfranchisement of higher-grade guards and drivers, as evidenced by the fact that the boards were to have representation from the "European and Anglo-Indian Defence Association"—an advocacy organization for members of these named communities in colonial India.[5] For a brief moment then, higher-grade, racially privileged railway employees in colonial India were invited into a conciliation scheme that paralleled the scheme being established at the same time in the metropole. But in colonial India, this proposed mechanism for labor-management negotiation was effectively a dead letter. Following the abandonment of the conciliation scheme in 1908, the colonial state and company authorities sought out alternative, less liberal methods for deterring strikes, ultimately settling upon a strategy for utilizing pension and gratuity funds as levers to enforce labor discipline. Access to retirement benefits was broadened to include the large majority of railway workers in colonial India, while rules were introduced clarifying that a worker's participation in strike action would effectively bar them from access to gratuity payments upon retirement, as the strike would reset the clock on their time served. Between 1911 and 1922, the year in which such no-strike clauses were abolished,[6] retirement benefits were one of the primary levers of labor discipline wielded against the broad majority of railway workers in colonial India, from entry-level workshop employees to drivers of passenger trains. Following the reform of railway retirement benefits in 1911, some number of Indian railway workers entered into alliance with the Amalgamated Society of Railway Servants of India and Burma, broadening somewhat the grade-based composition of this historically white laborist organization. Others continued to cleave to nationalist editors and leaders, relying on press organs to publicize grievances up through the Great War. These different approaches to ameliorating interlocking racial and class subordination would come into tension during a syndicalist strike in 1913.

CONVEYING GRIEVANCES AROUND THE TURN OF THE CENTURY

The periodical press had since the 1890s offered Indian railway workers a means of seeking redress for workplace grievances. But the press only served this function insofar as colonial state surveillance techniques made the contents of vernacular papers accessible to upper managers on the railways. Each week, translators employed by inspectors general of police composed "reports on native papers." These reports, which frequently ran to fifty or sixty pages, excerpted and translated into English select passages from a given administrative region's papers. Such textual selections, which often featured complaints or grievances, were grouped into distinct categories, such as "Railways and Communications, including Canals and Irrigation." State or company authorities would have been able to peruse this section each week in a matter of minutes, giving them a window onto the extent and nature of rail workers and passengers' frustrations. The fact that the grievances of workers were clubbed together with the grievances of passengers was significant, both in terms of how railway managers might have received these grievances and in terms of how this articulation shaped workers' entrance into oppositional political cultures. As we will see, the grievances articulated by or in relation to railway passengers helped frame the grievances that would be expressed by workers.

In her study of the experiences of women passengers in colonial India, Ritika Prasad has shown how a shift occurred around the turn of the century in the way vernacular papers framed railway outrages. Whereas earlier coverage of outrage cases had tended to frame these events with reference to conceptions of respectability, by the early twentieth century, outrage cases were more commonly taken as evidence of the state's complicity in "white violence"—a complicity shown insofar as European and Anglo-Indian perpetrators of violence faced at most incidental consequences for their actions. Press organs went so far as to call for women to arm themselves in self-defense against those who would violate their bodily autonomy.[7] This shift to a more militant register occurred around the same time as a change in how workers' experiences and grievances were conveyed in the vernacular and English-language press.

In discussing late-nineteenth-century outrage cases, Laura Bear highlights in particular the campaigns waged by Surendranath Banerjee in his paper, *The Bengalee*. She notes that, over the first years of the 1890s, Banerjee's coverage of railway outrages tended to follow a certain moralizing script: "The Indian women [discussed in these stories] appeared as respectable widows, young brides, and innocent village girls. They would often be rescued, if they were truly respectable, just in time."[8] These narratives of rescue anticipated some of the political demands put forward by Banerjee in an 1895 issue of *The Bengalee*, which included the hiring of "a better educated and a more respectable class of Hindoos and Mohamedans" who "would be married men possessed of greater self-restraint and less exposed to the temptations to which so many half-educated European and Eurasian striplings have fallen victim."[9] Here, as Bear notes, an argument against racially discriminatory hiring and promotion practices in the railway industry was routed through an argument for the essential respectability and protective orientation of married, formally educated Indian men.

For as much as the coverage of outrage cases in the press tended to be shaped by a class-, caste-, and gender-bound nationalist politics of respectability, the coverage of these cases in the 1890s sometimes exceeded the limits of this politics. Articles reported on acts of violence perpetrated by Indian men,[10] and coverage of certain cases of violence showed regard to women who might not have registered as respectable within prevailing cultural frameworks.[11] In 1895, Rajabala Dasi was violently raped by four European and Anglo-Indian guards in the residential quarters adjacent to the Asansol station. She managed to report the incident to a head-constable, receive medical attention, and identify the perpetrators of the assault. The case went to trial two months later and then the following month was heard by the high court. In covering the case, *The Bengalee* noted that Dasi was "a Boishnava by caste." Nationalist publishers, in discussing the Asansol outrage case, thus extended their regard to a woman who had separated herself from her family and was living an itinerant life, showing that narrow notions of respectability did not entirely govern the coverage of railway outrages in the vernacular and English-language press, especially from the mid-1890s. In the coverage of the Asansol outrage case, we can see early evidence for what Mrinalini Sinha, in her writing on anti-indenture politics, describes as a discursive democratization of the national cause, wherein *the people* are imagined through the figure of a "non-respectable" woman who has been harmed by those in power and who speaks back against her oppression. Insofar as the people were represented through such a figure and insofar as her voice was given credence, norms of respectability that would limit communities' circles of concern were put under pressure, if not fully reworked.

While such norms of respectability would not more meaningfully be dislodged prior to the anti-indenture movement, evidence for the preliminary democratization of the national cause over the late-1890s can also be seen in coverage of railway workers' movements, demands, and grievances. In the 1895 passage from *The Bengalee* quoted above,

Banerjee called for the employment of formally educated, married, and thus respectable Indian men. A July 1899 article in *The Samiran* (a Bengali weekly published in Calcutta) made a similar call but in a way that evinced a closer collaboration between the paper's editorial staff and rail workers employed in public-facing roles. The article notes that "ill-treatment of passengers by railway employes is so common because those employes are not themselves respectable men and do not, therefore, know how to treat respectable people. The pay and prospects in railway service are not such as to induce respectable men to enter it. And the hard work and ill-treatment by superiors to which railway employes are subjected positively deter respectable people from seeking service under railway administrations."[12] While Banerjee's framing of the issue of railway outrages in terms of the relative respectability of railway employees persists here, some of the concrete conditions of railway employment—low wages, supervisory violence—enter into the explanation for why "respectable men" are less likely to enter the service or to remain employed along the lines. The article then goes on to list seven grievances of "native railway servants," including:

1) Summary dismissal or fine on the slightest fault.
2) Absence of provision for old-age, when an employe becomes unfit for active service.
3) The necessity of being obsequious, not only to every European but also to everybody who wears European dress and to all superior officers.
4) Excessive labour and punishment on the slightest omission.
5) Difficulty of getting leave even on most urgent private affairs.
6) Absence of prospect, no one having any expectation of promotion who has no patron at the head office to back him.
7) Responsible work on miserably poor pay.

Here, a number of themes can be identified. First, there is a recognition of the problematic inaccessibility of upper managers to Indian rail workers. Upper managers were unlikely to serve as "patrons" who would support the promotion of Indian rail workers; they would not extend the benefits of provident funds to the majority of the workforce; they would not hear appeals when workers were summarily dismissed; and they were among those who expected nothing less than obsequiousness. This passage's account of Indian rail workers' conditions of labor makes clear that the characteristic features of "railway paternalism"—defined by a certain upper managerial discretion around the disciplining of workers and an investment in workers' social reproduction—were withheld from the majority of workers in colonial India as a matter of course. The regime of labor discipline to which they were subject was comparatively unforgiving and was characterized by a spectrum of indignities, from summary dismissal and an expectation of obsequiousness to fines and corporal punishment.[13] That "ill-treatment" at the hands of supervisors was highlighted in this 1899 article shows how workers were beginning to see themselves as subject to a sort of racialized violence akin to that on display in outrage cases. Indeed, the identical term—"ill-treatment"— was used in the article to describe the violence enacted against Indian passengers by public-facing railway workers and the violence enacted against Indian railway workers by their supervisors.

Between 1895 and 1899, then, we can note a shift in how the experiences of railway workers were portrayed in the vernacular press. By July of 1899, when *The Samiran* published its list of grievances, workers' perspectives on their conditions of labor more directly were being represented in the coverage of railway issues than had been the case in 1895. And, in concert with this shift, workers' vulnerability to managerial ill-treatment had come to be foregrounded in press coverage of railway matters. These democratizing shifts followed from an upsurge in collective organizing on the part of certain sectors of Indian railway workers. In particular, over the second half of the 1890s, Indian signal operators built effective fighting organizations and pursued a range of tactics to ameliorate their working conditions, culminating in May 1899 with a strike of signal operators employed by the Great Indian Peninsular Railway (GIPR). The GIPR signal operators' strike, in particular, drew editors of vernacular papers into relation with organized railway workers.[14] As they built relations with organized rail workers, editors came to express in writing a sense of responsibility for effectively representing workers' grievances to the public. Workers, in turn, seem to have built relations with such editors in part to bring pressure more effectively on managers while minimizing their own risk of facing retaliation. The relations forged over the last years of the 1890s between organized workers and sympathetic editors would be maintained into the first decades of the twentieth century, and editors of vernacular papers would come to take on an increasingly important role in mediating labor-management relations over this span.

In June 1899, the *Hindustani* (an Urdu-language paper based in Lucknow) published a defense of the recent strike of signal operators employed by the Great Indian Peninsular Railway. Their article insisted that workers had not struck capriciously, but rather had pursued for some years alternative means of resolving grievances: "They thought that they were overworked and underpaid, and more than once laid their grievances before the railway officers during the last two years in vain. Some signallers who made representations on the subject were severely dealt with and even fined."[15] A similar line was articulated as well by the *Hitavadi* (a Bengali weekly published in Calcutta): "The signallers of the Great Indian Peninsular Railway ... have been for the last two or three years dunning their grievances into the ears of the authorities but in vain. As a last resort, they struck work."[16] These passages cast into relief not only how ineffectual memorials to upper managers had been for GIPR signallers but also how managers retaliated against those who organized memorials by issuing fines and otherwise by ill-treating such employees. Such were the means by which Indian workers were effectively barred from petitioning their upper managers directly—a situation that spurred them to seek out third parties who might be able to convey grievances indirectly.

In 1897—two years before the 1899 strike—a group of signalers conveyed a grievance, perhaps through an intermediary, to William Wedderburn, member of Parliament for Banffshire, who asked on the floor of the House of Commons why Indian signal operators were not given the same housing allowances as European and Eurasian signal operators. Given Wedderburn's career in Bombay and his close working relationship with nationalist leader Gopal Gokhale, there is reason to think he may have received an appeal, directly or indirectly, from some of the same Bombay-based signallers who would strike on the GIPR two years later. But it is possible that the appeal may have come from elsewhere, as signal operators in Bengal and Assam also expressed dissatisfaction in 1899, via the mediation of the *Hitavadi*, over the discriminatory distribution of housing stock and allowances at their places of work.[17] In any case, Wedderburn's 1897 question in the House of Commons was forwarded along to the Public Works Department of the colonial state, which replied by insisting:

> There are practical difficulties in the way of requiring a Native Signaller, who as a rule is accompanied by his family, to occupy a set of quarters in a block occupied by Europeans and Eurasians. The Native Signallers would assert that their caste prejudices were ignored and violated, while the Europeans and Eurasians would contend that the comfort and cleanliness of their quarters were destroyed by the insanitary conditions of the Native Signallers' quarters.... [I]n places where Natives would have to occupy quarters in the same dormitories or blocks that are occupied by Christian Signallers, they live outside, and this they do from choice. We consider that it is impracticable to impose on Natives the condition as to compulsory occupation of

quarters when available, and this being so they have no claim to compensation when quarters are not provided.[18]

This passage asserts that upper managers were responsive to the expressed preferences both of European and of Indian railway workers, even as it concludes with the declaration that Indian signalers "*have no claim* to compensation when quarters are not provided," indicating a fundamental refusal to recognize Indian workers' housing needs.[19] The passage further illustrates how practices of racial segregation were justified by railway managers and colonial state officials. Discourses of religion and of public health were woven together in the making of segregated residential quarters. A Christian identity—often established or affirmed through marriage in a church—was a necessary condition for residence in nearly all railway colonies, at least until 1911. Given that superintendents were responsible for distributing housing in such colonies, a Christian identity was also a necessary condition for relating directly to upper managers around matters of housing. In the arena of housing, then, upper managers remained relatively inaccessible to the majority of railway workers in colonial India, and memorials to address housing discrimination appear to have been treated as out of order. In this context, recourse to third parties, combined with direct action on the shopfloor, formed a persistent pattern into the twentieth century—a pattern set during the 1899 signalers strike on the Great Indian Peninsular Railway.

Articles published in the vernacular press over the spring and summer of 1899 give some indication of how GIPR signalers established relations with supportive third parties in the context of their strike organizing.[20] With regard to the relations forged between striking GIPR signalers and nationalist leaders and editors, Bipan Chandra has observed that "almost all nationalist newspapers came out fully in support of the strike, with Tilak's newspapers *Mahratta* and *Kesari* campaigning for it for months. Public meetings and fund collections in aid of the strikers were organized in Bombay and Bengal by prominent nationalists like Pherozeshah Mehta, D. E. Wacha and Surendranath Tagore."[21] The support shown by nationalist leaders for the GIPR signalers strike itself became a matter of public debate and controversy, and sympathetic editors sought in their publications to clarify the nature of this support. In June 1899, the *Hitavadi* published an article that tried to clear up various misconceptions about the strike, including about strikers' demands, insisting that strikers had never demanded "that none but Brahmans should be employed as signallers."[22] The claim otherwise was "an invention, pure and simple, of some railway official of position." Moreover, the article notes, "the railway authorities have gone one step further. They have discovered a political purpose in this strike of the signallers. In their opinion, this strike is the result of a Brahmin conspiracy. It is even sought to connect Mr Tilak with this strike." While railway authorities apparently viewed the strike as following from caste-bound nationalist agitation, the editor of the *Hitavadi* insisted that the support shown for the strike by "the men of light and leading in Bombay" was not cause but effect. "The public" evidently were dissatisfied about the fact that GIPR "authorities [were] treating the native signallers in a different manner from that in which they treated the European guards." This discrepancy led "Mssrs. Wacha and Dwarakadas, and Dr. Ibrahimji, and others like them" to form "a committee for the relief of the poor signallers." The article reported: "The committee have already raised Rs 5,000 and many are paying subscriptions." The 1899 signalers strike thus fostered a degree of cross-class collaboration, not only in terms of fundraising but also, the *Hitavadi* informs us, in terms of advocacy: "The men of light and leading in Bombay have done something more to befriend the signallers. They have made representation to the Directors in England on their behalf." The editor suggests that these advocates should go further than they have in their representations to the Home Board: "They should also inform the Directors how the Railway authorities make a distinction of colour in their treatment of the Railway servants." We can thus see how the 1899 signalers strike not only fostered a degree of cross-class collaboration on the ground, but also gave rise, on the part of some nationalist leaders and editors, to a new sense of responsibility for representing the grievances of railway workers to the public and to railway authorities. This sense of responsibility appears to have animated the editor of the *Samiran*, who published in July of 1899 a list of grievances on behalf of "native railway servants."[23]

The editors of vernacular papers were not, however, unanimous in supporting the 1899 signalers strike. Over the course of June 1899, editors at *Al Bashir*, an Urdu-language periodical published in Etawah, and the *Hindustani* held a running debate on the question of whether the GIPR signalers had acted justly and thus whether it was appropriate for newspaper editors to support the strike. At one point in the exchange, the editor of Al Bashir insisted, "If the signallers had not demanded that none but Brahmans should be given higher appointments on the railway, as the *Hindustani* says they did not, it had better publish all the papers relating to the affair and thereby remove all misunderstanding from the public mind on the subject."²⁴ The *Hindustani* had observed the previous week that this demand was not among those included in the GIPR signalers' memorial and moreover that "the signallers on strike are not all Brahmans, but comprise Musalmans and Jews, Christians and Parsis."²⁵ The editor of *Al Bashir* expressed concern throughout the debate about the religious composition of the signaling workforce and called on the colonial state to ensure that "in future Hindus, Musalmans, Parsis and Christians are employed in equal numbers in all branches of the public service."²⁶ In making this appeal, the editor of *Al Bashir* picked up on the established nationalist demand for an end to racially discriminatory hiring and promotion practices in the industry, broadening the frame of this demand to take in as well the matter of preferential hiring practices for members of religiously defined communities.

The editor of the *Hindustani* replied to this appeal for employment parity in the following way: "The Hindustani has deemed it necessary to answer the comments of Al Bashir at some length in order to remove misapprehensions and to prevent the growth of an idea that the journals which lay claim to be the champions of the Muhammadan community are condemning the aggrieved signallers, a large proportion of whom are Hindus, so that some Musalmans may step into their shoes. Signalling is no child's play and young boys cannot learn it in a day."²⁷ Here, the editor of the *Hindustani* invoked a purported knowledge of the working conditions and on-the-job training of railway signalers in responding to the editor of *Al Bashir*'s call for employment parity. With this passage, we can see how the terms of debate in the vernacular press around labor matters were evolving, and how a certain rhetorical proximity to industrial workers was becoming an asset in such debates. While sympathetic editors took pains to insist that workers were acting of their own accord, they also, especially from 1899 or so, labored to demonstrate their familiarity with railway workers, and with the grievances and working conditions of this group. The pattern of interaction set in 1899 between editors and organized railway workers would continue into the early twentieth century, a time when labor and nationalist struggles were intensifying.

Grievances around housing and retirement benefits featured centrally in vernacular papers during the first decade of the twentieth century. In January 1905, the *Daily Hitavadi* noted that "the quarters which have been constructed [for Indian railway workers] at the Lilua station on the East Indian Railway ... have been pronounced by medical men as 'unfit for habitation.'"²⁸ Then again in June, the same paper followed up on the matter, noting that EIR authorities had compelled the "ticket-collectors attached to the Lilua station to live with their families in the most wretched and unhealthy quarters which have been built for them in that place.... The attention of the Agent of the Railway Company is drawn to the matter."[29] Addressing the managing agent, who occupied the highest managerial position in the company, the editors of the *Daily Hitavadi* construed this compelled residence in unsanitary housing as a form of "punishment and oppression" enacted by upper managers of the EIR.

Another site of exclusion and subordinate inclusion highlighted around the same time in vernacular periodicals was that of company-managed retirement benefits. In 1868, the East Indian Railway had established a provident fund to induce employees into long-term service and to establish an economic lever of control over such employees. In 1891, a provident institution partially modeled on that of the EIR was established on the Madras Railway. The regulations for this institution stipulated that those of "purely Asiatic descent" could participate in the fund, albeit at twice the rate of investment relative to other employees, and that a rail worker could be a member "whose salary is not less than 15 rupees a month, who is paid monthly, and who is entitled to not less than a month's notice before dismissal."[30] This regulation, while formally race-neutral, would have excluded the majority of Indian railway workers from the provident institution, as most workshop employees did not earn fifteen rupees a month and as many sectors of employees were classed as temporary incumbents and thus not guaranteed a month's notice.[31] In 1904, the *Basumati*, a Calcutta-based paper, noted that the EIR had reclassified those employed in its Press as "temporary incumbents" rather than "permanent officers of the Company," thus "depriving them of the benefits of the railway provident fund."[32] Then, during the strike on the EIR in the summer of 1906, retirement benefits were used as a lever to discourage striking and, evidently, to extract bribes. According to the *Daily Hitavadi*, certain strikers had been "informed that they had forfeited the bonuses and interest due on their deposits in the Provident Fund and others [had] been told that the question of their interest and bonuses was still undecided." The source for the story, we read, "went on to allege that there is a high-placed official in the Traffic Department, who is responsible for this differential treatment, and to hint that the favour of this official may be bought."[33] As Sumit Sarkar has observed, the Traffic Department head at the time, Mister Dring, was particularly "disliked by all sections of employees, Anglo-Indians not excepted."[34] These various sections of employees would take collective action, albeit along different timelines, during the strike wave that stretched from 1905 through 1907.

MAKING RAILWAY LABOR MOVEMENTS AFTER THE PARTITION OF BENGAL

In October 1905 the colonial state partitioned Bengal. The event of partition in 1905 spurred the formation of the Swadeshi movement—a movement that was particularly strong in and around Calcutta, where the East Indian Railway terminated. In the summer of 1906, clerks, stationmasters, signal operators, and other rail workers employed by the East Indian Railway struck work, and Swadeshi organizers traveled up the line, visiting Jamalpur, Asansol, and other major railway zones in an effort to establish a permanent union of railway workers. This was one of a number of occasions during the volatile post-1905 period when strike organizing intersected with the national movement. In these moments of intersection, as well as through more mundane interactions around workplace grievances, the relations between nationalist editors and organized groups of railway workers took on new dimensions. Nationalist editors and leaders not only conveyed workers' grievances through the medium of the vernacular press as they had from at least 1899, but in some cases also sought to foster solidarities across grade and sector.

The partition of Bengal formally took place on 16 October 1905. As Bipan Chandra has noted, "the national upsurge" on that day "included a spurt of working class strikes and hartals in Bengal." Railway carters and manual workers were among those who struck on 16 October in opposition to partition.[35] Engineering workshop employees at Liluah also had threatened to strike on 16 October, which resulted in their preemptively winning a holiday for the day of partition.[36] While nationalist-aligned strikes would set the pace of labor agitation over the following two years, anticolonial strikes were counterpointed by collective actions undertaken by higher-grade, racially privileged workers, whose strikes tended to be shorter, more targeted affairs. Just two weeks before the risings associated with the Partition of Bengal, as Sarkar observes, "there was a short but successful strike by the Anglo-Indian East Indian Railway guards on the question of overtime allowances."[37] Such non-nationalist-aligned strikes became occasions for nationalist editors to demonstrate their commitment to the cause of railway labor and to contest colonial interpretations of nationalist-aligned strikes. In November 1907, British and Anglo-Indian drivers, firemen, and guards struck on the East Indian Railway over economic grievances. The strike prompted the Railway Board and EIR authorities to establish conciliation boards—boards that would not last beyond the period of heightened strike activity. During this strike, the *Daily Hitavadi* observed:

> When the Bengalis working on the East Indian Railway struck work ... the noble white men pointed out the swadeshi and Banda Mataram as the cause of the strike, and nothing was left untried which was thought as likely to kill the swadeshi. But is the present great strike to be fathered on to the swadeshi also? Now it is the feringhees who have struck work, and so it will not do to blame the swadeshi. That is why nobody is expressing any opinion. Subordinate officers of the Railway have many real grievances which cannot be overlooked any more.[38]

Here the editor of the *Daily Hitavadi* at once contested colonial narratives about railway strikes while also implicitly making an argument about nationalists' relation to organized labor. Whereas colonial authorities had interpreted the 1906 EIR strike as essentially a Swadeshi conspiracy, thus denying the reality of workers' independent grievances and agency, the *Daily Hitavadi* argued that the 1907 strike of racially privileged railway workers demonstrated the reality of the grievances. And whereas colonial officials might tend to interpret nationalist papers' support for strikes as instrumental, here we can see that this support is based on principle. The strike of drivers and guards cannot have furthered the Swadeshi cause; yet nationalist editors were writing in favor of this strike. In addition to the *Daily Hitavadi*, the *Howrah Hitaishi* also wrote in support of the strike, arguing that the workers' "grievances are neither unjust nor unnatural. There is much in them which testifies to the grave injustice done to them by the authorities."[39] Here again, we can see how an appeal on the basis of editors' evident knowledge of railway working conditions had become rhetorically advantageous. These editors thus demonstrated their sense of responsibility to understand and represent workers' grievances, even when these grievances were not directly articulated with a challenge to colonial authority and when those striking had failed to show solidarity with Bengali strikers the previous year.

As Sarkar notes regarding the earlier strike, "it is ... understandable that the movement which evoked the most sustained nationalist interest and support was that of the Bengali Hindu station-masters and clerks of the EIR between July and September 1906. Nationalist involvement in labour affairs in fact reached a point of climax with this memorable two-month-long strike."⁴⁰ Sarkar has provided a thorough account of this strike, which drew nationalist editors and organizers into active roles as organizers. He describes how, during a particularly difficult stretch, organizers meeting in the offices of the *Sandhya* newspaper committed support for four hundred "starving" dismissed workers of the Howrah division—that is, workers closest in proximity to the paper's editorial offices. In addition to supporting striking workers in their city, a cohort of nationalist labor organizers traveled down the line to help found chapters of the railway union in towns with locomotive workshops and sheds. In Jamalpur, workshop employees seeking to assemble with nationalist organizers were met with extreme force at the factory gates and then faced a week-long lockout at the locomotive workshop. Macmillan, one of the sergeants who fired into the crowd of assembled workers, not only was not disciplined for his act of violence but actually received a promotion from the railway authorities.⁴¹ In terms of the strikers' demands, economic matters were linked with demands for an end to racial discrimination along the lines. Sarkar notes that a "memorial on behalf of 900 Asansol employees demanded reinstatement of their Howrah comrades, equal pay for Indian and white foremen, a 50 per cent rise in the wages of workshop hands, and grain compensation allowance."⁴² We can read a fair amount into these demands. The call for a grain compensation allowance reflects the high cost of food at the time. Most organizers during the 1905–7 strike wave demanded grain compensation allowances in addition to higher wages. The call for a 50 percent raise for workshop employees reflects the extent to which strike organizers were working to draw differently situated workers into the struggle. While relatively higher-grade clerks and station-masters had led the way in the summer of 1906, the representation of hyperexploited workshop employees emerged as a priority of strike organizers as the summer wore on. Not only were workshop hands' interests represented by strike organizers, but some of those who supervised workshop and other employees also saw their interests reflected in strikers' demands. Station-masters, shed foreman, and *mistris*—skilled mechanics—all supervised entry-level employees, whether at stations, in locomotive sheds, or in workshops, and strikers demanded equal compensation for Indian and European employees in these positions of relative authority. The call against racial discrimination and differential pay scales formed a key demand of the 1906 strike, and this demand was met with acute managerial intransigence. As Sarkar notes, following a meeting between strike organizers and managers in the summer of 1906, station-master Surendranath Mukherji was dismissed "for having dared to raise the question of racial discrimination at the meeting."[43] The demand that racial hierarchies of labor be unmade was particularly explosive because it raised fundamental questions about the nature of colonial rule. The railways were governed by the Railway Board of the colonial state, meaning that racial discrimination in the railway industry gave the lie to the colonial state's official commitment to nondiscrimination.

Railway workers and nationalist leaders' shared interest in contesting racial discrimination and labor hierarchization can help explain their alliance. I have sought to show not only how a shared opposition to racial discrimination and violence linked workers and editors but also how practical constraints and opportunities drew these groups together. Indian workers' inability to effectively petition managers and their exclusion from company-sponsored institutions of social reproduction helped compel them to find third parties who could amplify their grievances with the public and convey these grievances to upper managers. The vernacular press, insofar as it was surveilled by the colonial state, was well situated to serve this mediating function. Sumit Sarkar has argued that, while many clerks and other office-based railway workers belonged to "the fringes of bhadralok society," there was a fundamental gulf between the outlooks or "mentalities" of industrial railway labor and the bhadralok-dominated national movement.[44] Yet his own writings show how at times this gulf was bridged in practice, as rail workers—including workshop employees—sought out and made common cause with nationalist leaders during periods of mass mobilization. Laura Bear offers something of a counterpoint to Sarkar's argument for the gulf in outlooks between workshop employees and nationalist leaders, arguing that certain shared ideological investments in the moral health of the national body drew rail workers and nationalist leaders into alliance. Bear argues that workshop employees came to hold such investments in part through their encounters with paternalistic railway management. She notes that, during the 1906 strikes, we can see "an expansive meaning for the concept of *jati*. Idioms of jati began to acquire an association with a swadeshi community of common national interests tied together by a moral purity and moral sanctions. In this respect they echo the form, but not the content, of the idioms of race and nation in the railway hierarchy. The railway bureaucracy had made the practices of daily and family life among its European and Eurasian employees an emblem of the moral legitimacy of the Raj."⁴⁵ I wonder, however, how much such managerial discourse would have shaped the ideological investments of workshop employees, as these employees had long been cut out of company-sponsored institutions of social reproduction and thus were in a position to develop a politics of labor relatively free from managerial influence or persuasion, though not free from managerial violence. The "face" that the railway company presented to such workers was that of the truculent sergeant, whose looming frame blocked from view the at-times paternalistic upper managers of the firm. In 1906, in Jamalpur, workshop employees demanded the dismissal of Macmillan, a particularly despised representative of this former group.

In addition to the drawn-out strike on the EIR in the summer of 1906 and the lightning strikes of European and Anglo-Indian drivers and guards, the strike wave of 1905–7 included a range of other strikes, some of which were also aligned with nationalist upsurges. As Sarkar observes, the winter of 1907–8 saw "brief strikes by railway workshop hands at Samastipur (North Bihar), and by pointsmen at Chakradharpur on the Bengal-Nagpur line, and a bigger strike by the Indian (mainly Muslim) drivers and firemen of the Eastern Bengal State Railway." The latter strike "dragged on till the middle of February, and was eventually broken with the help of European drivers loaned from the army."⁴⁶ Finally, "in Rawalpindi, in Punjab, the arsenal and railway engineering workers went on strike as part of the 1907 upsurge in the Punjab which had led to the deportation of Lajpat Rai and Ajit Singh."⁴⁷ A few months after this upsurge, editors and organizers in the Punjab would also mobilize in response to an outrage case. In October 1907, a seventeen-year-old woman named Mussammat Viranwali survived rapes by a stationmaster and signal operator at the Rawalpindi station in the Punjab.⁴⁸ While she managed to tell her story to an officer of the colonial state, and while her assailants faced trial, the result of this trial was acquittal by an all-European jury. The case garnered a fair amount of publicity on the eve of a Railway Board inquiry into "outrages and thefts" on the lines—an inquiry prompted by a petition issued by the European and Anglo-Indian Defence Association that studiously avoided the question of outrages perpetrated by railway servants against women traveling in third-class carriages.⁴⁹ The Railway Board thus showed a fundamental disregard for Indian women travelers at a time when the violence faced by such women was being politicized by the vernacular press.

STATE INTERVENTIONS IN THE WAKE OF THE STRIKE WAVE

From 1906, in addition to engaging in an inquiry around "outrages and thefts" committed against passengers traveling in first- and second-class carriages, colonial officials also sought measures to curb strike action along the lines. Railway Board minutes indicate that, during the strike wave of 1905–7, the prospect of criminal liability for striking was considered and was even mooted with the secretary of state for India. But in January 1908, the secretary of state rejected reforms along these lines, suggesting that the government of India might instead "consider other measures, dealing for example with recruitment, conditions of engagement, provident funds, etc., which associated with Conciliation Boards may tend to produce the desired result." This reply set off a years-long negotiation internal to the railway bureaucracy that ultimately resulted in the reform of railway provident and gratuity policies. But by the time these policies finally were revised in 1911, conciliation boards had come and gone, meaning that the reform of retirement benefits was the only enduring measure, designed to prevent railway strikes, that was undertaken by the colonial state in the years following the 1905–7 strike wave.[50] The 1911 reform of retirement benefits was a watershed, as it established the first universal social benefit for Indian railway workers. But by making the gratuity payment contingent upon strike-free service, railway authorities at the same time codified Indian rail workers' civil disenfranchisement.

The secretary of state for India imagined the reform of provident funds ideally as a complement to conciliation boards. As discussed in chapter 4, such boards were established in Britain in 1907, so here at least the secretary of state envisioned the colonial state moving toward a new dispensation of labor relations roughly in step with the metropole. And as a matter of fact, conciliation boards had been established in 1907 for higher-grade, British and Anglo-Indian guards and drivers—workers who had struck that year. The racial exclusion built into these conciliation boards is evident in the fact that the "European and Anglo-Indian Defence Association" was to have representation on the boards.[51] As Laura Bear notes, drivers sought in board deliberations to establish greater authority over Indian firemen and to secure a change in the practice whereby they were "called into office to submit an explanation." There, the drivers explained, "we are spoken to as so many coolies and the threat is always held out to us of dismissal."[52] Of course, such personalized and discretion-laden discipline enacted by upper managers was quite distinct from how entry-level workshop employees and other workers classed as "menials" or "coolies" were governed. For such workers, sergeants' orders reigned, and these orders were backed up by the threat of violence. Regardless of how myopic drivers' demands may have been, the conciliation mechanism was soon abandoned by railway authorities, and this mechanism of relative workplace empowerment disappeared. I suspect that part of the reason why railway authorities abandoned the conciliation scheme so quickly was that they recognized there would be no formally race-neutral way to prevent this mechanism from being taken up by higher-grade Indian railway workers such as stationmasters and signal operators, as well as by firemen, shunters, *mistris*, pointsmen, clerks, and other sectors of workers. As we saw in chapter 4, the conciliation structure in Britain tended over time to incorporate an ever-widening circle of employees, whose representatives argued for their legitimate standing in relation to the entry requirements for such boards. In any case, with the abandonment of conciliation boards, a formal venue through which to ameliorate grievances was closed, ensuring that the social liberal dispensation in colonial India would be notably less liberal than in the metropole.

While they opted to close down conciliation boards, railway authorities continued to seek out alternative means to forestall strikes along the lines. In considering revising railway provident funds with an eye to making these funds more effective mechanisms of labor discipline, authorities confronted a conundrum. The funds had been built in such a way as to exclude the broad majority of Indian railway workers from their benefits. Most workshop employees did not earn the fifteen rupees a month required to be eligible for membership. But workshop employees were among those who had participated in the strike wave of 1905–7, so some inducement to loyalty on the part of such workers was desirable. In 1909, at a meeting of the Home Boards of some of the most prominent colonial Indian railways, the directors present identified a mechanism for including all Indian railway workers in retirement benefits without fundamentally remaking the membership basis of provident funds. They advocated

> not only increased subscriptions to the Provident Fund but also "that in addition to the benefits under the Provident Fund Rules the Directors may at their discretion grant from Revenue to an employe in the Indian staff, or to his widow and children dependent on him, for good and efficient service a bonus equal to half a month's actual pay at time of retirement for each year's

service subject to the provision that no bonus shall be given to an employe of under 15 years continuous service and that no bonus shall accrue for any year over 30 years service."[53]

This proposal, as written, would not be adopted by the Railway Board, as a number of directors of Indian railways who weren't present at the meeting objected to the terms of the resolution. But in 1911, the chairman of the Great Indian Peninsular Railway addressed his shareholders, noting that the proposed reform was being held up by the Railway Board—an address that got some publicity, and thus forced the hand of the colonial bureaucracy. Officials at the Railway Board also had one eye on the metropole, noting that "the men may demand also the improvement of the Provident Funds, especially when the events occurring at home are considered, *viz.*, the seamen's and dock strikes and the men going out on the Lancashire and Yorkshire Railways." In the end, the gratuity policy adopted in 1911 differed in a few ways from the initial proposal, in part by substituting "employee on monthly salary including menials" for "employee in the Indian staff." As the Railway Board noted, this revised formulation "would cover men like pointsmen, who often have long service and, receiving salaries less than Rs. 15, are not qualified to join the Provident Fund."[54] This act of substitution makes clear how the fifteen-rupee threshold for provident funds had long served as a formally race-neutral way to exclude most Indian railwaymen from social benefits. Two years after the gratuity policy was adopted, the agent of the East Indian Railway wrote to clarify with the Railway Board whether the policy applied to workshop and colliery employees who were paid on a piece-rate basis, were employed under subcontracting arrangements, and/or were paid weekly or bimonthly. The board affirmed the eligibility of these and nearly all other workshop and colliery employees, who numbered more than twenty-thousand individuals.[55]

While Home Board members had congratulated themselves in July 1909 for the "generous manner in which the subject [of gratuities] has been dealt with," their action was taken at the same time as they were receiving pressure from below and might have been a direct response to that pressure, which was not limited to the recent strikes. In April 1909, "cooly Mallappa Malkappa (Ticket No 2194) whilst on duty in the foundry shop of Hubly Workshops met with an accident owing to the breakage of the emery wheel in motion and died from the effects thereof." A few months later his father, Mallappa Narasapa Rajakhadi wrote to the agent of the Madras and Southern Mahratta Railway Company

(M&SMR) demanding five thousand rupees in damages for the death of his son. As this bereaved father wrote, "The man died at the shops while at work on the 16th April 1909 by the negligence of the Railway Company. He was the sole supporter of our family. Therefore I am entitled to damages which I claimed by application. No heed was taken of the same." Rajakhadi's threat of lawsuit prompted the agent of the M&SMR to request from the Railway Board the authority to grant a gratuity of six months' pay to the late Malkappa's family, amounting to a total of forty-eight rupees, which the board duly granted. The secretary of the Railway Board further informed the agents of all Indian railways that they were authorized to "grant gratuities to the widows or families of employes in case of death resulting from injuries received on duty up to six months' pay in each case, subject to a maximum of Rs. 200."[56] Thus, gratuities for fatally injured workshop employees already had been granted two years prior to the 1911 policy change that authorized gratuities both for fatally injured and for retiring workers.[57] The establishment of a new, more universal—if also punitive—gratuity policy in the wake of the 1905–7 strike wave thus was overdetermined; it had been brought about by the agency of various actors, from a bereaved father in Hubli to the secretary of state for India, and from striking workshop employees in Jamalpur to the chairman of the Great Indian Peninsular Railway.

The reform of railway retirement benefits in 1911 occurred simultaneous with an expansion of housing benefits to include at least certain sectors of Indian railway workers. As Laura Bear has shown, in 1911 Indian railwaymen employed at the Kharagpur workshops of the Bengal and Nagpur Railway were supplied with residential quarters. These quarters were set apart from the original railway colony and were designed to separate workers by "community."[58] In the years immediately following this expansion of housing benefits, mass eviction from company housing was adopted by managers as a common tactic against striking workers. Just as the 1911 reform of retirement benefits involved at once the universalization of a social benefit *and* the weaponization of this benefit in the interests of labor discipline, the expansion of housing benefits in 1911 gave managers another lever to pull in attempting to break strikes.

Between 1911 and 1922, housing and retirement benefits were weaponized on multiple occasions by company officials to break strikes along the lines. But in 1922, in the face of powerful, nationalist-aligned strikes, colonial officials evidently came to view these mechanisms of labor discipline as counterproductive. Evictions and the loss of retirement benefits, like other forms of victimization, seemed to be fueling strikes rather than suppressing them. In the spring and summer of 1922, authorities with the Railway Board moved to abolish the no-strikes clause of the gratuity policy and to reign in railway agents' authority to evict striking workers. In what follows, we will see how workers organized on the eve of WWI, how managers utilized revocable social benefits as tools of labor discipline between 1911 and 1922, and how these tools ultimately were at least partially dismantled by the colonial state under the pressure of strike action in 1922.

REVOCABLE SOCIAL BENEFITS AND THE SUPPRESSION OF STRIKES THROUGH THE GREAT WAR

In 1913, employees on the Madras Railway took strike action as part of a wider syndicalist work stoppage across the subcontinent. The strike was led by the Amalgamated Society of Railway Servants of India and Burma (ASRSIB) and occasioned the broadening of the base of the union. Much of the vernacular press opposed the strike, calling on Indian workers to keep some distance from the ASRSIB. Editors argued that Indian workers were more likely to lose retirement benefits than British and Anglo-Indian workers and that the latter could rely on pastors to mediate disputes with managers. Editors further argued that the ASRSIB was cynically championing the cause of Indian assistant stationmasters, whose interests would be better served by relying on the vernacular press as mediators.[59] Despite these arguments, some assistant stationmasters helped lead the strike. One of the leading organizers in southern India was a man named Margam Iyer, who was employed as an assistant stationmaster in Settigunta. As noted in a legal ruling, Iyer apparently "struck and left his employment, moving from station to station in the interests of the strike. . . . He was informed that his services were dispensed with and directed to vacate his staff quarters."[60] This directive came just hours before the district traffic superintendent appeared at Iyer's door flanked by police officers. Iyer was home at the time along with his wife and mother. The superintendent, Mr. Mercer, proceeded to hit Iyer with his walking stick, and "he and the police then expelled complainant forcibly from the house and kept him on the station platform till he could leave for Madras by train." For this act of violence, Superintendent Mercer was subsequently tried and convicted and was compelled to pay a three-hundred-rupee fine. He was, however, acquitted of "entry by might and house-breaking." Iyer appealed this acquittal, and his case was taken up by the Madras High Court, which ultimately opted not to revise the ruling of the lower court. Nevertheless, in making their decision, the high court held that grounds could have been found for convicting Mercer of "entry by might and house-breaking," given that he did not go through the proper legal channels for carrying out an eviction but instead acted with an "intention to cause fear or annoyance."

Iyer's case was highlighted in 1922 by striking workers on the North-Western Railway, who saw the case as supporting their demand for an end to evictions. Upon learning of this demand, the Railway Board requested a copy of the 1914 case from the Legislative Department, indicating that in 1922 the union knew more about the relevant case law than did the colonial bureaucracy. Upon reviewing the Madras High Court case, the Railway Board issued a directive to railway agents stipulating that any evictions of strikers should only be carried out "strictly through and in consultation with the civil authorities" and that ejectments "should be limited to those who are taking advantage of their occupation of railway quarters to intimidate those who have remained loyal . . ."[61] The directive arrived just a few days too late to the East Indian Railway headquarters, as the EIR had just that week evicted nearly thirty employees from company housing at Jhaja. The EIR agent replied to the Railway Board's directive in an ambiguous way, admitting that "it may be necessary later on to ask you to modify these instructions, but we will first give them a fair trial." As time passed, the Railway Board's call for targeted evictions was met with some protest by railway agents, who argued that they needed the power at least to threaten broad-based evictions in order to effectively weaponize housing against strikers. But the Railway Board's directive does seem to have curtailed evictions, which had become all too common over the previous year. During strikes in 1921, mass evictions had been carried out on the Burma Railway, the Oudh and Rohilkhand Railway, and the Assam Bengal Railway, provoking dissatisfaction among strikers and their supporters. The Railway Board moved to limit evictions soon after this form of victimization became an explicit matter of labor negotiations—and, implicitly, a matter of legal contestation—on the North-Western Railway in 1922. But at least between 1911 and 1922, evictions or the threat thereof had formed one of the key means of labor discipline in colonial India.

During this same span, colonial authorities and railway managers also deployed the gratuity policy in the service of labor discipline. We will recall that the 1911 gratuity policy stipulated that when an employee struck work, he would in consequence lose all the time he had accrued toward the fifteen year minimum threshold for receiving a gratuity payment upon retirement. For some employees, especially older employees, this consequence meant they would not receive a gratuity at all, and for nearly all other employees, the policy meant they would receive smaller gratuities than they would have had they not struck. The trouble with the policy, from a managerial perspective, was that once workers had struck, this lever of labor discipline lost most of its force. Why not strike again if one had already lost time toward the gratuity? Hence the need for some sort of work-around or exception that might reset the gratuity lever. In 1914, the agent of the Madras and Southern Mahratta Railway (M&SMR) wrote to the Railway Board requesting a special ruling on the question of whether strikes that had taken place before 1911 could be forgiven for the purposes of the gratuity. The situation the agent faced was as follows: In 1909, drivers and firemen on the M&SMR had taken strike action. Then again in 1913, during the buildup to the syndicalist strike discussed above, the same workers were "subjected to the greatest pressure by the Amalgamated Society of Railway Servants and others to induce them to throw in their lot with the strikers." The agent continues his report: "At a meeting I had with representatives of the men prior to the strike in 1913 I promised my best offices in securing immunity for them from the consequences of their conduct in 1909 in so far as the gratuities made admissible under the rules of 1911 were concerned, provided they remained loyal should the outbreak then threatening mature."[62] The men in question did indeed "render most valuable services to the Company" during the 1913 strike, and so the agent worked to uphold his side of the agreement. His request to forgive the 1909 strike was passed along via the Railway Board to the secretary of state for India, who did not officially condone the strike of 1909 but effectively enabled the Railway Board to disperse gratuities to the M&SMR drivers and firemen as if they had not struck in 1909. In order to induce workers not to strike in 1913, the agent thus felt the need to promise workers that they would retroactively be granted an exception to the gratuity policy, which demonstrates that this policy ironically tended to force managers and state officials to condone—in order more effectively to break—strikes.[63]

Again during the Great War, railway agents faced the conundrum of how to utilize the awkward mechanism of the gratuity policy to forestall or bring to a close railway strikes. In 1917, strikes broke out among workshop and traffic department employees of the Oudh and Rohilkhand Railway (ORR). The ORR agent interpreted these strikes as having political motivations, insisting that neither of the strikes "were based on genuine grievances." He continued, "the preposterous demands put forward by the men and the action of a certain Indian edited paper at the time made it palpably obvious that they were engineered by political agitators."[64] The agent claimed to have feared that sympathy strikes might break out on other lines and dealt punitively with strikers, dismissing on the spot any he suspected of being leaders. He then bargained with the remaining strikers in the traffic department, promising them that he would condone the strike for the purpose of the gratuity if they returned to work. He did not make a similar promise to workshop employees, which implies a differential treatment of traffic versus workshop employees at this time. As the president of the Railway Board noted, "the [workshop] staff cannot be looked on as so important; the railway could have continued running as we saw on the Great Indian Peninsula even if the shops had been shut down for a time." While workshop employees' interests were thus ignored, the agent's promise to traffic department employees seems to have helped break the strike. His promise also raised a problem for the Railway Board, which was faced with the question of whether to affirm the agent's decision to condone the strike for the purpose of gratuity. The Railway Board took the occasion to ask the secretary of state for general authority to condone strikes in the future, knowing that this would not be the last time that an exception to the gratuity policy would have to be made. The secretary of state granted this authority, and the Board duly endorsed the agent's decision to condone the strike for traffic department employees.

Given how central the gratuity policy had become to strike negotiations in the years after 1911, it is not surprising that workers in 1922 would insist as one of their primary demands that their strikes be condoned for purposes of gratuity and further that the gratuity policy be revised. In 1922 on the North-Western Railway, for example, strikers demanded increased pay, the condonation of their strike for the purposes of gratuity, that gratuities be treated as a "service award" and not a gift, that workers not be evicted from company-owned housing, the reinstatement of striking workers, and a number of other concessions.[65] Like the demands for reinstatement and against evictions, the demand for "condonation" can be seen as a demand that workers not face retaliation for striking. That is to say, the demand contained an implicit call for the legalization of strikes. When the colonial state was deliberating in 1922 about whether to abolish the no-strikes clause of the 1911 gratuity policy, some of those who weighed in on the question framed the matter in terms of this basic question of principle. The viceroy, for example, noted that the gratuity policy "is essentially a denial of right to strike: Thus it is entirely at variance with modern ideas as to rights of labour. It cuts at the root of all Trades Unionism, and Railway Unions as they gain cohesion must, as a mere matter of self-preservation, continue to go on attacking the system till they destroy it. As long as gratuity rules exist in their present form, therefore, they are a challenge to the Unions, and we must expect strikes until we alter the rules."[66]

The viceroy thus extrapolated from the contemporaneous situation on the East Indian Railway, where the EIR agent feared another strike unless the gratuity policy was revised, concluding that the punitive gratuity policy was more likely to fuel strikes than to forestall them. His telegram, from which the above excerpt was drawn, urgently called upon the secretary of state for India to revise the gratuity policy. During internal deliberations on the matter in Whitehall, Sir Louis James Kershaw, secretary of the Industries and Overseas Department of the India Office, composed a memo supporting the viceroy's request. "In many directions," he wrote, "the Government of India have deliberately set themselves to bring India abreast of Western countries in labour matters, and, whatever may be said in favour of the patriarchal view, it is now much too late to go back."[67] Kershaw went on to contrast this "patriarchal view" with "modern ideas," including the idea that workers had the right to strike. He thus laid out a historical polarity between patriarchal and modern approaches to railway governance, suggesting that the colonial Indian state lagged behind the British metropole in moving from one to the other. Kershaw appears to have seen in the gratuity policy the outlines of a paternalistic approach to management, wherein companies invested in workers' social reproduction as an inducement to loyalty and in lieu of union recognition. We have considered in this book the histories of railway paternalism in Britain and colonial India and have seen how established, paternalistic forms of management came into crisis after 1905.

The trouble with Kershaw's argument, in light of the preceding work, is that he appears to have viewed railway paternalism as a single thing, whose outlines in colony and metropole were broadly similar. This similarity would allow for a one-to-one comparison, whereby a territory's relative progress from paternalistic to modern labor relations could be charted and compared in two dimensions. But, as we have seen, paternalism was bifurcated into distinct colonial and metropolitan modes. In Britain, paternalism was yoked together with mutualism; there, workers' representatives were drawn into the comanagement of social benefits, with significant long-term consequences for working class composition. In India, even for racially privileged, higher-grade workers, paternalism was never linked with mutualist comanagement. And, more consequentially, paternalistic approaches to management were not—at least until 1911—applied to the majority of the workforce, who were governed at work through more starkly authoritarian practices and were generally denied social benefits. With the 1911 gratuity policy, a version of paternalism was at once generalized and made more punitive. The gratuity policy was conceived as a component part of a broader, empire-wide social-liberal turn. In metropole and colony alike, social-liberal governance aimed to forestall strikes and other forms of unrest, in part by drawing wider layers of the population into state-mediated social benefit programs. In the metropole, the state fostered workers' comanagement of insurance funds, while trade unionists were given a platform for representing workers' grievances. In colonial India, such a platform was pulled away almost as soon as it was built, while newly extended, revocable social benefits were employed as strike-deterring tools. Under the new social-liberal dispensation in colonial India, retirement and housing benefits were extended to Indian railway workers, but in a way that reiterated the denial of civil rights to such workers. These newly generalized social benefits were made to be more punitive than retirement or housing benefits had been when these benefits were largely reserved for British and Anglo-Indian employees. The strike-deterring tools established in 1911 could, however, be made to suffer a detournement: In the wake of the Great War, the punitive gratuity policy was jettisoned because it was effectively fueling strikes. In Britain and colonial India, labor movements during and after the Great War forced new dispensations of railway governance. But the story of how wartime and postwar struggles remade practices of railway governance in Britain and colonial India has been and must continue to be told elsewhere, as we've begun to run past the terminal station of this journey.

Conclusion

Respectability on the Line compares how railway labor history was made in Britain and colonial India from the 1840s through the Great War. This was the period during which paternalistic approaches to railway management prevailed, at least for the governance of certain sectors of workers. Those who managed the railways drew on models from across the Empire as they ordered their workforces, including in building residential zones and in establishing benefit funds. At the same time, they managed in ways that were influenced by and consistent with the respective patterns of governance in their locales. Distinct regimes of governance shaped the forms of organizing undertaken by different groups of railway workers—organizing that, in turn, helped remake structures of governance. The book compares how railway labor-management relations changed in Britain and colonial India up through the Great War, while also weaving these parallel narratives of change together into a cross-imperial history of railway labor.

There are essentially three major acts of comparison that I have undertaken in the preceding work. First, I have compared how paternalistic managerial techniques shaped relations of race, gender, and sexuality in and around early railway districts. Second, I have compared how the respective mechanisms for mediating railway grievances maintained (or not) by company executives helped give rise to distinct forms of labor organization and coalition building. And finally, I have compared how social struggles along the lines reciprocally interacted with the making of social-liberal governance in Britain and colonial India. For each of these stories, processes of borrowing or cross-imperial influence complicate the work of comparison.

In the first two sections of *Respectability on the Line*, we saw how paternalistic techniques of management in Britain and colonial India helped shape relations of race, gender, and sexuality in railway districts. Insofar as railway paternalism in colonial India involved the making of racially segregated institutions of social reproduction, this mode of management contributed to the racial hierarchization of the railway workforce. This hierarchization of the workforce was justified by a racial discourse of masculinity, which associated workplace responsibility with whiteness. Over the second half of the nineteenth century, discourses of race circulated from colony to metropole—including through trade unionist publications—contributing to the discursive racialization of grade-based hierarchies of labor in Britain. Notwithstanding this discursive racialization, institutions of social reproduction were comparatively "universalist" in the metropole, as they were at least formally accessible to all employees. Moreover, promotion through the ranks was possible for any worker in Britain, while in the colony, Indian workers faced a racial bar to promotion. These differences were significant in terms of the forms of labor organizing that emerged in colony versus metropole, as a white laborist project took shape to defend racial hierarchies of labor in 1870s colonial India, while a formally universalist union dominated by higher-grade workers emerged at the same time in Britain. In its public rhetoric, this latter union promoted the ideal of the paternal railwayman, which combined the longstanding breadwinner ideal with an orientation toward the paternalistic care of passengers and of vulnerable members of railway communities.

While railway workers' representatives thus embraced and bolstered the association of railway labor with respectable masculinity and the domestic ideal, on the ground this ideal was stretched within railway communities. The book's first section shows how paternalistic railway governance ironically helped facilitate homosexual subcultural formation in railway districts. The presence of homosexual subcultures in railway districts first became apparent to me as I read Henry Winship's scrapbook closely and saw that it seemed to encode the familial and erotic relations Winship maintained with a range of fellow workers along the infrastructures of the East Indian Railway. This source drew me to consider the conditions that would have enabled the making of male homosexual subcultures in segregated, colonial Indian railway districts. I came to see how company housing policies encouraged bachelor railwaymen to cohabit. Gender and racial divisions of labor ensured that these railwaymen would not be responsible for performing significant amounts of domestic labor and thus that they could be recognized as dual heads of household. Recruitment policies that prioritized the hiring of unmarried railwaymen in their mid-twenties ensured the reproduction of a substantial gender imbalance in railway districts and made workers who had avoided marriage uniquely qualified for work abroad. And company-funded institutions of "rational recreation"—from bathhouses and bands to theaters and libraries—enabled the making of intimate, everyday bonds between men. In presenting this research, I received comments and feedback to the effect that the sort of homosexual subcultural formation I described could only have happened in a colonial setting and surely did not happen in metropolitan railway towns, overseen as they purportedly were by norm-enforcing paternalistic managers. But was this so? Certainly not all of the enabling conditions noted above would have obtained in the metropole, but nevertheless there were some parallels in the railway workshop towns of Britain. Unlike in colonial India, railwaymen in metropolitan Britain generally seem not to have been able to cohabit as heads of household in company housing. But, as census records made clear, they were able to cohabit as boarders, especially in the homes of railway widows, who would have taken on substantial domestic labor responsibilities. While most would have boarded for a relatively brief period as they worked toward promotion and marriage, some evidently boarded well into their forties. A similar collection of institutions of rational recreation existed in British railway towns, including theaters, libraries, and bathhouses. And finally, at least until the second or third generation of railway communities, a meaningful gender imbalance existed in railway towns. Parallel, potentially enabling conditions therefore obtained. And indeed, memoirs, newspaper articles, and playbills suggest that, by the 1870s, bachelors formed a relatively distinct subculture in railway towns and that there were places where and times when homoerotic intimacies were permitted.

Having found evidence of nascent homosexual subcultural differentiation in the railway districts of Britain and colonial India, I was forced to think anew about railway paternalism in British imperial contexts. Perhaps railway paternalism, in its overlapping but also distinctive colonial and metropolitan manifestations, combined gender hierarchizing techniques of management with a permissive relation to the sexual and domestic lives of upper subordinate employees. In the metropole, techniques of management consistently compelled women into domestic service roles, whether by refusing to employ women in the industry or by structuring benefit funds in ways that perpetuated women's dependency on male breadwinners or their surrogates. In colonial India, policies designed to foster marriage between railway apprentices and graduates of orphan schools coexisted with sanctioned regimes of sex work in and around military cantonments. Hierarchizing gender relations thus were structured differently in colony and metropole, but a permissiveness toward gender and sexual nonconformity among upper subordinate employees was a broadly consistent pattern across these two sites. In thinking along these lines, comparison necessarily began to yield to an analysis of cross-imperial trends. Rather than two cases, I also had to think about Britain and colonial India as part of a unified, if uneven, field of historical activity. Paternalistic managers from colony and metropole were borrowing techniques of governance from one another, and perhaps this permissive stance toward upper subordinate employees was not just a consistent but also a shared feature of railway paternalism across the imperial field. Given that a shared print culture linked these two sites, the existence of advice literature for paternalistic managers and literary works portraying paternalistic governance offered one avenue for analyzing what was in part a cross-imperial culture of railway paternalism. And indeed, from the mid-nineteenth century, advice writing and works of literature seemed to promote a paternalism laced with a permissive relation toward sexual and gender nonconformity, at least for upper subordinate employees. Further comparative analysis will be necessary to place British imperial railway paternalism's relative permissiveness toward male homosexuality in relation to paternalistic managerial stances from other times and places. At first glance, it seems that British imperial railway paternalism differed from the Fordist governance to come somewhat later, as Ford's Department of Sociology more actively discouraged bachelorhood in its workforce.[1]

As discussed in chapter 1, the presence of significant numbers of widows in British railway towns—an enabling condition for the making of bachelor subcultures in these places—was an effect not only of high rates of accidental injury along the lines but also of mid-century transformations that rendered railway widows more dependent upon railway managers for continued support and housing tenancies. The revival of the deodand after 1838 gave railway widows the capacity, with the help of radical coroners, to extract significant payments from railway companies—payments that sometimes amounted to as much as five hundred pounds. Such payments ensured a certain independence for widows. But with the abolition of the deodand in 1846, widows were rendered more dependent upon railway managers for support. Managers tended to allow widows to retain tenancies so long as they could pay the rent, and company executives established contributory funds around the mid-century that provided a modicum of financial assistance for railway families. But these techniques of governance rendered railway widows dependent upon a breadwinning man, be he a boarder, new husband, or apprenticed son. Another way to frame this would be to say that this most grave of grievances—the accidental injury on the job of railway workers—became at the mid-century a matter mediated not by the state but instead by the company. Railway workers and widows lost the ability to press for recourse from the state and relied upon the company for whatever support they could secure. In particular, they relied upon company sponsored contributory funds—funds to which workers also contributed and upon whose boards workers' representatives sat. Railway paternalism thus entailed mechanisms for addressing certain workplace grievances within company-sponsored institutional settings. In addition to establishing contributory funds, paternalistic governors of British railway firms also fielded workers' petitions. As British railway workers moved toward unionization in the 1870s, they drew upon the mechanisms employers had established for mediating workplace grievances, issuing collective memorials to directors around wages and working hours and making benefit funds for railway widows in the image of company-sponsored contributory funds.

In colonial India, railway governance worked differently than in the metropole, and this was nowhere more evident than in the mechanisms managers established—or refused to establish—for the mediation of grievances. For British and Anglo-Indian employees—those permitted to reside and to attend social functions in railway colonies—provident funds provided a means for addressing workplace injuries, though workers' representatives did not play the same role on provident society boards as they did in the metropole. Racially privileged workers evidently also could get the attention of upper managers via the intervention of religious authorities in railway colonies. (This may have been true in the metropole as well and would perhaps help explain why support for unionization was strongest amongst nonconforming sectors of railway communities.[2]) For the majority of railway workers in colonial India though, both official and unofficial mechanisms for addressing grievances were notably lacking. The vast majority of Indian railway workers were not eligible for provident fund membership, and those who were eligible were slotted into a membership tier that offered comparatively paltry benefits. Provident fund rules and regulations were altered and made more exclusionary in their translation from metropole to colony. When Indian signal operators sought to petition managers in the 1890s for improved working and living conditions, their line managers imposed fines as punishment. Upper managers generally delegated to sergeants and other line managers the powers to discipline and dismiss Indian railway workers, and line managers fined and enacted physical violence against their subordinates with impunity. In the face of these conditions, groups of Indian railway workers began from the 1890s to rely on the vernacular press to communicate grievances to upper managers and to wider publics alike. This improvised method for mediating grievances brought at least certain sectors of Indian railway workers into close working relationships with nationalist leaders and editors—relationships that would be drawn upon during the Swadeshi-aligned strike wave of 1906. These relationships also seem to have influenced how workers framed their grievances, as workers came to echo a nationalist discourse on railway outrages in describing the "ill-treatment" they faced at the hands of supervisors.

Thinking comparatively, we can see that in both British and colonial Indian contexts, the way grievances were mediated played a significant role in determining how workers organized and built alliances. In Britain, paternalistic mechanisms for mediating grievances were adapted by early railway unionists, who utilized the tool of the petition and who modeled the benefit funds they established on company sponsored provident funds. In doing the latter, unionists asserted their self-conception as "paternal railwaymen"—a self-conception that tended to foster alliances with craft unionists and to promote a moralizing stance toward railway widows and other precarious members of railway communities. In colonial India, formal and informal mechanisms for mediating grievances were maintained in relation to racially privileged, higher-grade workers but were all but refused to Indian railway workers, who improvised an alternative means of mediating grievances and in doing so helped solidify an enduring alliance with the Indian national movement. This alliance would begin to be tested, however, in the wake of the 1911 reform of railway retirement benefits, when a more properly universal social benefit was established for workers in the railway industry, helping make the syndicalism of the ASRSIB a potentially appealing vehicle for at least a fraction of Indian railway workers. The reform of retirement benefits in 1911, a year which also saw the first experiments in company housing for Indian workshop employees, brings us to the third act of comparison undertaken in *Respectability on the Line*—that is, the comparison about how social struggles from below reciprocally shaped the turn to social-liberal forms of governance after 1906.

In both Britain and colonial India, social protest and strike organizing in the years 1905–7 helped spur a change in regimes of railway governance, as state agencies became more directly involved in overseeing labor-management relations. In the metropole, the Board of Trade established conciliation boards in 1907, while in 1911 the government drew railway companies and trade unions into the work of managing state approved insurance policies. These reforms compelled unions to build out their administrative and advocacy capacities, making them more bureaucratic but also broader-based entities in the process. In colonial India, Swadeshi-aligned strikes in 1906 spurred colonial officials to reform railway retirement benefits, at once universalizing this social benefit and establishing a strike-breaking lever over railway workers. In crafting their retirement gratuity policy, railway board officials understood themselves to be pursuing a suitably less liberal version of the social-liberal dispensation that had taken shape in the metropole. They were thus acting in a context shaped by the politics of the metropole, but the policy reform they crafted bore little resemblance to those pursued in metropolitan Britain. This difference is particularly salient when we consider that the railway board of the colonial state initially moved to establish conciliation boards along the lines of those established in Britain but quickly abandoned this mechanism of labor-management negotiation. The retirement gratuity policy seemed to offer managers a more effective, and less dialogical, lever of labor discipline. In the wake of WWI, however, the retirement gratuity policy was politicized by striking railway workers, who demanded that this benefit be guaranteed rather than made contingent upon "faithful service." Fearing that strike waves would continue if they failed to revise the policy, colonial officials scrapped the no-strikes stipulation in 1922. In metropolitan Britain, social liberal reforms also spurred labor radicalism along the lines, as the bureaucratic responsibilities imposed on unions by the 1911 National Insurance Act helped draw trade unionists toward amalgamation in 1913. As a party to the Triple Alliance, the resultant National Union of Railwayman contributed to making the post-WWI strike wave in Britain.

As we have seen in the above recapitulation of *Respectability on the Line*'s parallel narratives of labor history, there is no single approach to comparison pursued throughout the book. Especially because the story involves dynamics of cross-imperial influence, it is difficult to make comparison operate in the service of hypothesis testing.[3] Rather, what we are after is a fine-grained account of how early railway labor history was made differently across two sites within an uneven imperial field. As techniques of management were translated between colonial India and metropolitan Britain, they were adapted to align with the patterns of governance that defined these locales. Distinctive regimes of governance then differently conditioned the social movements from below that took shape in the late nineteenth century and that helped remake regimes of governance in the early twentieth century. Comparison allows us to track over time these differences and to grasp their consequences, even as we register dynamics of cross-imperial borrowing as well as parallel developments in colony and metropole.

The book has shown throughout the importance of dynamics in the sphere of social reproduction for the making of labor history. Through the first decades of the railways' existence, housing, provident, and retirement benefits formed central matters of concern in labor-management relations, whether we think of negotiations around widow's tenancies in early British railway towns or about large-scale labor unrest around the retirement gratuity in post-WWI India. Managers consistently sought to intervene in the domestic lives of at least some number of their subalterns, and these interventions (or the notable lack thereof) shaped the ways that railway workers and community members maintained family lives and built collective projects. *Respectability on the Line* has worked to keep in view some of the interplays between these different scales of social experience by considering how the shaping of domestic lives interacted with the making of social movements in Britain and colonial India. In Britain, we can see a certain disavowal at work in how trade unionists consistently projected the figure of the "paternal railwayman" in their public rhetoric even as housing and other arrangements enabled the reproduction of bachelor subcultures in railway districts. Bachelors and others whose lives didn't exemplify the domestic ideal helped make railway trade unionism in Britain, especially from 1906 up through the Great War, but the public rhetoric of unionists generally downplayed the domestic heterogeneity of railway communities. This rhetoric also set unionists on a path toward support during the interwar period for a masculinist politics of social welfare, which enthroned the male breadwinner–female homemaker domestic norm. In colonial India, struggles for access to quality housing and equal retirement benefits waged from the 1890s by Indian railway workers helped define some of the central flashpoints of labor-management conflict during the first two decades of the twentieth century. Struggles from below compelled the colonial state to intervene in railway labor relations, which they did by reforming the retirement gratuity policy. Retirement benefits bore directly on domestic matters, as many used their retirement gratuities to build a family home. In the years immediately following the Great War, different forms of unionism were consolidated in colonial India. On the East Indian Railway, nationalist aligned mass strikes politicized the retirement gratuity policy, while on the North Western Railway, a form of general unionism led the way.[4] The 1922 abolition of the retirement gratuity's no-strikes clause was taken by the viceroy and by Secretary Kershaw to signal the modernization of railway labor-management relations, insofar as this reform implicitly conceded to workers the right to strike over grievances. In this sense, the interwar period can be seen as a post-paternalistic period; but given how actively managers continued to shape the domestic lives of railway employees, we could perhaps also understand this and later periods as having been caught up in the afterlives of paternalism.

Respectability on the Line thus attends to the history of railway labor management relations from the 1840s through the Great War. This was the heyday of the liberal imperial era—an era that ultimately would not come to a close until midway through the interwar period. But liberal imperial modes of governance and labor management began to experience significant turbulence in the years immediately preceding WWI. Just as the Fordist era featured a distinctive regime of compensation characterized by wages that, for relatively enfranchised workers, kept up with productivity gains and that enabled mass consumption, the liberal imperial era featured distinctive, often paternalistic regimes of compensation—regimes that reproduced for an upper stratum of workers the conditions of possibility for respectable households. Such households generally were kept up by domestic specialists and featured at least one breadwinning head. These roles, as a rule, were gendered, even if they were not always filled by a husband and wife pairing. In colonial contexts, these roles were also racialized. Respectability was not simply a feature of domestic arrangements underwritten by particular regimes of compensation and reciprocally bound up with racial and gender hierarchization. Respectability also functioned as a flexible cultural norm that could be directed to various political ends.

As we have seen throughout the book, railway workers, their family members, and their allies mobilized norms of respectability in advancing various, sometimes countervailing, collective projects. By the early twentieth century, such collective projects were bringing into crisis established modes of railway management and governance. In colonial India, the stark, racializing divides in regimes of compensation began to be broken down under the pressure of nationalist-aligned unionism. By 1911, Indian railway workers and their family members won breakthroughs in terms of access to housing, both during their time of employment and afterwards. In metropolitan Britain, workers won labor rights and the right to manage state-regulated insurance funds—breakthroughs that bolstered industrial unionism and set the stage for the "modern" regime of labor management relations that would take shape in the immediate wake of WWI, when a form of sector-wide bargaining came to be practiced. In colonial India, the post-WWI dispensation was more ambiguous, as railway workers were partially able to overcome punitive strike-breaking tools even as unions were not formally recognized until 1926. After WWI, railway managers in colonial India also experimented with mechanisms to enable workers to voice shared grievances through recognized intermediaries.[5] While respectability as a cultural framework did not fade into obscurity in the interwar period as breadwinner politics continued to define railway unionists' advocacy in both Britain and colonial India, certain paternalistic managerial practices that had helped bolster frameworks of respectability were at least partially jettisoned in favor of features of "modern" labor management relations.[6] In this way, struggles to realize a broader-based politics of labor and to expand access to social benefits to those previously denied such access forced changes in modes of governance and management, while at the same time drawing in tow culturally dominant domestic norms. But then, in the early history of railway life and labor such domestic norms were at times distended, showing how a persistent and prevailing breadwinner politics was articulated in some way against variegated domestic arrangements on the ground. The conservative politics of gender and family that defined unionist advocacy is not, therefore, the whole story—other ways of living gender and family, and other ways of forging alliances, were cultivated in early railway communities and have left sufficient traces in the archives to be retrieved.

Notes

INTRODUCTION

1. IOR/L/PWD/6/849/1684, "No 8 Telegraph of 1897," 16 September 1897.

2. See Sushila Agrawal, *Press, Public-Opinion and Government in India* (Asha Publishing House, 1970), 235.

3. Inspector-General of Police, *Report on Native Papers for the Week Ending June 17, 1899* (Bengali Translator's Office), https://jstor.org/stable/saoa.crl.32979426.

4. Inspector-General of Police, *Report on Native Papers for the Week Ending August 26, 1899* (Bengali Translator's Office), https://jstor.org/stable/saoa.crl.32979436.

5. These conceptual categories are borrowed from the regulation school of social theory. See: Robert Boyer, *The Regulation School: A Critical Introduction* (Columbia University Press, 1990).

6. On the mid-century making of a stratum of working-class subjects concerned with practicing respectability, see Anna Clark, *The Struggle for the Breeches: Gender and the Making of the British Working Class* (University of California Press, 1997); John Foster, *Class Struggle and the Industrial Revolution: Early Industrial Capitalism in Three English Towns* (Weidenfeld and Nicolson, 1974), 203–50; Geoffrey Crossick, *An Artisan Elite in Victorian Society: Kentish London 1840–1880* (Croom Helm, 1978); Neville Kirk, *The Growth of Working Class Reformism in Mid-Victorian England* (University of Illinois Press, 1985), 174–240; P. Bailey, "'Will the Real Bill Banks Please Stand Up?' Towards a Role Analysis of Mid-Victorian Working-Class Respectability," *Journal of Social History*, 12, no. 3 (1979), 336–53. On mid-century

company paternalism in Britain, see: Patrick Joyce, *Work, Society and Politics* (Rutgers University Press, 1980); Sonya Rose, *Limited Livelihoods* (Routledge, 1992); Richard Price, *British Society, 1680–1880: Dynamism, Containment and Change* (Cambridge University Press, 1999); George Revill, "Liberalism and Paternalism: Politics and Corporate Culture in 'Railway Derby,' 1865–1875," *Social History* 24, no. 2 (May 1999); Frank McKenna, *The Railway Workers, 1840–1970* (Faber and Faber, 1980), 40–64.

7. Laura Bear, *Lines of the Nation: Indian Railway Workers, Bureaucracy, and the Intimate Historical Self* (Columbia University Press, 2007), 295.

8. On the organization of domestic labor in Jamalpur's official bungalows, see: Nitin Sinha, "Entering the Black Hole: Between 'Mini-England' and 'Smell Like Rotten Potato,' the Railway Workshop Town of Jamalpur, 1860s–1940s," *South Asian History and Culture* 3, no. 3 (2012), 332. As Sinha writes: "The most important site on which segregation was breached was the most private of all the spaces—the official bungalows. Each of these bungalows had three outhouses, one each for cook, sweeper and *dhobi* (washer man). One more class, which frequently visited the household was that of *mali* (gardener). For the purposes of attending to officials' private comfort and running household errands, the railway colony was frequently visited by the natives. For instance, the East Colony was dependent on the bazaar for its meat supply, which was hawked from door to door."

9. Sharon Marcus, *Between Women: Friendship, Desire, and Marriage in Victorian England* (Princeton University Press, 2007).

10. With respect to the "colonial urbanism" that characterized state and company efforts to organize and segregate space in Jamalpur, Nitin Sinha quotes Veena Oldenburg, whose "more telling contribution lies in mapping the influence of the 1857 'Mutiny' and the British fear of 'Indian towns' that considerably defined the contours of town planning . . . . [I]t is noteworthy that this fear was expressed even for towns such as Jamalpur, which had not existed during the time of the Mutiny." See Veena Talwar Oldenburg, *Making of Colonial Lucknow, 1856–1877* (Princeton University Press, 1984). Sinha, "Entering the Black Hole," 325.

11. Ian Kerr, "The Railway Workshops and Their Labour: Entering the Black Hole," in *27 Down: New Departures in Indian Railway Studies*, ed. Ian Kerr (Orient Longman, 2007), 231–76. In colonial India, the ratio of entry-level workshop employees to these skilled workers was higher than in the metropole.

12. Ian Kerr, *Building the Railways of the Raj, 1850–1900* (Oxford University Press, 1995).

13. NAI, Railway, Establishment, September 1913, 92–94 A, "Sanction to the proposal that piece-workers in the Locomotive Shops and daily rated employees in Collieries, East Indian Railway, be eligible for gratuities for good, efficient, faithful and continuous service." Of these 20,000 plus employees, 7,471worked through contracting arrangements and thus weren't eligible for the gratuity, but the EIR agent claimed that such contracting arrangements would soon be phased out (and indeed, these arrangements had in 1912 been ruled out of order by the Railway Board), so the premise of the correspondence was that these workers would soon come under the gratuity policy. The other exceptional case

was children employed in the collieries, who, the Railway Board ruled, could not build time for the gratuity until they had reached the age of maturity.

14. Simon Cordery, "Mutualism, Friendly Societies, and the Genesis of Railway Trade Unions," *Labour History Review* 67, no. 3 (2002): 263–79.

15. Ritika Prasad, *Tracks of Change: Railways and Everyday Life in Colonial India* (Cambridge University Press, 2015), 74–75. See also: Ritika Prasad, "Smoke and Mirrors: Railway Travel and Women in Colonial India," *South Asian History and Culture* 3, no. 1 (2012): 26–46; Manu Goswami, *Producing India: From Colonial Economy to National Space* (University of Chicago Press, 2004); Bear, *Lines of the Nation*, 56.

16. On the wider press coverage of white violence at the turn of the century, Prasad cites Elizabeth Kolsky, *Colonial Justice in British India: White Violence and the Rule of Law* (Cambridge University Press, 2010), 185–86.

17. Goswami, *Producing India*, 103–31. On the carceral violence European guards inflicted upon Indian travelers through enclosed, third-class carriages, see: Prasad, *Tracks of Change*, 23–57.

18. See, for example: Emma Finniswood, "Kitty's Sketches," *Railway Service Gazette*, no. 385 (1879).

19. Manu Goswami et al., "Introducing Critical Historical Studies," *Critical Historical Studies* 1, no. 1 (Spring 2014).

20. Mrinalini Sinha, "Anatomy of a Politics of the People," in *Political Imaginaries in Twentieth-Century India*, ed. Manu Goswami and Mrinalini Sinha (Bloomsbury, 2022), 31–49.

21. Sumit Sarkar, *The Swadeshi Movement in Bengal, 1903–1908* (Orient Blackswan, 1973), 215. Cf. Tithi Bhattacharya on the boundaries of bhadralok communities and the post-1905 wave of organizing: "The combined and uneven nature of development and assimilation produced the bhadralok as an ethic and a sentiment. This was to come to fruition in 1905 when zamindars, petty tenure holders, print and railway workers, and our historically neglected kerani, were to come together to give political shape to the battle cry of *Bande Mataram*. The nation was brought into being, not in the private world of the 'elite' as Chatterjee has argued, but in the ideological dissolution of class conflicts" (67). Tithi Bhattacharya, *The Sentinels of Culture: Class, Education, and the Colonial Intellectual in Bengal* (Oxford University Press, 2005).

22. Sarkar, *The Swadeshi Movement*, 220.

23. The analysis here is indebted to Timothy Alborn's broader account of how the NIA affected trade unions. Timothy Alborn, *Regulated Lives: Life Insurance and British Society, 1800–1914* (University of Toronto Press, 2009).

24. IOR/L/PWD/6/1106/1258, "Government of India, Railway Department, Enclosure No I to Despatch No. 30 Railway of 1911, Report by Railway Board."

25. W. E. B. Du Bois, "The African Roots of War," *The Atlantic Monthly*, May 1915.

CHAPTER 1. IMPERFECT TECHNOLOGIES OF MORALIZATION

1. P. W. Kingsford, *Victorian Railwaymen: The Emergence and Growth of Railway Labour, 1830–1870* (Frank Cass, 1970), xii.

2. TNA RAIL 414/527, George Hawkins, Traffic Manager, LB&SCR, "Circular No. 46," 19 April 1853.

3. Douglas Galton, Board of Trade, "Accident at New Cross on 13 April 1853," 27 April 1853."

4. TNA RAIL 414/527, "Circular No. 46," 19 April 1853.

5. Thomas Tredgold, *The Principles and Practice and Explanation of Locomotive Engines* (London, 1850), 15.

6. Elisabeth Cawthon, "New Life for the Deodand: Coroners' Inquests and Occupational Deaths in England, 1830–1946," *American Journal of Legal History* 33, no. 2 (1989): 137–47; Peter Bartrip and Sandra Burman, *The Wounded Soldiers of Industry: Industrial Compensation Policy, 1833–1897* (Oxford, 1983), 56–60; R. W. Kostal, *Law and English Railway Capitalism, 1825–1875* (Clarendon Press, 1994), 254–321.

7. W. A. Dinsdale, *History of Accident Insurance in Great Britain* (Stone and Cox, 1954), 55. Cf. F. Hayter Cox, *The Oldest Accident Office in the World: Being the Story of the Railway Passengers Assurance Company, 1849–1949* (1949), 21.

8. Aileen Fyfe, *Steam Powered Knowledge: William Chambers and the Business of Publishing, 1820–1860* (University of Chicago Press, 2012), 171.

9. TNA RAIL 236/647, "The Great Northern Railway Provident Society Rules, Article 44, 1852."

10. 1851 Census of England, Wiltshire, Swindon, District 8d.

11. Railway Regulation Act, chapter lv: 20, 30 July 1842.

12. TNA RAIL 220/4, "Report of directors to the tenth Annual General Meeting of the Grand Junction Railway, held at Liverpool," 1 August 1842. Quoted in F. C. Mather, "The Railways, the Electric Telegraph and Public Order during the Chartist Period, 1837–48," *History* 38, no. 132 (February 1953), 43.

13. British Transport Commission Archives R. 289/1; E. J. Cleather to R. Creed, dated 14 August 1842. Quoted in Mather, "The Railways, the Electric Telegraph," 44. Cleather served at this time as superintendent of the Grand Junction Railway, while Captain Mark Huish, formerly of the East India Company Army, served as the railway's secretary and general manager, having been appointed in 1841. Richard Creed, Cleather's addressee, served as secretary of the London and Birmingham Railway, while Lieutenant H. P. Bruyeres served above him as superintendent. *Robinson's Railway Directory* (Railway Times Office, 1841).

14. Diane Drummond, *Crewe: Railway Town, Company and People, 1840–1914* (Routledge, 2017), 9.

15. *Illustrated London News*, III, 23 December 1843. Quoted in Drummond, *Crewe*, 10.

16. On mid-century company paternalism, see: Joyce, *Work, Society and Politics*; Sonya Rose, *Limited Livelihoods*.

17. John Cattell and Keith Falconer, *Swindon: The Legacy of a Railway Town* (English Heritage, 1995), 36–67.

18. At Wellingborough, for example, managers with the Midlands Railway oversaw a building that appeared in census returns as the "Railway Engineman's Home." A half-dozen drivers and firemen lived there, along with the family responsible for acting as stewards of the home. See George Revill, "Paternalism,

Community and Corporate Culture: A Study of the Derby Headquarters of the Midland Railway Company and Its Workforce, 1840–1900" (doctoral thesis, Loughborough University of Technology, 1989), 53. 1881 Census of England, Northamptonshire, Wellingborough, District 17. For a broader view of the geography of railway housing, see Frank McKenna, "Victorian Railway Workers," *History Workshop Journal* 1 (Spring 1976), 37.

19. Richard Price, *British Society, 1680–1880* (Cambridge University Press, 1999), 307. On company paternalism, see also Joyce, *Work, Society and Politics*; Sonya Rose, *Limited Livelihoods*.

20. Arthur Helps, *The Claims of Labour: An Essay on the Duties of the Employers to the Employed and an Essay on the Means of Improving the Health and Increasing the Comfort of the Labouring Classes* (London, 1844), 80, 98.

21. Helps, *The Claims of Labour*, 52.

22. On Victorian-era cultural patterns of elliptical speech vis-à-vis gender and sexual nonconformity, see: H. G. Cocks, *Nameless Offenses: Homosexual Desire in the Nineteenth Century* (I. B. Tauris, 2003).

23. TNA RAIL 250/82. Quoted in Cattell and Falconer, *Swindon*, 43, 65.

24. TNA RAIL 252/334. Quoted in Cattell and Falconer, *Swindon*, 63.

25. Cattell and Falconer, *Swindon*, 55, 62.

26. John Cattell, "Edward Snell's Diary," *The Bath History Journal* 9, no. 5 (2002), 114. As Cattell notes, the first half of Snell's diaries, wherein these entries appear, remain unpublished and are held privately by Snell's descendants. The second half of Snell's diaries, which focus on his time in Australia, have been published. Edward Snell, *The Life and Adventures of Edward Snell: The Illustrated Diary of an Artist, Engineer and Adventurer in the Australian Colonies, 1849 to 1859*, ed. Tom Griffith and Alan Platt (Angus & Robertson and The Library Council of Victoria, 1988).

27. Cattell and Falconer, *Swindon*, 76–78.

28. Cattell and Falconer, *Swindon*, 81, 109–10. In 1868, the GWR provided startup funding for the Swindon Permanent Building Society, a cooperative housing society. By 1871, two hundred houses had been built by the society. Cattell and Falconer, *Swindon*, 104–7.

29. 1861 Census of England, Wiltshire, Swindon, Districts 13g and 14g; 1881 Census of England, Wiltshire, Swindon, Districts 20 and 21.

30. Cattell and Falconer, *Swindon*, 160–61.

31. "The Great Western Workshops at Swindon," *Swindon Advertiser and North Wilts Chronicle*, 1 May 1865.

32. For widow-run boarding houses in railway Derby, see Revill, "Paternalism, Community and Corporate Culture," 233. See also George Revill, "Liberalism and Paternalism."

33. 1881 Census of England, Wiltshire, Swindon, Districts 20 and 21.

34. On five-hundred-pound deodands for fatal railway accidents, see "The Late Railway Catastrophe," *The Standard* 6406, Wednesday, 5 February 1845, p. 6; "Railway Intelligence," *Blackburn Standard* 40, no. 525, (Wednesday, 5 February 1845; *Railway Chronicle*, 27 September 1845.

35. Cawthon, "New Life for the Deodand," 146. As Cawthon notes: "For despite employers' successes in invalidating the fines at Queen's Bench,

occasionally juries wielded threats of deodands skillfully enough to force employers to acknowledge their own negligence, as much for public relations' sake as for the purpose of avoiding larger fines. Juries, that is, might mention deodands pointedly in order to exact either concessions to public safety or gifts to the families of occupational accident victims."

36. Cawthon, "New Life for the Deodand," 146–47; Bartrip and Burman, *The Wounded Soldiers*, 56; Kostal, *Law and English Railway Capitalism*, 254–321.

37. Matthew Wilson Smith, "Victorian Railway Accident and the Melodramatic Imagination," *Modern Drama* 55, no. 4 (Winter 2012), 497–522; Kostal, *Law and English Railway Capitalism*, 254–321.

38. On populist rhetorics of the 1830s and '40s, see Gareth Stedman Jones, *Languages of Class: Studies in English Working Class History, 1832–1982* (Cambridge University Press, 1983); James Vernon, ed., *Re-Reading the Constitution: New Narratives in the Political History of England's Long Nineteenth Century* (Cambridge University Press, 1996).

39. *The Ghost of John Bull: Or, The Devils Railroad, A Marvellously Strange Narrative* (James Pattie, 1838).

40. *The Ghost of John Bull*, 2.

41. *The Ghost of John Bull*, 37.

42. On the popular resistance to railway companies' rights to acquire and lay tracks on privately owned land, see: Kostal, *Law and English Railway Capitalism*, 144–82.

43. *The Ghost of John Bull*, 59.

44. Smith, "Victorian Railway Accident and the Melodramatic Imagination," 497–522.

45. During the early months of 1850, immediately following the extension of policies to workers on comparable terms to those offered to passengers, at least three fully insured workers were killed and their widows were each offered five hundred pounds. In November 1850, the managers of the Railway Passengers Fund, evidently worried about runaway payments to workers and their heirs, established for workers "a fixed total disablement benefit of 20s per week (maximum £30)." Railway Passengers Assurance Company, *Claims and Compensation, From November 1849 to March, 1851*, p. 8; Dinsdale, *History of Accident Insurance*, 55; Cox, *Oldest Accident Office*, 21.

46. TNA RAIL 414/527, George Hawkins, Traffic Manager, LB&SCR, "Circulars Nos. 37 and 38," 1 March 1853.

47. TNA RAIL 236/647, "We are all aware," n.d.

48. In 1850, Sturrock helped draft the rules for the newly established GNR Locomotive Sick Society. Cordery, "Mutualism, Friendly Societies," 268.

49. Other early funds were The Derby Locomotive Friendly Society (1841), the London, Brighton & South Coast Railway Provident Society (1842), and the London and South Western Railway Friendly Society (1844). Max Riebenack, *Railway Provident Institutions in English-Speaking Countries* (Pennsylvania Railroad Company, 1905), 308. On the Great Western Railway Provident Society, see: E. T. MacDermot, *History of the Great Western Railway, Volume I* (Ian Allan, 1982), 359. As MacDermot notes, at first this society was voluntary, but by 1848 participation in the fund had become a mandatory condition of service.

50. Cordery, "Mutualism, Friendly Societies," 263–79. As Cordery notes: "For railwaymen, particularly those employed in better-paid grades, friendly society membership was a common expectation and a company benefit for which they petitioned. During the 1840s and 1850s, decades in which the railway industry expanded rapidly, friendly societies multiplied exponentially with the growth of affiliated orders such as the Oddfellows and Foresters. High accident and sickness rates endemic to railway labour encouraged wage workers to go 'fund mad' during those two decades. By 1870, some eighty railway friendly societies had been created, providing coverage to perhaps one half of the total railway workforce" (265). Also see Penelope Ismay, "Between Providence and Risk: Odd Fellows, Benevolence and the Social Limits of Actuarial Science, 1820s–1880s," *Past and Present* 226, no. 1 (February 2015).

51. Cordery, "Mutualism, Friendly Societies," 267–69. By 1850, as Cordery notes, the "patterns of railway governance, including the division of responsibility between management and men, had been set."

52. TNA RAIL 236/647, "The Great Northern Railway Provident Society Rules, Article 4, 1852."

53. The Great Western Railway Enginemen and Firemen's Mutual Assurance Sick and Superannuation Society, as well as its precursor in the 1850s, should be included in the short list of exceptional benefit funds that provided a widows fund in the 1850s. See: J. T. Lea, *The Great Western Railway Enginemen and Firemen's Mutual Assurance Sick and Superannuation Society, 1865–1965* (Swindon Signcraft, 1965), 1–3.

54. These allowance rates are for "Class C" members, who were to pay twelve shillings per week to retain their memberships. Upon accident-induced retirement, Class C members were promised weekly payments of seven shillings.

55. TNA RAIL 236/647, "The Great Northern Railway Provident Society Rules, Article 56, 1852."

56. TNA RAIL 236/647, "The Great Northern Railway Provident Society Rules, Articles 41–55, 1852."

57. TNA RAIL 236/647, "The Great Northern Railway Provident Society Rules, Article 31, 1852."

58. In addition to the Railway Guards' Universal Friendly Society, the other early, employee-run fund was the Locomotive Steam Enginemen and Firemen's Society. While the latter boasted six thousand members by 1870, the former could count nine hundred members at the time. Both were relatively exceptional for how early they offered widows funds. Kingsford, *Victorian Railwaymen*, 172–73.

59. Railway Guards' Universal Friendly Society, Minutes, 1849–1873; Rules, 1849–1863. Cited in Kingsford, *Victorian Railwaymen*, 173. Emphasis in original. Cf. *The Sixth Annual Report of the Society for the Relief of Distressed Widows, Applying within the First Month of Their Widowhood, Instituted October, 1923* (Henry Baylis, 1830).

60. Cox, *Oldest Accident Office*, 25.

61. Cox, *Oldest Accident Office*, 25.

62. Cox, *Oldest Accident Office*, 23–24.

63. Quoted in Martha Vicinus, *The Industrial Muse: A Study of Nineteenth Century British Working-Class Literature* (Harper and Row, 1974), 214.

Original source: Edwin Waugh et al., *Lancashire Dialect Poems, Sketches and Stories* (Abel Heywood and Son, 1915), 46.

64. Jessie's marriage plot, while somewhat disjointed, does conform to Sharon Marcus's account of the Victorian marriage plot, which, as she shows, is driven forward by intimate relations between women. Both in nursing her sister and in sharing a moment of grief with Mary, Jessie realizes intimate bonds with women in a way that precipitates her marriage to the Major. Sharon Marcus, *Between Women*.

65. Elizabeth Gaskell, *Cranford* (Penguin Books), 63.

66. Gaskell, *Cranford*, 60.

67. Gaskell, *Cranford*, 65.

68. Gaskell, *Cranford*, 70.

69. Gaskell, *Cranford*, 70.

70. Gaskell, *Cranford*, 187.

71. On the reciprocal influences of social reform and domestic literature, see Amanda Claybaugh, *The Novel of Purpose: Literature and Social Reform in the Anglo-American World* (Cornell University Press, 2007). On Gaskell and social reform, see Catherine Gallagher, *The Industrial Reformation of English Fiction: Social Discourse and Narrative Form 1832–1867* (University of Chicago Press, 1985), 62–87. For a source on Gaskell's relation to company paternalism, see W. R. Greg, "Mary Barton," *Edinburgh Review* (April 1849), 402–35, reprinted in: Elizabeth Gaskell, *Mary Barton: Authoritative Text, Contexts, Criticism*, ed. Thomas Recchio, 382–90 (Norton, 2008).

72. TNA RAIL 1014/3, "GWR hiring document for Joseph Bavis," 25 May 1843. See also: Kingsford, *Victorian Railwaymen*, 8.

73. On the former expression, see Frank McKenna, "Victorian Railway Workers," 27. On the latter expression, see Alison Light, *Common People: In Pursuit of My Ancestors* (University of Chicago Press, 2015), 111.

74. 1861 Census of England, Wiltshire, Swindon, Districts 13g and 14g; 1881 Census of England, Wiltshire, Swindon, Districts 20 and 21.

75. Frank McKenna, "Victorian Railway Workers," 44. On the responsibilities of the railway police in Crewe, see Drummond, *Crewe*, 147. On the role of railway inspectors, see *Hand-book Guide to Railway Situations*, 13.

76. TNA RAIL 414/527, George Hawkins, Traffic Manager, LB&SCR, "Circular No. 200, To Station Clerks, Guards, and Others," 24 November 1856.

77. Locomotive Superintendent Joseph Armstrong exerted this authority in 1872 when he threatened in a letter to the directors of the New Swindon Improvement Company that he would cut off the gas to the Mechanics Institution if the NSIC did not pay arrears to the Great Western for gas supplied to the shops in the market. He included in the same letter a demand that William Clements, the housekeeper of the institution, cease taking "tolls" from market stall vendors and hawkers. TNA RAIL 277/6, "Letter from Superintendent Armstrong to the Directors of the New Swindon Improvement Company," 2 December 1872.

78. RAIL 277/9 "GWRC to NSIC Lease," 3 October 1854.

79. Cattell and Falconer, *Swindon*, 66.

80. RAIL 277/9, "GWRC to NSIC Lease," 3 October 1854. Baths had been provided since 1845 in a courtyard immediately adjacent to the works, and evidently they were in high demand. Cattell and Falconer, *Swindon*, 66.

81. The 1881 census lists the following housekeepers for the Mechanics Institution: William Clements, a fifty-four-year-old widower, and his unmarried forty-year-old sister, Eliza. 1881 Census of England, Wiltshire, Swindon, District 21.

82. Cattell and Falconer, *Swindon*, 80.

83. RAIL 276/26.

84. RAIL 276/26, "Letter from Langdale to the Council of the Mechanics Institute, New Swindon," 14 September 1864.

85. Cattell and Falconer, *Swindon*, 111–12.

86. Alfred Williams, *Life in a Railway Factory* (Duckworth, 1920 [1915]), 481.

87. On the Turkish baths at Swindon and Crewe, see Malcolm Shifrin, *Victorian Turkish Baths* (Historic England, 2015).

88. Anthony Trollope, *Mary Gresley and An Editor's Tales* (Chapman and Hall, 1873), 71.

89. Trollope, *Mary Gresley*, 62.

90. Trollope, *Mary Gresley*, 85.

91. Trollope, *Mary Gresley*, 89.

92. Trollope, *Mary Gresley*, 93.

93. Trollope, *Mary Gresley*, 91–92.

94. On the mid-century making of a stratum of working-class subjects concerned with practicing respectability, see Foster, *Class Struggle and the Industrial Revolution*, 203–250; Crossick, *An Artisan Elite in Victorian Society*; Kirk, *The Growth of Working Class Reformism*, 174–240; Bailey, "'Will the Real Bill Banks Please Stand Up?'" 336–53. On registered and respectable working-class families and the 1867 Reform Act, see Catherine Hall, Keith McClelland, and Jane Rendall, *Defining the Victorian Nation: Class, Race, Gender and the British Reform Act of 1867* (Cambridge University Press, 2000).

95. An early example of this sort of cultural geography appears in Charles Booth's surveys. See Frank McKenna, "Victorian Railway Workers," 41. McKenna locates railway workers in the "respectable" districts mapped by Booth, while noting the strong association of railway labor with "cleanliness" and domestic respectability.

96. Another such committee was the quadrille band. See RAIL 276/22, "Rules for the Management of the Quadrille Band, in connection with the Mechanics Institution, " n.d.

97. RAIL 276/22, "New Swindon Mechanics Institution, Rules of the Amateur Dramatic Society," n.d.

98. RAIL 276/23.

99. RAIL 276/23, "Mechanics Institution, New Swindon. Great Attraction: Grand Dramatic Performance," 23 April 1873.

100. William Brough, *Prince Amabel* (T. H. Lacy, [1862?]), 12.

101. See for example: RAIL 276/23, "Mechanics Institution, New Swindon, Arthur Sketchley, Esq., *Mrs. Brown on Her Travels*, etc," 27 January 1875; and

RAIL 276/23, "Mechanics Institution, New Swindon, Drawing Room Entertainment, Messrs. Bruce and Verne," 24 January 1877.

102. Brough, *Prince Amabel*, 16.

103. Charles Upchurch has shown that the 1870 arraignment of Fanny Park and Stella Boulton occasioned the assembly of a group of individuals implicitly committed to the extension of liberal principles of governance to matters of gender and sexual nonconformity. A similar commitment appears to inform the script of *Prince Amabel*. Charles Upchurch, "Forgetting the Unthinkable: Cross-Dressers and British Society in the Case of the Queen vs. Boulton and Others," *Gender and History* 12, no. 1 (April 2000): 127–57.

104. Brough, *Prince Amabel*, 17.

105. RAIL 276/23, "Mechanics Institution, New Swindon, Arthur Sketchley, Esq., *Mrs. Brown on Her Travels*, etc," 27 January 1875.

106. On the history of the dame as a figure of drag performance, see: Jacob Bloomfield, *Drag: A British History* (University of California Press, 2023).

107. Williams, *Life in a Railway Factory*, 274–75.

108. "Married v. Single," *Swindon Advertiser and New Wilts Chronicle*, 27 August 1877.

109. See, for example, "Hungerford," *Swindon Advertiser and New Wilts Chronicle*, 9 February 1874.

110. See, for example: "A Secret: A Tale from the French," *Swindon Advertiser and North Wilts Chronicle*, 16 February 1874. The story had previously appeared in an 1857 edition of *Blackwood's Lady's Magazine*.

111. *Swindon Advertiser and North Wilts Chronicle*, 3 December 1866.

CHAPTER 2. STRAINS OF PERMISSIVENESS, FIELDS OF FORCE

1. IOR L/PJ/6/789/4145, "Letter from Bertha Haynes," 8 December 1906.

2. London Metropolitan Archives, P75/JN/014. I have not been able to locate a birth record for Bertha Haynes's child.

3. On the nature of this relationship, and on its vicissitudes, see: Ian Kerr, *Building the Railways of the Raj, 1850–1900* (Oxford University Press, 1995); John Hurd and Ian Kerr, *India's Railway History: A Research Handbook* (Brill, 2012); Damien Bailey and John McGuire, "Railways, Exchange Banks, and the World Economy: Capitalist Development in India, 1850–1873," in *27 Down: New Departures in Indian Railway Studies*, ed. Ian Kerr, 101–88 (Orient Longman, 2007); Bear, *Lines of the Nation*; Nitin Sinha, "Entering the Black Hole," 317–47.

4. Mary Lyndon Shanley, *Feminism, Marriage, and the Law in Victorian England, 1850–1895* (Princeton University Press, 1989); Melinda Cooper, "The Ethic of Family Responsibility: Reinventing the Poor Laws," *Family Values: Between Neoliberalism and the New Social Conservatism*, 67–118 (Zone Books, 2017). The legal reform most directly relevant to Bertha Haynes's case is the 1886 "Married Women (Maintenance in Case of Desertion) Act."

5. On paternalistic management practices in Victorian Britain, see: Rose, *Limited Livelihoods*, 22–49; Joyce, *Work, Society and Politics*. On paternalism in the management of British railway labor, see: Revill, "Liberalism and Paternalism";

Frank McKenna, *The Railway Workers, 1840–1970* (Faber and Faber, 1980), 40–64. On paternalism in the context of enclosed colonial zones, see: Ann Laura Stoler, *Along the Archival Grain: Epistemic Anxieties and Colonial Common Sense* (Princeton University Press, 2008); Bear, *Lines of the Nation*.

6. On the history of the regulationist regime in British imperial contexts, see: Philippa Levine, *Prostitution, Race and Politics: Policing Venereal Disease in the British Empire* (Routledge, 2003); Levine, "Venereal Disease, Prostitution, and the Politics of Empire: The Case of British India," *Journal of the History of Sexuality* 4, no. 4 (April 1994): 579–602; Antoinette Burton, *Burdens of History: British Feminists, Indian Women, and Imperial Culture, 1865–1915* (University of North Carolina Press, 1994); Lisa Lowe, *The Intimacies of Four Continents* (Duke University Press, 2015), 101–34; Judith Walkowitz, *Prostitution and Victorian Society: Women, Class, and the State* (Cambridge University Press, 1982).

7. On the persistence of the regulationist regime in India after its official repeal in 1888, see Burton, *Burdens of History*, 127–40.

8. Anjali Arondekar, *For the Record: On Sexuality and the Colonial Archive in India* (Duke University Press, 2009), 68n48; Levine, "Venereal Disease," 596.

9. G. Huddleston, *History of the East India Railway* (Thacker, 1906), 242.

10. Huddleston, *History of the East India Railway*, 241. After the uprisings of 1857 and 1858, as part of a strategy of counterinsurgency and moral reform, British officials aspired to establish European settlements in northern hill stations. Bear has shown how these aspirations also animated the thinking of railway officials, who sought out ways to establish salubrious settlements for European and Eurasian railwaymen at some remove from the metropolis. See: Bear, *Lines of the Nation*, 21–34; David Arnold, "White Colonization and Labour in Nineteenth-Century India," *Journal of Imperial and Commonwealth History* 11 (1983), 133–58.

11. Nitin Sinha, "Entering the Black Hole," 322–23.

12. In 1880, the EIR employed upwards of four hundred drivers, firemen, and shunters. While drivers and firemen worked on locomotives travelling between stations, shunters were responsible for transferring engines between stations, sheds, and yards and were thus more likely to work within a delimited area. A relatively standard career track linked these roles, and involved a passage from fireman, to shunter, and then to driver. See: Valerie Anderson, *The Eurasian Problem in Nineteenth-Century India* (doctorate thesis, SOAS, 2011), 252. Other grades of workers employed with the locomotive department included: clerks, gunners, and locomotive cleaners. In addition to the locomotive department, other major departments of the EIR included the carriages and wagons department, which operated workshops in Lillooah and the traffic department, which employed clerks, guards, ticket collectors, station-masters, and signalmen. In the late nineteenth century, the traffic department was housed alongside the locomotive department in Jamalpur, but the former department was later relocated to Calcutta. Huddleston, *History of the East India Railway*, 112.

13. Anderson, *Eurasian Problem*, 257.

14. United Grand Lodge of England Freemason Membership Registers, 1751–1921 (Lodge of Unity, Allahabad, no. 1698, folio 133). Haynes was "excluded" from the Allahabad lodge on 1 January 1908. The reason for his

exclusion was not indicated in the lodge's membership log. A reference to Allahabad appears in Bertha Haynes's letter, as she notes that her husband worked the line "running between Calcutta and Allahabad."

15. Further indication of such porosity is given by Nitin Sinha, who notes, "In 1906, the first Railway Young Men Christian Association for Europeans and Anglo-Indians was opened in Jamalpur. Situated on the line of the overnight rail trip from Calcutta it also had a sizeable community of floating members of the European and Anglo-Indian communities." Sinha, "Entering the Black Hole," 325.

16. As Laura Bear has shown, access to company-sponsored housing was restricted on the basis of race more than of role, as even higher-grade Indian railwaymen were not granted company housing by EIR managers up through the turn of the century. Bear, *Lines of the Nation*, 78–83. That said, as Bear shows in the same chapter, records associated with Jamalpur-based schools indicate that a very limited number of South Asian employees appear to have been able to secure housing in the railway colony.

17. As Anderson explains, housing in railway colonies was subsidized—or rather, housing was not distributed on the basis of market exchange. An individual railwayman's rent was determined as a fixed portion of his salary, while his access to housing was determined on the basis of "race" and grade. Anderson, *Eurasian Problem*, 247, 258–65.

18. See Sinha, "Entering the Black Hole"; Anderson, *Eurasian Problem*, 261–65; Bear, *Lines of the Nation*; Huddleston, *History of the East India Railway*, 242–44; Rudyard Kipling, "Among the Railway Folk," *From Sea to Sea* 2 (1889), 274–99.

19. Michel Foucault, "Of Other Spaces, Heterotopias," translated from *Architecture, Mouvement, Continuité* no. 5 (1984), 46–49. The closest Foucault comes to a general definition appears in the following lines: "One could describe, via the cluster of relations that allows them to be defined, the sites of temporary relaxation—cafes, cinemas, beaches. Likewise, one could describe, via its network of relations, the closed or semi-closed sites of rest—the house, the bedroom, the bed, et cetera. But among all these sites, I am interested in certain ones that have the curious property of being in relation with all the other sites, but in such a way as to suspend, neutralize, or invert the set of relations that they happen to designate, mirror, or reflect."

20. Kipling, "Among the Railway Folk."

21. Kipling, "Among the Railway Folk."

22. Kipling's railway colony thus blends the two faces of heterotopia sketched by Foucault, containing elements of the *crisis heterotopia* and the *heterotopia of deviance*. While *heterotopias of deviance* encompass the sorts of disciplinary institutions Foucault is known to have studied, *crisis heterotopias* are "privileged or sacred or forbidden places, reserved for individuals who are, in relation to society and to the human environment in which they live, in a state of crisis: adolescents, menstruating women, pregnant women, the elderly, etc." Foucault counterposed the two types of heterotopia in part along historical lines, suggesting that "in our society, these crisis heterotopias are persistently disappearing, though a few remnants can still be found, [including] the

boarding school, in its nineteenth century form, or military service for young men." An example Foucault offers of a composite heterotopia is the retirement home, as "after all, old age is a crisis, but is also a deviation since in our society where leisure is the rule, idleness is a sort of deviation." Michel Foucault, "Of Other Spaces, Heterotopias," 46–49.

23. On the patterns of family formation in a number of EIR railway colonies, see: Anderson, *Eurasian Problem*, 247–65. For anecdotes concerning late colonial family formation in railway colonies, some of which indicate an association between cohabitation and promotion, see: IOR/MSS EUR/R1-075, "Oral Biography Papers, Plain Tales from the Raj, 1972–1974"; IOR/MSS EUR/ T12-T15, "Plain Tales from the Raj, 1972–1974"; John Masters, *Bhowani Junction* (Viking Press, 1954); while it focuses on the making of military families in colonial India, see also: Durba Ghosh, *Sex and the Family in Colonial India* (Cambridge University Press, 2014); Erica Wald, *Vice in the Barracks: Medicine, the Military and the Making of Colonial India, 1780–1868* (Palgrave, 2014), 26–27. As Erica Wald has shown in relation to soldiers' marriages in colonial India, a young woman's graduation from an "orphan school" tended to mark her as eligible for a marriage proposal.

24. McKenna, *The Railway Workers*, 53.

25. On the organization of domestic labor in Jamalpur's official bungalows, see: Sinha, "Entering the Black Hole," 332. As he writes: "The most important site on which segregation was breached was the most private of all the spaces—the official bungalows. Each of these bungalows had three outhouses, one each for cook, sweeper and *dhobi* (washer man). One more class, which frequently visited the household was of that of *mali* (gardener). For the purposes of attending to officials' private comfort and running household errands, the railway colony was frequently visited by the natives. For instance, the East Colony was dependent on the bazaar for its meat supply, which was hawked from door to door."

26. British Library, Henry Robert Winship Collection, photo 798: 1860s. Based on evidence from the scrapbook, he seems to have returned to Newcastle sometime in the 1880s.

27. Winship Collection, photo 798 (29): 1860s.

28. Sharon Marcus's *The Drama of Celebrity* offers some guidance for how to conceptualize the formal elements of nineteenth-century scrapbooks. As Marcus notes, most scrapbookers confined themselves to the *resituation* of printed materials, which, if nothing else, registered their having attended to the images or clippings in question. In his scrapbook, Winship extensively resituated printed matter to various ends—often producing on a given page a distinctive field of resonance. But he also deployed written captions in ways that recast his original photographs, often—as here—into a domestic register. On *resituation*, see: Sharon Marcus *The Drama of Celebrity* (Princeton University Press, 2019), 99.

29. Winship Collection, photo 798 (75): 1860s. Emphasis added.

30. A Mister J. Lindley appears in the Howrah Amateur Theatre cast lists, which are included toward the end of Winship's scrapbook.

31. Winship Collection, photo 798: 1860s. Cases of cholera were not uncommon on the engineering works of the EIR. Perhaps the worst epidemic occurred

over the course of 1859, when nearly four thousand laborers on the EIR works died of cholera. Huddleston, *History of the East India Railway*, 25.

32. Winship Collection, photo 798 (26): 1860s.

33. I have discussed only a selection of the intimate portraits contained in the scrapbook. Unlike those that seem to position their subjects into domestic service roles, the portraits of M. Johnstone and T. L. Roberts are surrounded by clippings that seem to cast these men into spousal roles. In particular, Johnstone and Roberts's pages each include clippings that detail, in an ethnographic mode, the variety of marriage ceremonies and spousal relations maintained in different parts of the world. Winship Collection, photo 798 (8, 9): 1860s.

34. On the conventions of nineteenth-century ethnological works on India, see: C. A. Bayly, *Empire and Information: Intelligence Gathering and Social Communication in India, 1780–1870* (Cambridge University Press, 1999); Mark Brown, "Ethnology and Colonial Administration in Nineteenth-Century British India: The Question of Native Crime and Criminality," *The British Journal for the History of Science* 36, no. 2 (2003), 201–19.

35. Collection, Photo 798 (19, 20): 1860s.

36. Winship Collection, Photo 798 (33, 99): 1860s.

37. British engineers and inspectors involved in overseeing construction projects were notorious for the routine cruelties they enacted against those compelled to labor on the lines. Bear, *Lines of the Nation*, 64–70.

38. National Archives of India, Central India Agency, Railway, 1863, 94, "Impressment of Labourers"; NAI, Central India Agency, Railway, 1881–82, 239, "Disposal of Criminal Cases."

39. Winship Collection, photo 798 (10, 11): 1860s.

40. See, for example: Winship Collection, photo 798 (31, 32): 1860s. On the history of the construction of the EIR line, see Huddleston, *History of the East India Railway*, 28–47.

41. David Arnold, "White Colonization and Labour in Nineteenth-Century India," *Journal of Imperial and Commonwealth History* 11 (1983), 133–58; Bear, *Lines of the Nation*.

42. On labor-management antagonisms in this intensive phase of railway construction, see: Ian Kerr, "Working Class Protest in 19th Century India: Example of Railway Workers," *Economic and Political Weekly* 20, no. 4 (January 26, 1985): 34–40.

43. Huddleston, *History of the East India Railway*, 1–27.

44. Bear, *Lines of the Nation*, 21–34, 63–90; Harald Fischer-Tiné, *Low and Licentious Europeans: Race, Class, and "White Subalternity" in Colonial India*; Satoshi Mizutani, *The Meaning of White: Race, Class and the 'Domiciled Community' in British India, 1858–1930* (Oxford University Press, 2012).

45. For the establishment of paternalistic institutions in Swindon, see: TNA/RAIL 276–78. See also Revill, "Liberalism and Paternalism"; Frank McKenna, *The Railway Workers*, 40–64.

46. On "rational recreation," see: Bear, *Lines of the Nation*, 74–75. IOR/L/PWD/6/716/1376, "EIR Provident Fund Rules, Sanction to Certain Alterations, 1906."

47. For an example of the government's outright refusal to authorize company funds for the provision of a particular institution, in this case hotels in railway districts, see: Sinha, "Entering the Black Hole," 329, 330.

48. IOR/L/PWD/5/1, "From Captain F.S. Taylor," 28 January 1863. While the promotion of temperance in their subordinates was something company managers and colonial state officials both pursued, here as well there seems to have been a tacit acceptance of subordinates' drinking. Apparently, on the Jubbalpore line, a Mister Kellner was granted by the railway agent the right to sell alcohol in his station-based refreshment rooms. NAI, Central India Agency, Railway, 1867, 108, "Liqueur shops near the railway on the Jubbalpore line."

49. Revill, "Paternalism, Community and Corporate Culture," 41–42, 276.

50. Levine, *Prostitution, Race, and Politics*, 40.

51. Jessica Hinchy, *Governing Gender and Sexuality in Colonial India: The Hijra, c. 1850–1900* (Cambridge University Press, 2019), 36–41; Jessica Hinchey, "The Eunuch Archive: Colonial Records of Non-Normative Gender and Sexuality in India," *Culture, Theory and Critique* 58, no. 2 (2017); Anjali Arondekar, *For the Record*.

52. Levine, "Venereal Disease," 586–88.

53. Bear, *Lines of the Nation*, 80.

54. In addition to the formation of intimate bonds between cohabiting bachelors, which forms the central focus of this chapter, and in addition to the hiring of regulated sex workers, rail managers permitted heterosexual cohabitation absent a formal marriage relation—colloquially referred to as a *nika* marriage. Moreover, managers monitored cases of servants bringing Indian women into colonies on behalf of railwaymen under the pretext that they were said to be servants' spouses. It is grim but important to note that it is not clear whether managers drew a line of distinction between coerced and at least relatively consensual sexual relations or not, as their approach to the governance of their upper subordinates in relation to these two ethically distinct sorts of acts was broadly consistent. They routinely composed reports exonerating upper subordinates accused of having sexually assaulted Indian passengers. Under the rule of railway paternalism, managers not infrequently prioritized gathering information and inducing a sense of loyalty in their upper subordinates rather than punishing them for breaches of official moral codes, even when those harmed were pressing their claims. Bear, *Lines of the Nation*, 80. Cf. Ghosh, *Sex and the Family*; IOR/L/PJ/6/848/453, "Summary of the Proceedings of the Rawalpindi Outrage Case," November 1907. For an affirmative justification of the above-mentioned approach to discipline in railway contexts, see: Michael Reynolds, *Engine-Driving Life: Stirring Adventures and Incidents in the Lives of Locomotive Engine-Drivers* (London, 1881).

55. Arondekar, *For the Record*, 68n48; Levine, "Venereal Disease," 596. The full quote from which this excerpt is drawn reads as follows: "Philippa Levine's illuminating argument on the connections between 'sexually transmitted diseases and the business of politics and governance' in post-Mutiny British India is worth summarizing here. For Levine, the success of the script of colonial governance, especially as it skirts the threat of homosexuality among its armed forces

in India, depends primarily on its management of the debates around venereal diseases. Levine adds that such a shift of focus to the effects of venereal disease as the emerging threat to the empire is particularly critical to understanding the 'centrality of sexual politics in the maintenance of empire.' 'Without available women, soldiers unable to control their passions in the tropical heat of the East would turn to rape—or worse to one another. The constant haunting fear of homosexuality, the presence of which would undermine the manly adventure of conquest, underscores the whole debate on prostitution in this era, despite a conspicuous reluctance to discuss the question in official circles."

56. Arondekar, *For the Record*, 56–58. Arondekar also highlights the somewhat more public case of Archdeacon William Noyes of Rangoon, who was charged with "having behaved with improper familiarity and indecency towards certain private soldiers," and was convicted at a court martial in 1893. While there was some consideration of bringing charges as well under the penal code, this course was dismissed for a purported lack of evidence, suggesting that British colonists were, as a rule, shielded from prosecution under the sodomy statutes of the penal code.

57. England and Wales, National Probate Calendar, Index of Wills and Administrations (1926); LBSC Railway Employment Records, Locomotive Department (1881), 111.

58. IOR/L/PWD/6/315/2589, "Report by the Consulting Engineer," 7 January 1890.

59. IOR/L/PWD/5/31, "Regulations relating to recruiting of Locomotive and Carriage and Wagon Departments of Indian State Railways, 1903–1935." The policy prioritizing unmarried men was officially scrapped during WWI, at least with respect to the Indian State Railways. But the prioritization of single men, at least by non-state railways, remained in evidence after the war: IOR/L/PWD/6/1051/4771, "Statement of vacant appointments for which covenanted hands are required to be recruited from England," 9 October 1919.

60. IOR/L/PWD/6/315/2589, "Memorandum by the Director General of Stores," 2 December 1889.

61. On managerial "common sense" with respect to married workers' demoralization, see: IOR/L/PWD/6/1102/1258, "GOI Finance Department, Enclosure to dispatch No 190 of 1919: Report by the Railway Board."

62. British Library, MSS EUR/F133/42: 1861–1862.

63. Carolyn Steedman, "The Magistrates," *Dust: The Archive and Cultural History* (Rutgers University Press, 2002), 38–65.

64. Steedman, *Dust*, 47.

65. Marcus, *Between Women*.

66. Hinchy, "The Eunuch Archive," 6.

CHAPTER 3. PATERNAL FIGURES

1. Lambeth Palace Library. W. Temple 46, f. 24.

2. "The Family of the Bishop of London are Staying with Mr Langdon, the station master," *Carlisle Patriot*, Friday, 21 May 1886. The *Carlisle Patriot*'s first editor, Robert Perring, was from Devon, and the paper generally aligned

itself with the established church; perhaps these facts help explain the *Carlisle Patriot*'s interest in the social calendar of a railway family living on the opposite edge of the country. While Frederick Temple served as archbishop of Canterbury from 1896 to 1902, William served in the same post from 1942 to 1944.

3. Roger Langdon et al., *The Life of Roger Langdon* (Elliot Stock, 1909), 5.

4. Langdon et al., *The Life of Roger Langdon*, 5. "When Miss Ellen Langdon desired me to undertake this portion of the work I felt honoured, though diffident. A feeling that it was my clear duty to pay any mark of respect I could to the memory of this worthy man decided me to accept her invitation." Henry evidently was troubled by the question of how best to honor the memory of a beloved father and railwayman—a question that perhaps pressed upon him as well in his personal life. In 1908, Henry's brother, C. A. Lambert, was promoted to district superintendent of the North Eastern Railway at Hull. C. A. had thus successfully followed in their father's footsteps, while Henry was living the comparatively comfortable life of a London-based solicitor.

5. Langdon et al., *The Life of Roger Langdon*, 5.

6. Langdon et al., *The Life of Roger Langdon*, 72.

7. Langdon et al., *The Life of Roger Langdon*, 79.

8. Langdon et al., *The Life of Roger Langdon*, 5.

9. Drummond, *Crewe*, 77.

10. Catherine Hall, "Rethinking Imperial Histories: The Reform Act of 1867," *New Left Review* 1, no. 208 (November/December 1994), 18.

11. ASRS, *The General Secretary's Report to the Annual General Meeting at Cardiff* (October 5, 1880), 14.

12. Anna Clark, *The Struggle for the Breeches: Gender and the Making of the British Working Class* (University of California Press, 1997).

13. Simon Cordery, "Mutualism, Friendly Societies, and the Genesis of Railway Trade Unions," *Labour History Review*, 67, no. 3 (2002), 263–79.

14. On the refounding of the ASRSI, see: Lajpat Jagga, "Colonial Railwaymen and British Rule: A Probe into Railway Labour and Agitation in India, 1919-1922," *Studies in History* III, nos. 1–2 (1981), 115.

15. Edwin Phillips, *Full Report of the First General Delegate Meeting of the Amalgamated Society of Railway Servants, together with a Concise History of the Union from its Commencement* (ASRS Society Office, 1872).

16. James Cronin, "Strikes and Power in Britain, 1870-1920," in *Strikes, Wars, and Revolutions in an International Perspective: Strike Waves in the Late Nineteenth and Early Twentieth Centuries*, ed. Leopold H. Haimson and Charles Tilly (Cambridge University Press, 2002), 93–94.

17. Kingsford, *Victorian Railwaymen*, 64–65.

18. Philip Bagwell, *The Railwaymen: The History of the National Union of Railwaymen* (George Allen & Unwin, 1963), 66.

19. Charles Bassett-Vincent, *An Authentic History of Railway Trade Unionism* (Derby, 1963 [1902]).

20. On this political conjuncture, see: Eric Hobsbawm, *Industry and Empire: The Making of Modern English Society*, vol. 2, *1750 to the Present Day* (Pantheon Books, 1968), 101–5; Keith McClelland, "Rational and Respectable Men: Gender, the Working Class, and Citizenship in Britain, 1850–1867," in *Gender*

and Class in Modern Europe, ed. Laura Frader and Sonya Rose (Cornell University Press, 1996), 280–93; Catherine Hall, "Rethinking Imperial Histories," 3–29. For an account of the ascendancy of liberal constitutionalism across Europe at this moment, see Geoff Eley, *Forging Democracy: The History of the Left in Europe, 1850–2000* (Oxford University Press, 2002), 38–39.

21. For the former, see: R. J. Irving, "The Profitability and Performance of British Railways, 1870–1914," *The Economic History Review, New Series* 31, no. 1 (February, 1978), 46–66. As Philip Bagwell notes, the pre-1873 boom was a key enabling context for railway unionism. Bagwell, *The Railwaymen*, 66.

22. Irving, "Profitability and Performance," 53.

23. Jack Simmons, *The Express Train and Other Railway Studies* (David St. John Thomas, 1994), 221. I haven't yet been able to locate comparable statistics for total employment levels over this period. Kingsford includes a table that spans 1856 to 1876, which indicates that the overall number of railway employees multiplied by 2.55 over this span—two-thirds of the period Simmons considers. This would suggest a comparatively slower rate of employment growth, making for a more intensive pace of work. Kingsford further shows that the number of passengers conveyed per servant increased from 1,283 in 1860 to 1,660 in 1873, showing from another angle the extent of speedup over the late-1860s and early 1870s. Kingsford, *Victorian Railwaymen*, 47, 63. R.J. Irving argues that speedup was an effect of competitive pressures, especially in the first years of the 1870s, when rail managers sought to compete for passengers by offering faster and more frequent trains. Irving, "Profitability and Performance," 53.

24. As Wilson notes, continuous brake technology and block signaling systems were not legally mandated until 1889, in the immediate aftermath of the Armagh disaster of 12 June 1889. H. Raynar Wilson, *Railway Accidents, Legislation and Statistics 1825–1924* (Raynar Wilson, 1925), 26–27; Kingsford, *Victorian Railwaymen*, 27–28.

25. During this time, the Board of Trade took on an additional inspector to handle the rising annual rate of accidents—a measure that reached its peak in 1873. This statistical measure is not entirely reliable, especially as labor organizing effectively pressured the state in 1871 to mandate inspections not only for accidents affecting passengers but also for those that solely affected rail workers, meaning that reports conducted on either side of this threshold are not commensurate. Nevertheless, the period immediately preceding this change was marked by a dramatic increase in recorded accidents as well, suggesting that the spike in officially recorded accidents was not, above all, a function of shifts in the parameters of record keeping. Between 1871 and 1890, the large plurality of accidents (921 of 2,473) occurred because of "collisions within fixed signals at stations or sidings." Especially prominent were accidents involving rear-end collisions, the recorded causes of which included problems with brake power, problems with securing intervals between trains or signaling, the defective arrangement of signals or points, excessive speed, and negligence. Simmons, *The Express Train*, 215, 247; Wilson, *Railway Accidents*, 28, 47.

26. *Railway Service Gazette*, no. 1, Saturday, 3 February 1872.

27. *Railway Service Gazette*, no. 28, Saturday, 10 August 1872, 13–14.

28. *Railway Service Gazette*, no. 28, Saturday, 10 August 1872, 2.

29. *Railway Service Gazette*, no. 27, Saturday, 3 August 1872, 13.

30. On promises for sympathy action from London car men, see: "Railway Servants." Times [London, England] 22 July 1872: 12. The Times Digital Archive. Web. 18 Aug. 2015.

31. See, for example: "The Strike And Lock-Out." *Times* [London, England] 26 July 1872: 12, The Times Digital Archive, 18 Aug. 2015.

32. *Railway Service Gazette*, no. 27, Saturday, 3 August 1872, 1.

33. *Railway Service Gazette*, no. 27, Saturday, 3 August 1872, 2.

34. *Railway Service Gazette*, no. 28, Saturday, 10 August 1872, 1–2. For public criticisms of the Broad Street Strike through the Fall of 1872, see: *Railway Service Gazette*, no. 49, Saturday, 4 January 1873, 1.

35. Cordery, "Mutualism, Friendly Societies," 263.

36. Bassett-Vincent, *Authentic History*, 61.

37. Bassett-Vincent, *Authentic History*, 64.

38. Quoted in: "The Derby Orphanage: Its History," *Railway Review*, 27 April 1888.

39. ASRS, *The General Secretary's Report*, 14.

40. See, for example, the report from the Manchester branch: *Railway Service Gazette*, no. 316, 15 February 1878, 4–5. A resolution passed by the Clapham Junction branch in 1878 also conveys some indication of unionists' frustrations with the selection processes used by the Derby committee: "The secretary called attention to a resolution passed at the last meeting of the metropolitan sub-committee, recommending that the children of subscribers should be admitted without election when there are not more of such candidates than there are vacancies to be filled up, and that the children of non-subscribers should not be submitted for election until the children of subscribers had been provided for; and a resolution was passed unanimously approving of this principle." *Railway Service Gazette*, 19 July 1878, 4. On Manchester unionists' arguments for the inadequacy of the orphanage in addressing the crisis of reproduction faced by railway widows, see: *Railway Service Gazette*, no. 311, 11 January 1878; *Railway Service Gazette*, no. 397, 5 September 1879, 1.

41. Fred Evans, *The Duty of the Society to the Orphans of Members* (February, 1879), 2. This report was first read at the Executive Committee on 2 April 1878.

42. *Railway Service Gazette*, no. 397, 5 September 1879, 1.

43. ASRS, Annual General Meeting, 5 October 1880, 5–6.

44. ASRS, Executive Committee Meeting, 4 May 1881.

45. ASRS, Agenda of Annual General Meeting, 1880, 17–18.

Rule xx.7: It shall be the duty of the secretary, or other officer appointed by the branch, to ascertain the condition of the orphans aided from the fund, and from time to time to report to the branch or to the Executive Committee as to their cleanliness, clothing, schooling, and general treatment. Should it be found that from any cause the orphans are neglected and the moneys not applied to their benefit by their guardian, the Executive Committee reserves to itself the right to withhold the moneys from the guardian, and to authorize the branch officers to expend the allowances in food and clothing for the children. . . .

xx.9: Should the mother of any orphan or family of orphans remarry, the children shall cease to be entitled to the benefit. Should the mother of a family receiving the benefit of the fund be guilty of immorality, the Executive Committee shall have power, on the representation of the branch, to withhold payment of the benefit while the children remain with the mother, or to apply it for the benefit of the children if separated from the mother. Should a mother of children on the fund desert them, the provisions of this clause and of Clause 8 shall apply to such children.

46. We can draw a parallel between the patriarchal presumption of control over women's labor encoded here and an 1878 editorial in the *Railway Service Gazette*, which argued against women's enfranchisement on the grounds that "to this day women are protected in the same way that property generally is protected. There is an understanding between men not to injure women just as there is an understanding not to trespass on each others' lands." *Railway Service Gazette*, no. 335, 28 June 1878, 1.

47. ASRS, Minutes of the Meeting of the Executive Committee, with a Copy of the General Office Financial Statements, 21 July 1880, 4.

48. ASRS, Minutes of the Meeting of the Executive Committee, 5.

49. ASRS, Minutes of the Executive Committee Meeting (May 1887), 4.

50. ASRS, Minutes of the Executive Committee Meeting (February 1887), 5.

51. ASRS, Minutes of the Executive Committee Meeting (May 1887), 4.

52. Charles Dickens, *Dombey and Son* (Clarendon Press, 1974 [1848]), 274–75.

53. On the appropriation of melodramatic rhythms and rhetorical forms in Dickens's *Dombey and Son*, see William Axton, *Circle of Fire: Dickens' Vision and Style and the Victorian Popular Theater* (University of Kentucky Press, 1966), 219–61.

54. Kostal, *Law and English Railway Capitalism*, 254–321.

55. Jamie Bronstein, *Caught in the Machinery: Workplace Accidents and Injured Workers in Nineteenth-Century Britain* (Stanford University Press, 2008); Elisabeth Cawthon, *Job Accidents and the Law in England's Early Railway Age* (Edwin Mellen, 1997); P. W. J. Bartrip and S. B. Burman, *The Wounded Soldiers of Industry* (Clarendon Press, 1983); Kostal, *Law and English Railway Capitalism*.

56. Dorothy W. Collin, "The Composition and Publication of Elizabeth Gaskell's Cranford," *Bulletin of John Rylands II Library of Manchester* 69 (1986): 59–95; Elizabeth Gaskell, *Cranford*.

57. Ellen Wood, *Oswald Cray* (1901 [1864]), 86–7.

58. "The Influence of Railway Travelling on Public Health," *The Lancet* (1862), 65–66. James Ogden Fletcher. *Railways in Their Medical Aspects* (London, 1867), 34–35.

59. Marshall M. Kirkman, *Railway Service: Trains and Stations; Describing the Manner of Operating Trains, and the Duties of Train and Station Officials* (New York, 1878), 156–57.

60. John Carter, *On the Influence of Education and Training in Preventing Diseases of the Nervous System* (London, 1855), 152–53.

61. [A Signalman], *A Voice from the Signal-Box: Or, Railway Accidents and their Causes* (Longmans, Green, 1874).

62. Langdon et al., *The Life of Roger Langdon*, 88.

63. Langdon et al., *The Life of Roger Langdon* (1909), 94.

64. *The Principal Causes of Railway Accidents, with Proposed Remedies, by a Railway Servant of Fifteen Years Experience* (Edinburgh, 1873).
65. J. Leahcimrac, *John Ingram: Or, Railway Life behind the Curtain* (Holmes, 1889).
66. Finniswood wrote under the pseudonym of Eona, and over her lifetime would publish a number of other short stories and poems, many of which concerned life in railway communities.
67. "Kitty's Sketches," *Railway Service Gazette,* 385, (1879), 5.
68. "Kitty's Sketches," 5.
69. *Railway Service Gazette,* 16 August 1878, 3. On Asian racialization in the context of late nineteenth-century campaigns of exclusion, see: Iyko Day, *Alien Capital: Asian Racialization and the Logic of Settler Colonial Capitalism* (Duke University Press, 2016).
70. Jonathan Hyslop, "The Imperial Working Class Makes Itself 'White': White Labourism in Britain, Australia, and South Africa Before the First World War," *Journal of Historical Sociology* 12, no. 4 (1999).
71. *Railway Service Gazette,* 16 May 1879, 2.
72. Not including perquisites.
73. IOR: MSS EUR C612.
74. IOR/L/PWD/6/1051, "Machine Shop Foremen required for Kanchrapara Workshops," 1919.
75. Mike Savage, "Discipline, Surveillance and the 'Career': Employment on the Great Western Railway, 1833-1914," in *Foucault, Management and Organization Theory,* ed. Alan McKinlay and Ken Starkey (Sage Publications, 1998), 85. On internal labor markets in the early British rail industry, see also: Peter Howlett, "Evidence of the Existence of an Internal Labour Market in the Great Eastern Railway Company, 1875-1905," *Business History* 42, no. 1 (January 2000), 21-30.
76. UK Appointments to Indian Railways, 1849-1925, Index to Names in L/AG/46. IOR Lists 205, OIOC Reading Room.
77. Freemason membership records from the 1910s give a number of examples of British men who were promoted to the role of driver after three or four years of working under contract as firemen. United Grand Lodge of England Freemason Membership Registers, 1751-1921.
78. K. M. Hassan, *Report on the Representation of Muslims and Other Minority Communities in the Subordinate Railway Service* (Government of India Press, 1932).
79. John W. Mitchell, *The Wheels of India* (London, 1934), 49.
80. Kerr, ed., *Railways in Modern India*; Lajpat Jagga, "Colonial Railwaymen and British Rule"; Goswami, *Producing India*, 103-31.
81. Mitchell, *The Wheels of India*, 59-62; Bear, *Lines of the Nation*; Goswami, *Producing India*, 103-31; "The Amalgamated Society of Railway Servants in India," *The Times of India*, 17 August 1874, 3.
82. Goswami, *Producing India*, 103-31; Bear, *Lines of the Nation*; Mrinalini Sinha, *Colonial Masculinity: The "Manly Englishman" and the "Effeminate Bengali" in the Late Nineteenth Century* (Manchester University Press, 1995).

83. Quoted in Goswami, *Producing India*, 115.

84. *Railway Service Gazette*, no. 317, 22 February 1878, 3: "The Amalgamated Society of Railway Servants in India is in liquidation. A new society has been formed, the first meeting of whose executive committee took place on Jan. 3. The editor of the *Indian Railway Service Gazette* offers a reward of fifty rupees to the persons who will furnish that paper with 'the greatest number of correct statements of different accidents' during the year."

85. IOR/L/PWD/3/72, "Mayo et al, Letter to the Duke of Argyll, Secretary of State for India," 6 January 1871. Data recorded on 30 September 1870. The aggregate numbers across the various rail companies overseen by the PWD were as follows: Traffic Department, 1,340 Europeans and East Indians; Carriage and Wagon Department, 133 Europeans and East Indians; Locomotive Department, 2,285 Europeans and East Indians.

86. East India Railway Company, *EIR Alphabetical List of Europeans and East Indians in the Company's Service* (EIRC Press, Calcutta, 31 December 1888).

87. For a piece of narrative propaganda published in the *Indian Railway Service Gazette* that attempted to dramatize the risks purportedly associated with the employment of South Asian men as drivers, see the reprinted article: "An East Indian Railway Story," *The Pontiac Commercial* 1:46 (Pontiac, MI, May 1877), 3.

88. W. Trant, "Trades Unionism in India," *Fortnightly Review* 32 (London, 1879), 270–71. Formatting added.

89. Elsewhere, Trant writes: "I have italicised the word Christian, because to my mind its appearance in the rule was one of the greatest elements of weakness in the constitution of the society. It must not for one moment be supposed to have a religious signification. It simply meant that 'no natives need apply.' I ought, perhaps, to have mentioned before that one of the great incentives to the formation of the Amalgamated Society of Railway Servants in India, was the strong inclination shown on the part of the railway companies gradually to educate the natives to occupy positions as engine-drivers, stokers, guards, and in other capacities." Trant, "Trades Unionism in India," 270.

90. Trant, "Trades Unionism in India," 268.

91. In addition to Trant, see also: "The Amalgamated Society of Railway Servants in India," *The Times of India*, 17 August 1874, 3.

92. Trant, "Trades Unionism in India," 271.

93. Trant, "Trades Unionism in India," 274.

94. "From the Indian Railway Service Gazette, 'Inattention of Railway Men,'" *Brotherhood of Locomotive Engineers' Monthly Journal* 12, no. 8 (August 1878 [1877]): 353.

95. Jagga, "Colonial Railwaymen and British Rule," 115–17; Rules of the Amalgamated Society of Railway Servants of India and Burma (1907).

CHAPTER 4. LABORING BEHIND THE CURTAIN

1. TNA, MT 2185/3.
2. TNA, MT 6/2129/4.
3. The correlation between public-facing and conciliation-grade workers was not exact. Many of those included in conciliation grades—goods drivers

or platelayers, for example—would not substantially have interfaced with the wider public. And, as an August 1911 appeal from a restaurant car conductor for inclusion in the conciliation scheme makes plain, not all of those who interfaced with the public were construed as engaged in the "manipulation of traffic." MT 6/2018/5. Nevertheless, the higher-grade workers who most exemplified railway labor for the traveling public—drivers, firemen, guards, porters, and signalmen—were core members of conciliation grades, and were leaders of railway craft unionism.

4. Leahcimrac, *John Ingram*.
5. Leahcimrac, *John Ingram*, 48–49.
6. McKenna, *The Railway Workers*, 65–81.
7. Leahcimrac, *John Ingram* (1889), 157.
8. *The Railway Express*, 1:1 (Thursday, October 9, 1890), 1–3.
9. Bagwell, *The Railwaymen*, vol. 1 (Routledge, 1963), 132.
10. *The Railway Express*, 1:1 (Thursday, October 9, 1890), 4.
11. Bagwell, *The Railwaymen*, 149. For a report from the 1890s, see: ASRS, *List of Donations, Subscriptions, &c. to the Orphan Fund of the ASRS* (Co-Operative Printing Society, 1893). "During 1893, the 250 additional children that have been placed on the fund gives a total of 1,597 that have received weekly allowances since its establishment" (3).
12. On the 1890 strike wave, and on other strike waves in Britain from 1870 through 1920, see: Cronin, "Strikes and Power in Britain."
13. Bagwell, *The Railwaymen*, 146. While not a central front in the industrial war, company housing occasionally became a flashpoint in late nineteenth-century battles between railway families and company directors. The low quality of company-owned housing also appears as a grievance in early editions of *The Railway Express*.
14. Bagwell, *The Railwaymen*, 144.
15. For statistics outlining the relatively low level of organization in 1897 of porters and permanent-way employees, see: Bagwell, *The Railwaymen*, 183.
16. Sheila Rowbotham, *Edward Carpenter: A Life of Liberty and Love* (Verso, 2008), 509.
17. Bagwell, *The Railwaymen*, 263.
18. G. D. H. Cole and R. Page Arnot, *Trade Unionism on the Railways: Its History and Problems* (Fabian Research Department and Allen and Unwin, 1917), 11.
19. Frank Bealey and Henry Pelling, *Labour and Politics, 1900—1906* (Macmillan, 1958), 23.
20. Bealey and Pelling, *Labour and Politics*, 23.
21. On the crossimperial formation of white labourism in the first decade of the twentieth century, see Jonathan Hyslop's essays.
22. For the former argument, see Bealey and Pelling, *Labour and Politics*, 265. For the latter, see Henry Pelling, "The Working Class and the Origins of the Welfare State," *Popular Politics and Society in Late Victorian Britain* (Macmillan, 1979), 1–18.
23. Bealey and Pelling, *Labour and Politics*, 264–65.
24. Pelling, "The Working Class and the Origins of the Welfare State," 1–18.

25. Arthur Marwick, "The Labour Party and the Welfare State in Britain, 1900–1948," *American Historical Review*, 73, no. 2 (December, 1967), 380–403.

26. TNA, RAIL 1014/3, GWR Relics, V3, 37B, "Circular No 2105, from General Manager Inglish, 24 October 1907."

27. Bagwell, *The Railwaymen*, 269.

28. Bagwell, *The Railwaymen*, 277.

29. TNA, MT/6/1859/6, "Letter from R Pullen to Board of Trade, 6 November 1908."

30. Bagwell interprets workers' rising disillusionment after 1910 as following in part from the increase that year in company income and dividends—an increase that did not translate into improved working conditions or compensation. Bagwell, *The Railwaymen*, 284.

31. Ralph Darlington, *Labour Revolt in Britain, 1910–1914* (Pluto, 2023), 95. See also Bagwell, *The Railwaymen*, 327.

32. Bagwell, *The Railwaymen*, 304.

33. TNA, MT 2078/4, 10 Nov 1911.

34. Bagwell, *The Railwaymen*, 291–93.

35. Bagwell, *The Railwaymen*, 292.

36. James Cronin, *Industrial Conflict in Modern Britain* (Rowman and Littlefield, 1979), 100.

37. Bagwell, *The Railwaymen*, 294–95.

38. McKenna, *The Railway Workers*, 73–74.

39. Rail workers' reliance on mass pickets in 1911 is consistent with Geoff Eley's argument in *Forging Democracy* about the importance of municipal associations and solidarities in the history of early twentieth-century European labor and socialist organizing. Eley, *Forging Democracy*. For some sense of the variety of picket and sabotage efforts undertaken during the 1911 strike and of railway workers' reliance on extra-industry associations, see: Holton, *British Syndicalism 1900–1914* (Pluto, 1976), 89–110.

40. Edwards, *Remembrance of a Riot* (Llanelli Borough Council, 1988), 41–2. For a description of picketers' tactics in holding off police attempts to break the picket, see: 49–50.

41. Edwards, *Remembrance of a Riot*, 62–63.

42. Edwards, *Remembrance of a Riot*, 46.

43. Edwards, *Remembrance of a Riot*, 48.

44. Edwards, *Remembrance of a Riot*, 45–46.

45. An illustration of the latter can be found in Keir Hardie's polemics against the Liberal Party: "The Liberals have made noises about Welsh nationalism, but has one of them been heard to say a word of pity or sympathy for the ageing mother and father who are weeping their hearts out in a lonely home in Llanelly for a young Welsh lad shot through the heart? No, none of them . . ." Edwards, *Remembrance of a Riot*, 148.

46. Edwards, *Remembrance of a Riot*, 148. The official spelling of the town's name changed in 1966 from Llanelly to Llanelli. There is a different, smaller town in South Wales that is currently named Llanelly.

47. Bagwell, *The Railwaymen*, 333–34.

48. Bentley Gilbert, "Winston Churchill versus the Webbs: The Origins of British Unemployment Insurance," *The American Historical Review* 71 no. 3 (April, 1966), 853.

49. Timothy Alborn, "Senses of Belonging: The Politics of Working-Class Insurance in Britain, 1880–1914," *The Journal of Modern History* 73, no. 3 (September, 2001), 561–602; Bentley Gilbert, "The British National Insurance Act of 1911 and the Commercial Insurance Lobby," *Journal of British Studies* 4, no. 2 (May, 1965), 147.

50. George Alcock, *Fifty Years of Railway Trade Unionism* (Co-Operative Printing Society, 1922), 419.

51. Alborn, "Senses of Belonging," 565.

52. Alcock, *Fifty Years*, 419.

53. Alcock, *Fifty Years*, 419–22.

54. Bagwell, *The Railwaymen*, 336.

55. MRC, MSS 127/GR/4/5.

56. Bagwell, *The Railwaymen*, 330.

57. Rosa Matheson, *The Fair Sex: Women and the Great Western Railway* (The History Press, 2011); Bagwell, *The Railwaymen*, 345.

CHAPTER 5. CONVEYING GRIEVANCES IN THE VERNACULAR

1. IOR/L/PWD/6/797/1302.

2. For the latter strike wave, see: Nitin Sinha, "The World of Workers' Politics: Some Issues of Railway Workers in Colonial India, 1918–1922," *Modern Asian Studies* 42, no. 5 (September 2008), 999–1033.

3. For a useful conceptual distinction between paternalism and mutualism in the context of metropolitan railway labor relations, see Cordery, "Mutualism, Friendly Societies," 263–79.

4. IOR/L/PWD/6/716/1376.

5. IOR/L/PWD/6/755/37, "The Gazette of India," 14 December 1907; IOR/L/PWD/6/761/881, "Establishment of Conciliation Boards and question of legislation against strikes," 2 May 1908; IOR/L/PWD/6/752/2349. Bear discusses these conciliation board deliberations, which featured drivers attempting unsuccessfully to secure more authority over Indian firemen. Bear, *Lines of the Nation*, 97.

6. IOR/L/PWD/6/1106/1258.

7. Ritika Prasad, "Smoke and Mirrors: Railway Travel and Women in Colonial India," *South Asian History and Culture* 3, no. 1 (2012), 26–46.

8. Bear, *Lines of the Nation* (2007), 55.

9. Bear, *Lines of the Nation* (2007), 56.

10. See for example: Inspector-General of Police, *Report on Native Papers in Bengal for the Week Ending June 17, 1899* (Bengali Translator's Office), https://jstor.org/stable/saoa.crl.32979426.

11. Cf. Sinha on the press coverage of violence against indentured women in early twentieth century India. Sinha, "Anatomy of a Politics of the People," 31–49

12. Inspector-General of Police, *Report on Native Papers in Bengal for the Week Ending August 26, 1899* (Bengali Translator's Office), https://jstor.org/stable/saoa.crl.32979436.

13. For a discussion of the role of violence in railway labor-management relations, see David Arnold, "Industrial Violence in Colonial India," *Comparative Studies in Society and History* 22, no. 2 (April 1980), 234–55.

14. For a brief discussion of these interactions, see: Sarkar, *The Swadeshi Movement*, 192.

15. *Selections from the Vernacular Newspapers Published in the Panjab, North-Western Provinces, Oudh, Central Provinces and Berar*, 14 June 1899, https://jstor.org/stable/saoa.crl.25057467.

16. Inspector-General of Police, *Report on Native Papers in Bengal for the Week Ending June 3, 1899* (Bengali Translator's Office), https://jstor.org/stable/saoa.crl.32979424.

17. Inspector-General of Police, *Report on Native Papers in Bengal for the Week Ending June 10, 1899* (Bengali Translator's Office), https://jstor.org/stable/saoa.crl.32979425.

18. IOR/L/PWD/6/849/1684, "No 8 Telegraph of 1897," 16 September 1897.

19. On the denial of housing allowances to Indian signal operators, see also: *Report on Native Papers for the Week Ending May 30, 1903* (Bengali Translator's Office), https://jstor.org/stable/saoa.crl.26165599. "The Hitavadi of the 22nd May writes as follows. . . . Again, even those European and Eurasian signallers, who live in their own houses or make a profit by letting out portions of their houses, receive house-allowances. Names of such officers may be given if required. But poor native signallers receive no house allowances even if they live in rented houses."

20. For a discussion of the 1899 signalers strike in relation to the national movement, see: Jagga, "Colonial Railwaymen and British Rule," 115–17.

21. Bipan Chandra, *India's Struggle for Independence* (India Penguin, 1988), 359–60.

22. Inspector-General of Police, *Report on Native Papers in Bengal for the Week Ending June 17, 1899* (Bengali Translator's Office), https://jstor.org/stable/saoa.crl.32979426.

23. For published grievances on behalf of Indian railway workers in the summer of 1899—in this case on behalf of signalers in Assam and Bengal—see also: Inspector-General of Police, *Report on Native Papers for the Week Ending June 10, 1899*, (Bengali Translator's Office) https://jstor.org/stable/saoa.crl.32979425. Sumit Sarkar has highlighted some of the early, scattered efforts of nationalist organizers to support workers' organizing. Sarkar, *The Swadeshi Movement*, 190–1.

24. *Selections from the Vernacular Newspapers Published in the Panjab, North-Western Provinces, Oudh, Central Provinces and Berar*, 28 June 1899, https://jstor.org/stable/saoa.crl.25057469.

25. *Selections from the Vernacular Newspapers Published in the Panjab, North-Western Provinces, Oudh, Central Provinces and Berar*, 14 June 1899, https://jstor.org/stable/saoa.crl.25057467.

26. *Selections from the Vernacular Newspapers Published in the Panjab, North-Western Provinces, Oudh, Central Provinces and Berar*, 28 June 1899, https://jstor.org/stable/saoa.crl.25057469.

27. *Selections from the Vernacular Newspapers Published in the Panjab, North-Western Provinces, Oudh, Central Provinces and Berar*, 14 June 1899, https://jstor.org/stable/saoa.crl.25057467.

28. Inspector-General of Police, *Report on Native Papers in Bengal for the Week Ending February 4, 1905* (Bengali Translator's Office), 107, https://jstor.org/stable/saoa.crl.33176775.

29. Inspector-General of Police, *Report on Native Papers in Bengal for the Week Ending June 10, 1905* (Bengali Translator's Office), 559, https://jstor.org/stable/saoa.crl.33176793.

30. The National Archives of India, Public Works Department, Account Railway A, December 1891, 33, "Madras Railway Provident Institution, Rules and Regulations."

31. In 1909, the father of an Indian railway worker killed on the job at the Hubli workshops threatened to file suit against the Madras and Southern Mahratta Railway. In the exchange that followed, the agent of the M&SMR noted that the fatally injured railwayman, Mallappa Malkappa, had been earning 8 rupees per month. The National Archives of India, Railway, Establishment, November 1909, 26–30.

32. Inspector-General of Police, *Report on Native Papers for the Week Ending June 4, 1904* (Bengali Translator's Office), 514, https://jstor.org/stable/saoa.crl.33176740.

33. Inspector-General of Police, *Report on Native Papers for the Week Ending August 18, 1906* (Bengali Translator's Office), 743–44, https://jstor.org/stable/saoa.crl.33176855.

34. Sarkar, *The Swadeshi Movement*, 216.
35. Chandra, *India's Struggle for Independence*, 361–62.
36. Sarkar, *The Swadeshi Movement*, 204.
37. Sarkar, *The Swadeshi Movement*, 202.
38. Inspector-General of Police, *Report on Native Papers for the Week Ending November 30, 1907*, (Bengali Translator's Office), 1349, https://jstor.org/stable/saoa.crl.33176922.

39. Inspector-General of Police, *Report on Native Papers for the Week Ending November 30, 1907*, (Bengali Translator's Office), https://jstor.org/stable/saoa.crl.33176922.

40. Sarkar, *The Swadeshi Movement*, 215.
41. Sarkar, *The Swadeshi Movement*, 222.
42. Sarkar, *The Swadeshi Movement*, 219.
43. Sarkar, *The Swadeshi Movement*, 216.
44. Sumit Sarkar, "The Conditions and Nature of Subaltern Militancy: Bengal from Swadeshi to Non-Cooperation, c 1905–22," in *Subaltern Studies III: Writings on South Asian History and Society*, ed. Ranajit Guha (New Delhi, 1984), 273, 277.

45. Bear writes that during the 1906 strike at the Kharagpur workshops, "those who didn't strike were threatened with being made to eat cow or pig

flesh." In this time, she argues, we can see "an expansive meaning for the concept of *jati*. Idioms of jati began to acquire an association with a swadeshi community of common national interests tied together by a moral purity and moral sanctions. In this respect they echo the form, but not the content, of the idioms of race and nation in the railway hierarchy. The railway bureaucracy had made the practices of daily and family life among its European and Eurasian employees an emblem of the moral legitimacy of the Raj. These Indian employees were attempting to forge a counterversion of this moral purity of political communities with a more democratic impulse than the versions of jati among Bengali nationalists in the 1890s. In this community, as in the railway's paternalist practices, obligations to a national and political community are of the same kind as those you owe to your family and social community." Here, Bear sketches out a process of political democratization, wherein workers' "counterversion" in 1906 reflected more democratic impulses than the "versions of jati among Bengali nationalists in the 1890s." With respect to the latter, Bear is primarily referencing the above-discussed writings of Banerjee on railway outrages. We have seen how nationalist editors' closer engagement with railway labor after 1899 helped bring about this democratization of the national cause, at least with respect to industrial labor. Bear, *Lines of the Nation*, 96.

46. Sarkar, *The Swadeshi Movement*, 226.
47. Chandra, *India's Struggle for Independence*, 362.
48. IOR/L/PWD/723/453.
49. NAI, Railway, Traffic, April 1909, 20–81, A, "Measures to prevent outrages and thefts in running trains." The inquiry was spurred by an October 1907 telegram sent to the Railway Board by a representative of the "European and Anglo-Indian Defence Association." The telegram noted "the growing frequency and gravity of outrages in railway trains and the anxiety to the public mind arising therefrom" and called on the Railway Board to initiate reforms to assuage this anxiety. The telegram had its intended effect as the Railway Board initiated a years-long process of reform with the following aims: insulating first- and second-class passengers from bystanders along the tracks, enabling women traveling in first- and second-class carriages to lock their compartment doors at night, making lines of communication between passengers and guards more seamless, and involving the police in the hiring process for menial employees.
50. IOR/L/PWD/6/1106/1258, "Government of India, Railway Department, Enclosure No I to Despatch No. 30 Railway of 1911, Report by Railway Board."
51. IOR/L/PWD/6/755/37.
52. Bear, *Lines of the Nation*, 97.
53. IOR/L/PWD/6/1106/1258, "Government of India, Railway Department."
54. IOR/L/PWD/6/1106/1258, "Government of India, Railway Department."
55. NAI, Railway, Establishment, Sept 1913, 92–94 A, "Sanction to the proposal that piece-workers in the Locomotive Shops and daily rated employees in Collieries, East Indian Railway, be eligible for gratuities for good, efficient, faithful and continuous service." Of these twenty-thousand plus employees, 7,471 worked through contracting arrangements and thus weren't eligible for the gratuity, but the EIR agent claimed that such contracting arrangements would soon be phased out (and indeed, in 1912, these arrangements had been

ruled out of order by the Railway Board), so the premise of the correspondence was that these workers would soon come under the gratuity policy. The other exceptional case was children employed in the collieries, who, the Railway Board ruled, could not build time for the gratuity until they had reached the age of maturity.

56. NAI, Railway, Establishment, November 1909, 26–30, "Grant of six months pay to the legal heirs of the deceased cooly Mallappa Malkappa, Hubli Workshops."

57. On the granting of gratuities to the families of fatally injured railway workers before 1911, see also: NAI, Railway, Establishment, Feb 1910, 13–16, A, "Agents power to grant gratuity to widows or families of deceased railway servants."

58. Bear, *Lines of the Nation*, 98.

59. *Report on Native Papers in the Madras Presidency*, May 3, 1913, https://jstor.org/stable/saoa.crl.30368035; *Report on Native Papers in the Madras Presidency*, June 14, 1913, https://jstor.org/stable/saoa.crl.30368070.

60. NAI, Railway, Establishment, June 1922, E 1–8 B, "Power of Railway Administration to Evict Strikers from Railway Quarters, Stations, Buildings, etc. under Section 138 of the Railway Act."

61. NAI Railway, Establishment, June 1922, E 1–8 B, "Power of Railway Administration to Evict Strikers," "Confidential directive from Railway Board Secretary Waghorn to East Indian Railway Agent Colvin, 18th March 1922."

62. NAI, Railway, Establishment, August 1914, 105–106 A, "Condonation of the break in service for purposes of gratuity of men who struck work on the Madras and Southern Mahratta Railway during the strike of 1909, but who remained loyal during the strike which occurred in 1913."

63. See also: NAI, Railway, Establishment, Sept 1915, 18–20 A, "Sanction of the Secretary of State to the condonation of a break in the service of certain employes of the Burma Railways who went on strike in June 1913, for the purposes of calculating retiring gratuities for good, efficient, faithful and continuous service." An alternative arrangement with the same effect was arrived at for employees who struck work in 1913 on the Great Indian Peninsular Railway. Rather than have their strike condoned for the purpose of the gratuity, the Railway Board in this case authorized the GIPR agent to issue retiring workers who had struck work in 1913 gratuities for inadequate provident fund payments, thus substituting one gratuity for the other. See: NAI, Railway, Establishment, April 1915, 13–15 A, "Grant of permission to the Agent, Great Indian Peninsular Railway, to make the compensation gratuity rules applicable to the men of that railway who were re-engaged after the strike of 1913, provided that their service has been in other respects good and faithful."

64. NAI, Railway, Financial, February 1920, 571 F-17 / 1–7 A, "Secretary of State's sanction to grant the Government of India power to waive the penalty for breaks of service in connection with a strike for purposes of gratuity subject to a report of the circumstances in each case being made to him."

65. NAI, Railway, Establishment, June 1922, E 1–8 B, "Power of Railway Administration to Evict Strikers from Railway Quarters, Stations, Buildings, etc. under Section 138 of the Railway Act."

66. IOR/L/PWD/6/1106/1258, "Viceroy, Railway Department, to Secretary of State for India, 10th May, 1922."

67. IOR/L/PWD/6/1106/1258.

CONCLUSION

1. Clarence Hooker, "Ford's Sociology Department and the Americanization Campaign and the Manufacture of Popular Culture among Assembly Line Workers, c. 1910–1917," *Journal of American Culture*, 20, no. 1 (Spring 1997), 47–53. Quoted in Chris Chitty, *Sexual Hegemony: Statecraft, Sodomy, and Capital in the Rise of the World System* (Duke University Press, 2020), 172.

2. On the relationship between religious affiliation and unionism in railway Crewe, see Drummond, *Crewe*, 282–322.

3. On comparison as hypothesis testing, see: William H. Sewell Jr., "Marc Bloch and the Logic of Comparative History," *History and Theory* 6, no. 2 (1967), 208–18.

4. On early 1920s railway unionism in colonial India, see: Ahmad Azhar, *Revolution in Reform: Trade Unionism in Lahore, c. 1920–70* (Orient Blackswan, 2019); Nitin Sinha, "The World of Workers' Politics," 999–1033; Jagga, "Colonial Railwaymen and British Rule," 103–45; Silas Webb, "'Pet ke waaste': Rights, Resistance and the East Indian Railway Strike, 1922," *Indian Economic and Social History Review* 51, no. 1 (2014), 71–94.

5. Bear, *Lines of the Nation*, 110.

6. For breadwinner politics in Britain, see: Susan Pedersen, *Family, Dependence, and the Origins of the Welfare State: Britain and France, 1914–1945* (Cambridge University Press, 1995). For colonial India, see: N.-W.R. Union, *Memorandum for The Royal Commission on Labour in India* (Lahore, 1929).

Bibliography

ARCHIVAL SOURCES

Major Collections

British Library, London
British Library Newspapers Collection, Colindale
India Office Records (IOR), British Library, London
The National Archives of India (NAI), Delhi
The National Archives of the United Kingdom (TNA), London
South Asian Open Archives (SAOA)
University of Warwick Modern Records Centre (UWMRC), Warwick

Other Document Sources

British Transport Commission Archives
Lambeth Palace Library
London Metropolitan Archives
National Probate Calendar for England and Wales

Newspapers and Periodicals

Blackburn Standard
Brotherhood of Locomotive Engineers' Monthly Journal
Carlisle Patriot
Edinburgh Review
Fortnightly Review

Gazette of India, The
Illustrated London News
Indian Railway Service Gazette
Lancet, The
Pontiac Commercial, The
Railway Chronicle
Railway Express, The
Railway Review
Railway Service Gazette
Standard, The
Swindon Advertiser and North Wilts Chronicle
Times of India
Times of London

PRIMARY SOURCES

1851 Census of England, UK National Archives.
1861 Census of England, UK National Archives.
1881 Census of England, UK National Archives.
[A Signalman]. *A Voice from the Signal-Box: Or, Railway Accidents and Their Causes*. Longmans, Green, 1874.
ASRS (Amalgamated Society of Railway Servants). Minutes of the Meeting of the Executive Committee, with a Copy of the General Office Financial Statements, 21 July 1880).
ASRS. *The General Secretary's Report to the Annual General Meeting at Cardiff*, 5 October 1880.
ASRS. Agenda of Annual General Meeting, 1880.
ASRS. Annual General Meeting, 5 October 1880.
ASRS. Executive Committee Meeting, 4 May 1881.
ASRS. Minutes of the Executive Committee Meeting, May 1887.
ASRS. Minutes of the Executive Committee Meeting, February 1887.
ASRS. *List of Donations, Subscriptions, &c. to the Orphan Fund of the ASRS*. Co-operative Printing Society, 1893.
Bassett-Vincent, Charles. *An Authentic History of Railway Trade Unionism*. Derby, 1963 [1902].
Brough, William. *Prince Amabel*. T. H. Lacy, [1862?].
Carter, John. *On the Influence of Education and Training in Preventing Diseases of the Nervous System*. London, 1855.
Dickens, Charles. *Dombey and Son*. Oxford: Clarendon Press, 1974 (1848).
Du Bois, W. E. B. "The African Roots of War." *The Atlantic Monthly*, May 1915.
EIRC (East India Railway Company). *EIR Alphabetical List of Europeans and East Indians in the Company's Service*. EIRC Press, Calcutta, 31 December 1888.
Evans, Fred. *The Duty of the Society to the Orphans of Members*, February, 1879.
Fletcher, James Ogden. *Railways in Their Medical Aspects*. London, 1867.

Galton, Douglas. "Accident at New Cross on 13 April 1853, Dated 27 April, 1853."
Gaskell, Elizabeth. *Cranford*. Penguin Books, 2005.
The Ghost of John Bull: Or, The Devils Railroad, A Marvellously Strange Narrative James Pattie, 1838.
Greg, W. R. "Mary Barton." *Edinburgh Review* (April 1849).
Hand-book Guide to Railway Situations. Cassell, Petter and Galpin, 1861.
Hassan, K. M. *Report on the Representation of Muslims and Other Minority Communities in the Subordinate Railway Service*. Government of India Press, 1932.
Helps, Arthur. *The Claims of Labour: An Essay on the Duties of the Employers to the Employed and an Essay on the Means of Improving the Health and Increasing the Comfort of the Labouring Classes*. London, 1844.
Huddleston, G. *History of the East India Railway*. Thacker, 1906.
Kipling, Rudyard. "Among the Railway Folk." *From Sea to Sea*, 2 (1889), 274–99.
Kirkman, Marshall M. *Railway Service: Trains and Stations; Describing the Manner of Operating Trains, and the Duties of Train and Station Officials*. New York, 1878.
Langdon, Roger, Ellen Langdon, and Henry Lambert. *The Life of Roger Langdon*. Elliot Stock, 1909.
Leahcimrac, J. *John Ingram: Or, Railway Life behind the Curtain*. Holmes, 1889.
London, Brighton, and South Coast Railway Employment Records. Locomotive Department, 1881.
Masters, John. *Bhowani Junction*. Viking Press, 1954.
Mitchell, John W. *The Wheels of India*. London, 1934.
North-Western Railway Union. *Memorandum for The Royal Commission on Labour in India*. Lahore, 1929.
Phillips, Edwin. *Full Report of the First General Delegate Meeting of the Amalgamated Society of Railway Servants, Together with a Concise History of the Union from its Commencement*. ASRS Society Office, 1872.
The Principal Causes of Railway Accidents, with Proposed Remedies, by a Railway Servant of Fifteen Years Experience. Edinburgh, 1873.
Railway Guards' Universal Friendly Society. Minutes, 1849–1873.
Railway Guards' Universal Friendly Society. Rules, 1849–1863.
Railway Passengers Assurance Company. *Claims and Compensation, from November 1849 to March, 1851*.
Railway Regulation Act. Chapter I.V:20. 30 July 1842.
Reynolds, Michael. *Engine-Driving Life: Stirring Adventures and Incidents in the Lives of Locomotive Engine-Drivers*. London, 1881.
Robinson's Railway Directory. Railway Times Office, 1841.
Snell, Edward. *The Life and Adventures of Edward Snell: The Illustrated Diary of an Artist, Engineer and Adventurer in the Australian Colonies, 1849 to 1859*, edited by Tom Griffith and Alan Platt. Angus & Robertson and The Library Council of Victoria, 1988.

The Sixth Annual Report of the Society for the Relief of Distressed Widows, Applying within the First Month of their Widowhood, Instituted October, 1923. Henry Baylis, 1830.
Trant, W. "Trades Unionism in India," *Fortnightly Review* 32. London, 1879.
Tredgold, Thomas, *The Principles and Practice and Explanation of Locomotive Engines.* London, 1850.
Trollope, Anthony. *Mary Gresley and An Editor's Tales.* Chapman and Hall, 1873.
United Grand Lodge of England Freemason Membership Registers, 1751–1921.
Williams, Alfred, *Life in a Railway Factory.* Duckworth, 1920 [1915].
Wood, Ellen, *Oswald Cray.* 1901 [1864].

SECONDARY SOURCES

Agrawal, Sushila. *Press, Public-Opinion and Government in India.* Asha Publishing House, 1970.
Alborn, Timothy. "Senses of Belonging: The Politics of Working-Class Insurance in Britain, 1880–1914." *The Journal of Modern History* 73, no. 3 (2001): 561–602.
Alborn, Timothy. *Regulated Lives: Life Insurance and British Society, 1800–1914.* University of Toronto Press, 2009.
Alcock, George. *Fifty Years of Railway Trade Unionism.* Co-Operative Printing Society, 1922.
Anderson, Valerie. *The Eurasian Problem in Nineteenth-Century India.* Doctoral thesis, SOAS, 2011.
Arnold, David. "Industrial Violence in Colonial India." *Comparative Studies in Society and History* 22, no. 2 (April 1980): 234–55.
Arnold, David. "White Colonization and Labour in Nineteenth-Century India." *Journal of Imperial and Commonwealth History* 11 (1983): 133–58.
Arondekar, Anjali. *For the Record: On Sexuality and the Colonial Archive in India.* Duke University Press, 2009.
Axton, William. *Circle of Fire: Dickens' Vision and Style and the Victorian Popular Theater.* University of Kentucky Press, 1966.
Azhar, Ahmad. *Revolution in Reform: Trade Unionism in Lahore, c. 1920–70.* Orient Blackswan, 2019.
Bagwell, Philip. *The Railwaymen: The History of the National Union of Railwaymen.* George Allen & Unwin, 1963.
Bailey, Damien, and John McGuire. "Railways, Exchange Banks, and the World Economy: Capitalist Development in India, 1850–1873." In *27 Down: New Departures in Indian Railway Studies*, edited by Ian Kerr. Orient Longman, 2007.
Bailey, P. "'Will the Real Bill Banks Please Stand Up?' Towards a Role Analysis of Mid-Victorian Working-Class Respectability." *Journal of Social History* 12, no. 3 (1979): 336–53.
Bartrip, Peter, and Sandra Burman. *The Wounded Soldiers of Industry: Industrial Compensation Policy, 1833–1897.* Oxford University Press, 1983.

Bayly, C. A. *Empire and Information: Intelligence Gathering and Social Communication in India, 1780–1870*. Cambridge University Press, 1999.
Bealey, Frank, and Henry Pelling. *Labour and Politics, 1900–1906*. Macmillan, 1958.
Bear, Laura. *Lines of the Nation: Indian Railway Workers, Bureaucracy, and the Intimate Historical Self*. Columbia University Press, 2007.
Bhattacharya, Tithi. *The Sentinels of Culture: Class, Education, and the Colonial Intellectual in Bengal (1848-85)*. Oxford University Press, 2005.
Bloomfield, Jacob. *Drag: A British History*. University of California Press, 2023.
Boyer, Robert. *The Regulation School: A Critical Introduction*. Columbia University Press, 1990.
Bronstein, Jamie. *Caught in the Machinery: Workplace Accidents and Injured Workers in Nineteenth-Century Britain*. Stanford University Press, 2008.
Brown, Mark. "Ethnology and Colonial Administration in Nineteenth-Century British India: The Question of Native Crime and Criminality." *The British Journal for the History of Science* 36, no. 2 (2003): 201–19.
Burton, Antoinette. *Burdens of History: British Feminists, Indian Women, and Imperial Culture, 1865–1915*. University of North Carolina Press, 1994.
Cattell, John. "Edward Snell's Diary," *The Bath History Journal* 9, no. 5 (2002).
Cattell, John, and Keith Falconer. *Swindon: The Legacy of a Railway Town*. English Heritage, 1995.
Cawthon, Elisabeth. "New Life for the Deodand: Coroners' Inquests and Occupational Deaths in England, 1830–1946." *American Journal of Legal History*. 33, no. 2 (1989): 137–47.
Cawthon, Elisabeth. *Job Accidents and the Law in England's Early Railway Age*. Edwin Mellen Press, 1997.
Chandra, Bipin. *India's Struggle for Independence*. Penguin, 1988.
Chitty, Chris. *Sexual Hegemony: Statecraft, Sodomy, and Capital in the Rise of the World System*. Duke University Press, 2020.
Clark, Anna. *The Struggle for the Breeches: Gender and the Making of the British Working Class*. University of California Press, 1997.
Claybaugh, Amanda. *The Novel of Purpose: Literature and Social Reform in the Anglo-American World*. Cornell University Press, 2007.
Cocks, H. G. *Nameless Offenses: Homosexual Desire in the Nineteenth Century*. I. B. Tauris, 2003.
Cole, G. D. H, and R. Page Arnot. *Trade Unionism on the Railways: Its History and Problems*. Fabian Research Department and Allen and Unwin, 1917.
Collin, Dorothy, W. "The Composition and Publication of Elizabeth Gaskell's Cranford." *Bulletin of John Rylands II Library of Manchester* 69 (1986): 59–95.
Cooper, Melinda. *Family Values: Between Neoliberalism and the New Social Conservatism*. Zone Books, 2017.
Cordery, Simon. "Mutualism, Friendly Societies, and the Genesis of Railway Trade Unions." *Labour History Review* 67, no. 3 (2002): 263–79.
Cox, F. Hayter. *The Oldest Accident Office in the World: Being the Story of the Railway Passengers Assurance Company, 1849–1949*. RPAC, 1949.

Cronin, James. *Industrial Conflict in Modern Britain*. Rowman and Littlefield, 1979.
Cronin, James. "Strikes and Power in Britain, 1870–1920." In *Strikes, Wars, and Revolutions in an International Perspective: Strike Waves in the Late Nineteenth and Early Twentieth Centuries*, edited by Haimson and Tilly. Cambridge University Press, 2002.
Crossick, Geoffrey. *An Artisan Elite in Victorian Society: Kentish London 1840–1880*. Croom Helm, 1978.
Darlington, Ralph. *Labour Revolt in Britain, 1910–1914*. Pluto, 2023.
Day, Iyko. *Alien Capital: Asian Racialization and the Logic of Settler Colonial Capitalism*. Duke University Press, 2016.
Dinsdale, W. A. *History of Accident Insurance in Great Britain*. Stone and Cox, 1954.
Drummond, Diane. *Crewe: Railway Town, Company and People, 1840–1914*. Routledge, 2017.
Edwards, John. *Remembrance of a Riot*. Llanelli Borough Council, 1988.
Eley, Geoff. *Forging Democracy: The History of the Left in Europe, 1850–2000*. Oxford University Press, 2002.
Fischer-Tiné, Harald. *Low and Licentious Europeans: Race, Class, and "White Subalternity" in Colonial India*. Orient Blackswan, 2009.
Foster, John. *Class Struggle and the Industrial Revolution: Early Industrial Capitalism in Three English Towns*. Weidenfeld and Nicolson, 1974.
Foucault, Michel. "Of Other Spaces, Heterotopias." Translated from *Architecture, Mouvement, Continuité* 5 (1984): 46–49.
Fyfe, Aileen. *Steam Powered Knowledge: William Chambers and the Business of Publishing, 1820–1860*. University of Chicago Press, 2012.
Gallagher, Catherine. *The Industrial Reformation of English Fiction: Social Discourse and Narrative Form 1832–1867*. University of Chicago Press, 1985.
Gaskell, Elizabeth. *Mary Barton: Authoritative Text, Contexts, Criticism*, edited by Thomas Recchio. Norton, 2008.
Ghosh, Durba. *Sex and the Family in Colonial India*. Cambridge University Press, 2014.
Gilbert, Bentley. "The British National Insurance Act of 1911 and the Commercial Insurance Lobby." *Journal of British Studies* 4, no. 2 (1965).
Gilbert, Bentley. "Winston Churchill versus the Webbs: The Origins of British Unemployment Insurance." *The American Historical Review* 71, no. 3 (1966).
Goswami, Manu. *Producing India: From Colonial Economy to National Space*. University of Chicago Press, 2004.
Goswami, Manu, Moishe Postone, Andrew Sartori, and William H. Sewell Jr. "Introducing Critical Historical Studies." *Critical Historical Studies* 1, no. 1 (2014).
Hall, Catherine. "Rethinking Imperial Histories: The Reform Act of 1867." *New Left Review* 1, no. 208 (1994).
Hall, Catherine, Keith McClelland and Jane Rendall. *Defining the Victorian Nation: Class, Race, Gender and the British Reform Act of 1867*. Cambridge University Press, 2000.

Hinchy, Jessica. "The Eunuch Archive: Colonial Records of Non-Normative Gender and Sexuality in India." *Culture, Theory and Critique* 58, no. 2 (2017).
Hinchy, Jessica. *Governing Gender and Sexuality in Colonial India: The Hijra, c. 1850–1900*. Cambridge University Press, 2019.
Hobsbawm, Eric. *Industry and Empire: The Making of Modern English Society*, vol. 2 *1750 to the Present Day*. Pantheon Books, 1968.
Holton, Bob, *British Syndicalism 1900–1914*. Pluto, 1976.
Hooker, Clarence. "Ford's Sociology Department and the Americanization Campaign and the Manufacture of Popular Culture Among Assembly Line Workers, c. 1910–1917." *Journal of American Culture* 20, no. 1 (1997).
Howlett, Peter. "Evidence of the Existence of an Internal Labour Market in the Great Eastern Railway Company, 1875–1905." *Business History* 42, no. 1 (2000): 21–30.
Hurd, John, and Ian Kerr. *India's Railway History: A Research Handbook*. Brill, 2012.
Hyslop, Jonathan. "The Imperial Working Class Makes Itself 'White': White Labourism in Britain, Australia, and South Africa Before the First World War." *Journal of Historical Sociology* 12, no. 4 (1999).
Hyslop, Jonathan. "The World Voyage of Keir Hardie: Indian Nationalism, Zulu Insurgency and the British Labour Diaspora 1907–1908." *Journal of Global History* 1 (2006): 343–62.
Hyslop, Jonathan. "The Strange Death of Liberal England and the Strange Birth of Illiberal South Africa: British Trade Unionists, Indian Labourers and Afrikaner Rebels, 1910–1914." *Labour History Review* 79, no. 1 (2014): 97–120.
Irving, R. J. "The Profitability and Performance of British Railways, 1870–1914." *The Economic History Review*, New Series 31, no. 1 (1978): 46–66.
Ismay, Penelope. "Between Providence and Risk: Odd Fellows, Benevolence and the Social Limits of Actuarial Science, 1820s–1880s." *Past and Present* 226, no. 1 (February 2015).
Jagga, Lajpat. "Colonial Railwaymen and British Rule: A Probe into Railway Labour and Agitation in India, 1919–1922." *Studies in History* 111, no. 1–2 (1981).
Jones, Gareth Stedman. *Languages of Class: Studies in English Working Class History, 1832–1982*. Cambridge University Press, 1983.
Joyce, Patrick. *Work, Society and Politics*. Rutgers University Press, 1980.
Kerr, Ian. "Working Class Protest in 19th Century India: Example of Railway Workers." *Economic and Political Weekly* 20, no. 4 (1985): 34–40.
Kerr, Ian. *Building the Railways of the Raj, 1850–1900*. Oxford University Press, 1995.
Kerr, Ian, ed. *Railways in Modern India* (Oxford University Press, 2001).
Kerr, Ian. "The Railway Workshops and Their Labour: Entering the Black Hole." In *27 Down: New Departures in Indian Railway Studies*, edited by Ian Kerr. Orient Longman, 2007.
Kingsford, P. W. *Victorian Railwaymen: The Emergence and Growth of Railway Labour, 1830–1870*. Frank Cass, 1970.

Kirk, Neville. *The Growth of Working Class Reformism in Mid-Victorian England*. University of Illinois Press, 1985.

Kolsky, Elizabeth. *Colonial Justice in British India: White Violence and the Rule of Law*. Cambridge University Press, 2010.

Kostal, R. W. *Law and English Railway Capitalism, 1825–1875*. Clarendon Press, 1994.

Lea, J. T. *The Great Western Railway Enginemen and Firemen's Mutual Assurance Sick and Superannuation Society, 1865–1965*. Swindon Signcraft, 1965.

Levine, Philippa. *Prostitution, Race and Politics: Policing Venereal Disease in the British Empire*. Routledge, 2003.

Levine, Philippa. "Venereal Disease, Prostitution, and the Politics of Empire: The Case of British India." *Journal of the History of Sexuality* 4, no. 4 (1994): 579–602.

Light, Alison. *Common People: In Pursuit of My Ancestors*. University of Chicago Press, 2015.

Lowe, Lisa. *The Intimacies of Four Continents*. Duke University Press, 2015.

MacDermot, E. T. *History of the Great Western Railway*, vol. 1. Ian Allan, 1982.

Marcus, Sharon. *Between Women: Friendship, Desire, and Marriage in Victorian England*. Princeton University Press, 2007.

Marcus, Sharon. *The Drama of Celebrity*. Princeton University Press, 2019.

Marwick, Arthur. "The Labour Party and the Welfare State in Britain, 1900–1948." *American Historical Review* 73, no. 2 (1967): 380–403.

Mather, F. C. "The Railways, the Electric Telegraph and Public Order during the Chartist Period, 1837–48." *History* 38, no. 132 (1953).

Matheson, Rosa. *The Fair Sex: Women and the Great Western Railway*. The History Press, 2011.

McClelland, Keith. "Rational and Respectable Men: Gender, the Working Class, and Citizenship in Britain, 1850–1867." *Gender and Class in Modern Europe*, edited by Laura Frader and Sonya Rose. Cornell University Press, 1996.

McKenna, Frank. "Victorian Railway Workers," *History Workshop Journal* 1 (Spring 1976).

McKenna, Frank. *The Railway Workers, 1840–1970*. Faber and Faber, 1980.

Mizutani, Satoshi. *The Meaning of White: Race, Class and the 'Domiciled Community' in British India, 1858–1930*. Oxford University Press, 2012.

Oldenburg, Veena Talwar. *Making of Colonial Lucknow, 1856–1877*. Princeton University Press, 1984.

Pedersen, Susan. *Family, Dependence, and the Origins of the Welfare State: Britain and France, 1914–1945*. Cambridge University Press, 1995.

Pelling, Henry. "The Working Class and the Origins of the Welfare State." *Popular Politics and Society in Late Victorian Britain*. Macmillan, 1979.

Prasad, Ritika. "Smoke and Mirrors: Railway Travel and Women in Colonial India." *South Asian History and Culture* 3, no. 1 (2012): 26–46.

Prasad, Ritika. *Tracks of Change: Railways and Everyday Life in Colonial India*. Cambridge University Press, 2015.

Price, Richard. *British Society, 1680–1880: Dynamism, Containment and Change*. Cambridge University Press, 1999.

Revill, George. "Paternalism, Community and Corporate Culture: A Study of the Derby Headquarters of the Midland Railway Company and Its Workforce, 1840–1900." Doctoral thesis, Loughborough University of Technology, 1989.

Revill, George. "Liberalism and Paternalism: Politics and Corporate Culture in 'Railway Derby,' 1865–1875." *Social History* 24, no. 2 (1999).

Riebenack, Max. *Railway Provident Institutions in English-Speaking Countries*. Pennsylvania Railroad Company, 1905.

Rose, Sonya. *Limited Livelihoods*. Routledge, 1992.

Rowbotham, Sheila. *Edward Carpenter: A Life of Liberty and Love*. Verso, 2008.

Sarkar, Sumit. *The Swadeshi Movement in Bengal, 1903–1908*. Orient Blackswan, 1973.

Sarkar, Sumit. "The Conditions and Nature of Subaltern Militancy: Bengal from Swadeshi to Non-Cooperation, c. 1905–22." In *Subaltern Studies III: Writings on South Asian History and Society*, edited by Ranajit Guha. New Delhi, 1984.

Savage, Mike. "Discipline, Surveillance and the 'Career': Employment on the Great Western Railway, 1833–1914." In *Foucault, Management and Organization Theory*, edited by Alan McKinlay and Ken Starkey. Sage Publications, 1998.

Sewell, Jr., William H. "Marc Bloch and the Logic of Comparative History." *History and Theory* 6, no. 2 (1967).

Shanley, Mary Lyndon. *Feminism, Marriage, and the Law in Victorian England, 1850–1895*. Princeton University Press, 1989.

Shifrin, Malcolm. *Victorian Turkish Baths*. Historic England, 2015.

Simmons, Jack. *The Express Train and Other Railway Studies*. David St. John Thomas, 1994.

Sinha, Mrinalini. *Colonial Masculinity: The "Manly Englishman" and the "Effeminate Bengali" in the Late Nineteenth Century*. Manchester University Press, 1995.

Sinha, Mrinalini. "Anatomy of a Politics of the People." In *Political Imaginaries in Twentieth-Century India*, edited by Manu Goswami and Mrinalini Sinha. Bloomsbury, 2022.

Sinha, Nitin. "The World of Workers' Politics: Some Issues of Railway Workers in Colonial India, 1918–1922." *Modern Asian Studies* 42, no. 5 (2008): 999–1033.

Sinha, Nitin. "Entering the Black Hole: Between 'Mini-England' and 'Smell Like Rotten Potato', the Railway Workshop Town of Jamalpur, 1860s–1940s." *South Asian History and Culture* 3, no. 3 (2012).

Smith, Matthew Wilson. "Victorian Railway Accident and the Melodramatic Imagination," *Modern Drama* 55, no. 4 (Winter 2012).

Steedman, Carolyn. *Dust: The Archive and Cultural History*. Rutgers University Press, 2002.

Stoler, Ann Laura. *Along the Archival Grain: Epistemic Anxieties and Colonial Common Sense*. Princeton University Press, 2008.

Upchurch, Charles. "Forgetting the Unthinkable: Cross-Dressers and British Society in the Case of the Queen vs. Boulton and Others." *Gender and History* 12, no. 1 (2000): 127–57.

Vernon, James, ed., *Re-Reading the Constitution: New Narratives in the Political History of England's Long Nineteenth Century*. Cambridge University Press, 1996.

Vicinus, Martha. *The Industrial Muse: A Study of Nineteenth Century British Working-Class Literature*. Harper and Row, 1974.

Wald, Erica. *Vice in the Barracks: Medicine, the Military and the Making of Colonial India, 1780–1868*. Palgrave, 2014.

Walkowitz, Judith. *Prostitution and Victorian Society: Women, Class, and the State*. Cambridge University Press, 1982.

Waugh, Edwin, et al. *Lancashire Dialect Poems, Sketches and Stories*. Abel Heywood, 1915.

Webb, Silas. "'Pet ke waaste': Rights, Resistance and the East Indian Railway Strike, 1922." *Indian Economic and Social History Review* 51, no. 1 (2014): 71–94.

Wilson, H. Raynar. *Railway Accidents, Legislation and Statistics 1825–1924*. Raynar Wilson Company, 1925.

Index

advertisement, labor recruitment and, 101–3
"The African Roots of War" (Du Bois), 16
Al Bashir, 142–43
Alcock, George, 127–28
Amalgamated Society of Railway Servants (ASRS), 8–9, 79, 84, 112, 135, 166–67; Britain, making railway unionism in, 86–94; clerical workers and, 127–28; formation of National Union of Railwaymen (NUR), 126–31; GRWU and all grades unionism, 116–18; Orphan Fund, 85–86, 89–94; politics of railway labor (1889-1914), 112–13; response to LNWR porters strike, 89
Amalgamated Society of Railway Servants of India (ASRSI), 100–108, 105*fig*
Amalgamated Society of Railway Servants of India and Burma (ASRSIB), 154
Anglo-Indians: ASRSI union membership and, 79, 106; conciliation boards and, 135, 150; employment barriers, 103–4; Kipling's vision of railway colony as industrial romance, 57–58; racialized discrimination and, 1–2, 7, 8, 103–4, 144, 154, 159; segregated railway districts, 51, 56–57, 68, 134, 165; strikes by, 145–46, 149, 150; violence by, 136, 137
anti-indenture movement, 12–13, 137–38
Arnot, R. Page, 118

Arondekar, Anjali, 70
ASRS. *See* Amalgamated Society of Railway Servants (ASRS)
ASRSI. *See* Amalgamated Society of Railway Servants of India (ASRSI)
ASRSIB. *See* Amalgamated Society of Railway Servants of India and Burma (ASRSIB)
Assam Bengal Railway, 155
Associated Society of Locomotive Engineers and Firemen (ASLEF), 117, 126
Atkins, F. T., 107–8

bachelors, 162–63; bachelors' balls, 48–49; as boarders, 26–27; cohabitation by, 6; India, railway colony housing and, 54–55, 71–72, 74; railway company recruitment policies and, 71–75; railway towns, paternalism in, 5–6; widow-bachelor households, 22–23, 27–28, 38–39, 49–50
Bagwell, Philip, 87, 116, 121, 126
Banerjee, Surendranath, 136–37, 138
Barnden, Henry, 20
Bass, Michael Thomas, 86
Bassett-Vincent, Charles, 84, 90
Basumati, 144
bathhouses, 40–44
Bealey, Frank, 118–19
Bear, Laura, 6, 136–37, 148, 150–51

Bell, Richard, 119
benefit funds, 95, 177nn50–58; benefits claimants and unions boards, conflict between, 85–86; early trade unionism, 9; India, funds as means to enforce labor discipline, 135, 144–45, 153–54; moralization of funds for widows and orphans, 92–94, 164–65; mutualist organizations as example for union-run funds, 84–85; as self-help initiatives, 119–20
Bengal: partition of, 145–49; vernacular press, 2
Bengal and Nagpur Railway, 153
The Bengalee, 136–37
Benthamite moralizing, 24
Bevan, John, 124–25
block system for signaling, 87
boarding houses: making of sexual cultures in Swindon, 38–39, 49–50; railway widows as operators of, 22–23, 27–28, 38–39, 49–50; Swindon, high rents and overcrowding, 25–27
Board of Trade, 20, 111–12, 118; in 1911 railway strike, 122; conciliation boards and, 121, 167; politics of railway labor (1889-1914), 113, 119; social liberal governance efforts, 126–27
bookstalls on rail lines, 22
braking technology, 87
breadwinner ideal, 84, 85, 117, 162, 168–69
Britain: craft unions in, 79; distribution of benefits to workers, 7–8; early trade unionism, 8–9; making railway unionism in, 86–94; mid-century contributory schemes, 30–38; national railway strike (1911), 122–26; origins of railway paternalism in, 23–30, 162; rhetorics of railway masculinity, 10–11; social liberal approaches to governance, 13–16, 118–22, 167
British workers, in India: rebuilding railway labor in the 1860s, 67–75; segregated railway districts, 56–57
Browne, T. R., 56
Brunel, Isambard, 25
Burma Railway, 155
Burns, John, 116

Campbell, D. W., 56
Campbell, J., 61–62, 63, 64*fig*
capital accumulation, 3, 11–12
capitalism, history of labor under, 11–12

career advancement, 181n12; course of normative life and, 58–59; Henry Winship's scrapbook, EIR engineer, 59–67, 61*fig*, 64*fig*, 66*fig*; labor migrants, pace of promotion and, 102–4; race and career advancement, 103–8, 105*fig*; railway company recruitment policies, 71–75
Carpenter, Edward, 118
Carter, John, 96
Cawthon, Elizabeth, 28
Chakradharpur, 149
Chandra, Bipan, 141, 145
charity, 33, 84–85, 90–91. *See also* benefit funds
Chartist strike waves, 24
Chester and Crewe Railway, 23–24
children: family law in Victorian Britain, 53–54; Labor Representation Committee Manifesto (1906), 119–20; legitimacy of, 32 51–52; orphanages and orphans funds, 9, 32, 33, 84–85, 90–94, 151; as part of the paternal identity of rail workers, 82–84, 85, 90–94, 98–99, 108, 124–25; in "The Turkish Bath" story, 42–43; workhouses, 84
Chinese workers, 100
Christianity, 106–7
churches, 22–23
The Claims of Labour (Helps), 24, 28
Clark, Anna, 84, 85
Clarke, Seymour, 31, 39
class: company paternalism and, 24–25; depictions of in *Mrs. Brown and her Travels*, 47–48; depictions of in "The Turkish Bath" story, 42–44; distribution of social benefits, 158–59; "George Stephenson class," paternal railwaymen as, 83–84; India, racial exclusions in conciliation boards, 150–51; labor-management conciliation boards and, 113; national railway strike (1911), class antagonisms and, 125–26; norms of masculinity and femininity, 10, 84–86, 97–100; ordering railway labor, 6–8; paternalist social institutions as working-class improvement, 49–50; public facing and behind the scenes railway labor, 112–13; railway towns, housing arrangements in, 25–26; respectability as cultural concept, 2–3, 5; sympathetic strikes, structural power of workers and, 123–26, 142; Victorian era working-class history, 84–86; white

laborism, 106, 108; working-class widows, paternalistic views of, 32–35, 84–86, 91–95, 164–65. *See also* nationalist-aligned unionism, India
Cleather, Edward, 23
clergy, 69–70
clerical workers, 127–28
Cole, G. D. H., 118
Cole, George, 72–73
Cole, Lucy, 72–73
colonial officials: efforts to curb strikes, 150–59, 167; fear of homosexuality, 71; hijras, criminalization of, 70–71, 74–75; India, discriminatory practice for railway labor, 104; interventions in family life, 51–55
conciliation boards. *See* labor-management conciliation boards
conjuncture, concept of, 12
contagious diseases (CD) regime, 70, 75
Cordery, Simon, 9, 31–32, 84–85
corporate governance, separation of ownership and management, 4
craft unions, 3; benefits claimants and unions boards, conflict between, 85–86; Britain, making railway unionism in, 86–94; early trade unionism, 8–9, 79; National Union of Railwaymen, formation of, 126, 130; new unionism of General Railway Workers' Union (GRWU), 116–18; politics of railway labor (1889-1914), 112–13; railway workers as paternal figures, 82–86, 125, 166; social liberalism and rise of all-grades unionism, 118–22; union leaders as guardians of widows and children, 83–84; widows and orphans funds, 89–94, 164–65
Cramp, C. T., 118
Cranford (Gaskell), 20–21, 34, 35–38, 49–50, 95
Creed, Richard, 25
Crewe, railway town, 23–24, 81
Criminal Tribes Act (CTA) (1871), 74–75
Critical Historical Studies, 12
Cronin, James, 123

Daily Hitavadi, 143–44, 146
Dalton, Mary, 22–23
Dasi, Rajabala, 137
Davies, John, 124–25
deodand, 28–30, 94–95, 165
Derby, 84, 86, 89–91
Devon, 81, 97–99
Dickens, Charles, 94–95

dockworkers' strike (1911), 122
Dombey and Son (Dickens), 94–95
domestic life, 4–6; Edward Snell's diary on, 26; employer and colonial officials interventions in, 51–55; family law reform, Victorian Britain, 53–54; Henry Winship's scrapbook, EIR engineer, 59–67, 61fig, 64fig, 66fig, 162–63; India, railway colony as heterotopia, 55–59, 182n19, 182n22; India, railway paternalism in, 54–55; long-distance relationships, 72–73; paternal status as unmoored from family situation, 83–84; railway towns, paternalism in, 4–6; surveillance of, railway governance and, 39. *See also* paternalism; railway towns / colonies
drag performances, 46, 47–48, 65, 74–75
Du Bois, W. E. B., 16

Eastern Bengal State Railway, 149, 155
East Indian Railway (EIR), 52, 181n12; career advancement and, 103–8, 105fig; gratuity policy, debate about changes to, 158; Henry Winship's scrapbook, EIR engineer, 59–67, 61fig, 64fig, 66fig, 162–63; housing conditions, 143–44, 182n16; India, rebuilding railway labor in the 1860s, 68–75; labor agreements, 101–3; management structure, 4; provident fund, 134, 144; strike (1905), 145; strike (1906), 13, 144, 145; strike (1907), 145–46. *See also* Jamalpur, EIR railway colony
East Indian Society, 107
Edinburgh & Glasgow Railway (EGR), 34, 58–59
Edwardian era, respectability as cultural concept, 2–3
EIR. *See* East Indian Railway (EIR)
EIR Volunteer Rifles, 57
employers: *The Claims of Labour* (Helps), 24–25, 28; interventions in family life, 51–55; labor, recruitment of, 54–55, 71–75, 101, 102–3, 112, 116, 150, 163. *See also* labor-management conciliation boards; paternalism; specific railway company names
employment, labor agreements, 101–3
European and Anglo-Indian Defence Association, 135, 150–51

family law, 53–54
family life. *See* domestic life; paternalism

fictional depictions of railway workers: *Cranford* (Gaskell), 20–21, 34, 35–38, 49–50, 95; *The Ghost of John Bull*, 29, 34; *John Ingram: Or, Railway Life behind the Curtain* (Leahcimrac), 113–16; "Kitty's Sketches," 99–100; *Mrs. Brown on Her Travels*, 47–50; *Oswald Cray* (Wood), 95–96; rhetorics of masculinity, 10–11, 82–84, 108, 162; widow-bachelor domestic form in, 49–50
Field, James, 71–72
Fifty Years of Trade Unionism (Alcock), 127–28
Finniswood, Emma, 99–100
Fordism, 164, 169
Fortnightly Review, 106
Foucault, Michel, 182n19, 182n21

Gaskell, Elizabeth, 20–21, 35–38, 49–50, 95
gender: divisions of labor, 82–83; hijras, 70–71, 74–75; making of sexual cultures in Swindon, 38–50; male breadwinner, female domestic norm, 84, 85, 117, 162, 168–69; masculinity of railway unionist discourse, 130–31; nonconformity, 25, 37, 163–64 (*See also* homosexuality); performances by Swindon Amateur Dramatic Society, 46–50; respectability as cultural concept, 2–3; rhetorics of railway masculinity, 10–11, 82–84, 108, 162
General Railway Workers' Union (GRWU), 14, 112–13; all grades unionism and gendering of railway labor, 115–18; formation of National Union of Railwaymen (NUR), 126–31
George Stephenson class, 83
The Ghost of John Bull: Or, The Devil's Railroad, a Marvelously Strange Narrative (1838), 29, 34
GNR. *See* Great Northern Railway (GNR)
Gokhale, Gopal, 140
Goswami, Manu, 11, 12
Grand Junction Railway, troop transport on, 23–24
gratuity funds, 172n13; India, funds as means to enforce labor discipline, 135, 144–45, 153–54, 169; India, revocable social benefits and suppression of strikes through the Great War, 155–59; India, state intervention in wake of strike wave (1905-7), 151–54; as paternalistic approach to management, 158–59

Great Central Railway, 120
Great Indian Peninsular Railway (GIPR), 71–72, 153; career advancement and, 103–8, 105*fig*; signal operator strike (1899), 139–43; strike of 1899, nationalist movement and, 132; worker strike (1899), 1–2
Great Northern Railway (GNR), 96; provident fund of, 31–32; rules relating to railway widows, 22–23, 164–65
Great Western Magazine, 81
Great Western Provident Society, 31
Great Western Railway (GWR): benefit societies of, 124; career advancement and, 103; contributory funds of, 31–32; *The Life of Roger Langdon* (Langdon), 80–81; management structure, 4; Swindon Mechanics Institution, 40–50, 41*fig*, 45*fig*; railway towns, housing rent rates, 25–26; Swindon railway town, paternalism and, 5–6
Griffiths, Thomas, 15
GRWU. *See* General Railway Workers' Union (GRWU)
GWR. *See* Great Western Railway (GWR)

Hall, M., 61
Hall, Stuart, 12
Hallam, Mrs. C. E. S., 90
Harding, John, 27
Harding, Susan, 27
Hawkins, George, 19–20, 30–31, 39
Haynes, Bertha, 51–55
Haynes, W. J., 51–55, 56
Helps, Arthur, 24, 28, 37
Hendry, Susan, 22–23
heterotopia, railway colony as, 55–75, 182n19, 182n22
hijras, 70–71, 74–75
Hinchy, Jessica, 74
Hindustani, 139–40, 142–43
history of labor under capitalism, 11–12
History Workshop Journal, 114–15
Hitavadi, 2, 140, 141–42
Home Board, 2, 4, 142, 151–52
homosexuality, 6, 178n64, 185n55; bachelors, cohabitation by, 6, 71–72, 74, 163; government regulation of sex workers, 54–55; Henry Winship's scrapbook and, 59–67, 61*fig*, 64*fig*, 66*fig*, 75, 162–63; hijras, criminalization of, 70–71, 74–75; railway company recruitment policies and, 71–75
Horne, Leonard, 111

Household Words, 20–21, 95
housing, 172n8; bachelors, cohabitation by, 6, 71–72, 74, 163; career advancement and, 58–59; company housing allowances, 7–8; ordering of railway labor, 6–8; overcrowding, 25–27; racialized discrimination in, 1–2; railway towns, design of, 24; railway widows as tenants in railway towns, 22–23, 38–39, 164–65; rents in railway towns, 25; service bonus as means to purchase a home, 15
housing, Britain: GWR's workshop town of Swindon, 5–6; making of sexual cultures in Swindon, 38–50; paternalism in railway towns, 25–30; Springburn Hill, EGR railway district, 58–59
housing, India: bachelor housing in, 54–55; Christian identity as condition for housing, 141; EIR, substandard housing, 143–44; eviction of striking workers, 154–55; racial discrimination in, 140–41; segregated railway districts, 57, 168–69; signal operators lack of housing, 140–41; state intervention in wake of strike wave (1905-7), 153–54
How Five Bachelors Kept House, 49–50
Howrah Hitaishi, 146
Humphries, Charles, 111
Hyslop, Jonathan, 100

Illman, Charles, 71–72
ILP. *See* Independent Labour Party (ILP)
imperialism, 3–4, 12, 16, 161–64, 168, 169; cultural norms, print media and, 10; railways as key infrastructures of imperial power, 104; white laborism and, 100
Imperial Japanese Government Railways, 100–101
indentured workers, 12–13, 119, 137
Independent Labour Party (ILP), 118
India, 172n8; craft unions and racialized discourse of paternal responsibility, 85–86; craft unions in, 79; Criminal Tribes Act (CTA) (1871), 74–75; democratizing the national movement in, 12–13; discriminatory distribution of social benefits, 7–8, 134, 165–66, 168–69; early trade unionism, 8–9; gratuity system as strike deterrent, 158–59, 169; hijras, regulation of, 70–71, 74–75; mass labor unrest (1905-7), 134–35; nationalist-aligned unionism, 132–35, 170; partition of Bengal, railway labor movements and, 145–49; post-World War I labor shortages, 102; racialization of paternal responsibility, 100–108, 105*fig*; railway colony as heterotopia, 55–59, 182n19, 182n22; railway construction, history of, 51; railway labor agreements, 101–3; rebuilding railway labor in the 1860s, 67–75; registered sex workers in, 54; revocable social benefits and suppression of strikes, 154–59; rhetorics of railway masculinity, 10–11; social liberal approaches to governance, 13–16; state intervention in wake of strike wave (1905-7), 150–54; vernacular press and conveying of labor grievances, 133–45, 165–67
Indian National Congress, 1
Indian Railway Service Gazette, 108
Indians, racialized discrimination and, 1–2
industrial unionism: all-grades unionism and gendering of railway labor, 113–18; National Insurance Act and NUR, 126–31; national railway strike (1911), 122–26; politics of railway labor (1889-1914), 112–13; social liberalism and rise of all-grades unionism, 118–22
industrial workplaces, political culture in, 5–6
injured workers. *See* workplace injuries
insurance: benefit funds, worker contributions to, 95; contested claims, 34; elimination of policies (1850), 30; health insurance, 120, 127; National Insurance Act (1911), 14, 113, 120, 126–31, 167, 170; National Union of Railwaymen (NUR) and, 126–31, 167; Railway Passengers' Assurance Company, 21–22; unemployment insurance, 120
Irving, R. J., 87
Iyer, Margam, 154–55

Jamalpur, EIR railway colony, 6, 153, 172n8, 182n16; as heterotopia, 55–59, 182n19, 182n22; ordering railway labor, 6–8; rebuilding railway labor in the 1860s, 69; Rudyard Kipling's views of, 57–58; strikes at, 147, 149; workers employed, data on, 56
Japanese workers, 100–101
jati, 148, 198n45
Jermyn Street Hammam, 42
John, John, 124
John Ingram: Or, Railway Life behind the Curtain (Leahcimrac), 113–16
Johnson, Matilda, 22–23

Kerr, Ian, 7
Kershaw, Louis James, 158, 169
Kesari, 133, 141
Kharagpur, 153
Khilifat movement, 15
Kingsford, Peter, 33
Kipling, Rudyard, 57–58, 59, 182n21
"Kitty's Sketches," 99–100

labor: all-grades unionism and gendering of railway labor, 113–18; company benefits for, 7–8; cultivation of respectable workforces, 2; EIR strike (1906), 13; history of labor under capitalism, 11–12; India, rebuilding railway labor in the 1860s, 67–75; India, revocable social benefits and suppression of strikes, 154–59; India, segregated railway districts, 56–57; India, state intervention in wake of strike wave (1905-7), 150–54; India, subcontracting in, 51; India, vernacular press and conveying of labor grievances, 133–45, 165–67; insurance payouts, 21–23; labor agreements, 101–3; mass labor unrest (1905-7), 3; national railway strike (1911), 122–26; ordering railway labor, 6–8; partition of Bengal, railway labor movements and, 145–49; railway company recruitment policies and, 71–75; reciprocal sympathy strikes, 14; recruitment of, 54–55, 71–75, 101, 102–3, 112, 116, 150, 163; rights of, Taff Vale decision, 113, 118. *See also* railway workers; trade unions; unions; specific union names
labor-management conciliation boards, Britain, 113; as means to deflect union recognition, 120–21; social liberal governance and, 118–22, 167
labor-management conciliation boards, India: partition of Bengal, railway labor movements and, 146; racial discrimination and, 135; state intervention in wake of strike wave (1905-7), 150–54
Labour party, turn toward social liberalism, 118–22
Labour Representation Committee (LRC), 113, 118, 119–20
Lambert, Henry, 80–81, 82, 98
Langdon, Ellen, 80, 82, 97–99
Langdon, Roger, 80–81, 82
Langley, Baxter, 89
LBR. *See* London and Birmingham Railway (LBR)

LB&SCR. *See* London, Brighton, and South Coast Railway (LB&SCR)
Leahcimrac, J., 113–14
Levine, Philippa, 70
LGBTQ persons, 6, 70–71, 74–75. *See also* homosexuality
liberal imperial regime, 3
Liberal party, turn toward social liberalism, 118–22, 167
Life in a Railway Factory (Williams), 41, 48–50
life insurance, 95. *See also* benefit funds; widows
The Life of Roger Langdon (Langdon), 80–81, 97–99
Llanelli, South Wales, 124–25
Lloyd George, David, 13, 14, 118, 120
LNWR. *See* London and North Western Railway (LNWR)
Locomotive Steam Enginemen and Fireman's Society, 107
London, Brighton, and South Coast Railway (LB&SCR), 19–20, 30–31, 121
London and Birmingham Railway (LBR), 23, 25
London and North Western Railway (LNWR), porters strike, 88–89
LRC. *See* Labour Representation Committee (LRC)
Lyall, C. J., 52–53

Madras and Southern Mahratta Railway Company (M&SMR), 153, 156
Madras Railway, 144, 154
The Mahratta, 133, 141
Malkappa, Mallappa, 152–53
managers: managerial practices and shaping of early trade unionism, 8–9; paternalism and, 5–6. *See also* paternalism
Manchester and Birmingham Railway, 23–24
Marcus, Sharon, 6, 74
marriage, 185n54; elasticity of, Victorian era, 6; rituals of, 106–7
Mary Queen of Scots, 63, 64fig
masculinity, rhetorics of, 10–11, 82–84, 108, 162
mass pickets, national railway strike (1911), 123–26
Mays, John, 27
Mays, Mary, 27
McKenna, Frank, 58, 114–15
mechanics institutions, 5, 22–23; GWR's workshop in Swindon, paternalism and, 5–6; in Jamalpur, India, 57–58;

membership as paternalistic benefit, 7–8; Swindon, 40–50, 41*fig*, 45*fig*; Swindon, making of sexual cultures, 38–50
Mehta, Pherozeshah, 141
men, rhetorics of railway masculinity, 10–11, 82–84, 108, 162
mid-nineteenth-century conjuncture, 12, 16
military: British colonial governance, 68; contagious diseases (CD) regime, 70; EIR Volunteer Rifles, 57; India, cantonments near railways, 54–55; troop transport by railway companies, 23–24; use of in national railway strike (1911), 124–26
Mitchell, John, 103
mode of regulation, 3
Moore, Thomas, 60
moralizing bureaucracy, 6; Britain, mid-century contributory schemes and moralization of widows, 30–38, 164–65; India, rebuilding railway labor in the 1860s, 68–75; paternalistic institutions for injured workers and their families, 22–23
Morley, John, 133
Mowatt, J. R., 32
Mrs. Brown on her Travels, 47–48, 49–50
"Mrs. Shuttle Worsted" (Staton), 35
mutualist organizations, 9, 84–85, 130, 134–35, 159. *See also* benefit funds

national conciliation boards. *See* labor-management conciliation boards
National Insurance Act (NIA) (1911), 14, 113, 120, 126–31, 167
nationalist-aligned unionism, India, 132–35; democratizing the national movement, 12–13; partition of Bengal, railway labor movements and, 145–49; rhetorics of railway masculinity, 11; support for worker strike against GIPR (1899), 2
National Union of Railwaymen (NUR), 14; formation of, 113, 125–26, 167; national insurance and, 126–31
"Nature" (Moore), 60
New Swindon. See Swindon, GWR railway town
New Swindon Improvement Company (NSIC), 39–40
New Swindon Mechanics Institution, 40–50, 41*fig*, 45*fig*
NIA. *See* National Insurance Act (NIA) (1911)
Non-Cooperation movement, 15

North-Western Provinces (NWP), 74
North-Western Railway, 155, 157
NSIC. *See* New Swindon Improvement Company (NSIC)
NUR. *See* National Union of Railwaymen (NUR)

orphan funds, 84; ASRS Orphan Fund, 85–86, 89–94; as paternal agency, 85–86
Oswald Cray (Wood), 95–96
Oudh and Rohilkhand Railway (ORR), 155, 156–57

Parliamentary Committee on Colonisation (1958), 68
Partition of Bengal, 13
paternal figures: ASRS as surrogate father for orphans, 92–94; Britain, making railway unionism in, 86–94; India, racialization of paternal responsibility, 100–108, 105*fig*; paternal status as unmoored from family situation, 83–84; in print culture, 81, 82–83, 94–100; public-facing roles on the railway, 112; railwayman as, 2–3; Roger Langdon, 80–81
paternalism: applied differently in Britain and India, 158–59, 162, 168–70; Arthur Helps suggestions for managers, 24–25, 28; employer and colonial officials interventions in family life, 54; patriarchal and modern views of railway governance, 158–59; political organizing, shaping of, 8–9; projects of working-class improvement, 48–50; rhetorics of railway masculinity, 10–11, 82–84, 108, 162. *See also* domestic life
paternalism, Britain: GWR's workshop town of Swindon and, 5–6; making of sexual cultures in Swindon, 38–50; mid-century contributory schemes and moralization of widows, 30–38, 164–65; origins of railway paternalism, 23–30, 158–59; support for injured railwaymen and their families, 22–23
paternalism, India, 51–55, 158–59; railway paternalism, withholding of, 138–39; rebuilding railway labor in the 1860s, 68–75
Pelling, Henry, 118–19
"A Penitent's Hymn," 62
pensions: India, pension funds as means to enforce labor discipline, 135, 144–45, 153–54; India, revocable social benefits

pensions (*continued*)
    and suppression of strikes, 154–59;
    social liberalism and, 120
periodicals. *See* fictional depictions of
    railway workers; vernacular press
piece-work arrangements, 7
Plug Plot strikes, 23
political culture: democratizing the national
    movement, 12–13; of working class, 5
Poor Law Amendment Act (1834), 84
Post Magazine, 34, 35
Postone, Moishe, 12
Prasad, Ritika, 10, 136
press. *See* vernacular press
Price, Richard, 24
Prince Amabel, 46–47, 49–50
print culture: *John Ingram: Or, Railway Life
    behind the Curtain* (Leahcimrac),
    113–16; paternal railwayman in
    Victorian print, 94–100; railway labor
    and paternal obligation, 82–83. *See also*
    fictional depictions of railway workers;
    vernacular press
provident funds, 5, 22–23; benefit payout
    from, 14–15; Britain, mid-century
    contributory schemes and moralization
    of widows, 31–38, 164–65; EIR
    governance of, 134, 144; India, state
    intervention in wake of strike wave
    (1905-7), 150–54; membership as
    paternalistic benefit, 7–8, 30; organi-
    zation of, 9
public drunkenness, 68–69
public-facing workers: paternal responsi-
    bility and, 79–80, 96, 112; respectability
    of, 5, 9, 82–83, 138; rhetorics of railway
    masculinity, 10–11; uniforms of, 82–83;
    in Victorian print culture, 94–100, 112,
    116; white supremacist labor regimes,
    105–6
Pullen, R., 121
Punch, 35
Punjab, 149

racialized groups, 1–2; anti-Asian sentiment,
    100–101; craft unions and racialized
    discourse of paternal responsibility,
    85–86, 162; discriminatory distribution
    of social benefits, 7–8, 162; housing
    discrimination and, 1–2; racialization of
    paternal responsibility, 100–108, 105*fig*,
    162; respectability as cultural concept,
    2–3; segregated railway districts, 56–57,
    183n25; strikes and racial

discrimination, 147–48; worker
    recruitment and, 54–55
Rai, Lajpat, 149
Railway Clerks Association (RCA), 117
The Railway Express, 116
Railway Guards Friendly Society, 35
Railway Guards Universal Friendly
    Society, 33
railway industry: accidents, rates of, 86–88,
    188n25; executives, paternalism and,
    5–6; increasing profits of in early 1870s,
    86–87; speculative stock bubble (1846),
    94–95; troop transport by, 23–24
Railway Life behind the Curtain, 99
Railway Passengers' Assurance Company,
    21–22, 34, 176n45
Railway Servants' Orphanage, 89–94
Railway Service Gazette, 10, 84, 87, 89,
    91–92, 99–101
railway towns / colonies, 5; colonial
    urbanism and town planning, 172n10;
    design of, 24; as heterotopias, 55–75,
    182n19, 182n22; housing arrangements
    in, 25–30; railway widows as long-term
    tenants, 22–23, 38–39; regulation of,
    94–95; segregation in, 51. *See also*
    domestic life; housing
railway workers: ordering of, 6–8; popular
    belief of being impervious to pain,
    96–97; railway company recruitment
    policies and, 71–75; reading on the job,
    20–21; recruitment of, 54–55, 71–75,
    101, 102–3, 112, 116, 150, 163;
    rhetorics of railway masculinity, 10–11,
    82–84, 108, 162. *See also* fictional
    depictions of railway workers; labor;
    railway towns / colonies; strikes by
    workers; unions
The Railway Workers (McKenna), 114–15
Rajakhadi, Mallappa Narasapa, 152–53
Rawalpindi, 149
RCA. *See* Railway Clerks Association (RCA)
Rebecca riots, 23
recruiters, 102
religion: Christian identity as condition for
    housing, 141; preferential hiring
    practices, 142–43
religious instruction, 69–70
rent, company housing and, 25–26
respectability: as a contested term, 2; as
    cultural concept, power of, 2–3, 169–70;
    as described in Anthony Trollope's "The
    Turkish Bath," 42–44; domestic life and,
    4–6, 58–59, 168–70, 185n54; GWR

hiring requirements, 38; India, rebuilding railway labor in the 1860s, 68–75; India, vernacular press coverage of experience of women passengers, 136–37; India, vernacular press view of railway employees, 138; Kipling's vision of railway colony as industrial romance, 57–58; project of working-class improvement, 48–50; respectable workforces, cultivation of, 2; uniforms as badges of respectability, 82–83
retirement benefits, 14–15; pension funds as means to enforce labor discipline, 135, 144–45, 153–54, 169; revocable social benefits and suppression of strikes, 154–59, 166–67; state intervention in wake of strike wave (1905-7), 150–54; striking and loss of benefits, 13, 14–15
Robertson, Thomas, 101–2
"Rock'd in the Cradle of the Deep" (Willard), 60
Rolland, Stuart, 42
Rose, George, 47–48
Royal Commission on Trade Unions (1867–9), 86

Saint Paul's Magazine, 42
Samastipur, 149
The Samiran, 2, 138, 139, 142
Sandhya, 147
Sanghani, K. S., 133
Sanjivani, 10
Sarkar, Sumit, 13, 144–45, 146–47, 148, 149
Sartori, Andrew, 12
Savage, Mike, 103
savings banks, 22–23, 30–38, 95
SDF. *See* Social Democratic Federation (SDF)
Second Reform Act, 83
self-help, language of, 84, 91, 119–20
Seneca, 65
Settigunta, 154
Sewell, William H. Jr., 12
sexuality: making of sexual cultures in Swindon, 38–50; performances by Swindon Amateur Dramatic Society, 46–50; sexual nonconformity, 25, 37. *See also* homosexuality; transgender people
sexually transmitted disease, 68–69, 70, 75, 186n55
sexual violence: in fictional portrayals of rail travel, 100; rhetorics of railway masculinity, 10–11; vernacular press reports of railway outrages, 136–39, 149

sex workers, 54, 69–70, 74–75
Shakespeare, William, 98–99
signal operators: block system for signaling, 87; GIPR strike (1899), 139–43; housing benefits for, 1–2; *John Ingram: Or, Railway Life behind the Curtain* (Leahcimrac), 113–16; *The Railway Workers* (McKenna), 114–15
Singh, Ajit, 149
Sinha, Mrinalini, 12–13, 137
Sketchley, Arthur, 47–48
Snell, Edward, 26
"Snowed Up," 96–97
Social Democratic Federation (SDF), 118
social institutions: India, segregated railway districts, 57; paternalism of, 22, 48, 84. *See also* Winship, Henry
social liberalism, in Britain, 13–16; emergence of railway conciliation boards and, 118–22, 167; National Insurance Act (1911), 126–31; politics of railway labor (1889-1914), 113; shaping of labor unions and, 13–16
social liberalism, in India, 13–16
Springburn Hill, Glasgow, 58–59
Squance, W. J. R., 111
Staton, J. T., 35
Steedman, Carolyn, 73
Stephen, J. F., 75
Stewart, Thomas, 61–65
strikes by workers: Britain, origins of paternalism, 23–24; EIR strike (1906), 13; gratuity system as strike deterrent, comparison with Britain and India, 158–59, 169; India, GIPR strike (1899), 1–2; India, revocable social benefits and suppression of strikes, 154–59; India, state intervention in wake of strike wave (1905-7), 150–54; labor-management conciliation boards, as means to deflect strikes, 120–21; LNWR porters strike, 88–89; national railway strike (1911), 113, 122–26; national strike wave (1890), 117; partition of Bengal, railway labor movements and, 145–49; rail managers' threats against striking workers, 120; sympathetic strikes, 14, 123, 125, 156–57, 167; Taff Vale Railway strike (1900), 113; violence and, 147
Sturrock, Archibald, 25–26, 31
subcontracting arrangements, 7, 51
surveillance: of gender nonconformity, 74; railway governance and, 39; of

surveillance *(continued)*
    vernacular press in India, 136; of widows and orphans, 93–94, 164–65
Swadeshi, 13, 173n21, 198n45
Swadeshi movement, 145, 173n21
Swindon, GWR railway town, 5–6, 23–24, 81; all grades unionism, 116–17; boarding arrangements in, 27–28; high rents and overcrowding, 25–27; housing arrangements, 25–26; Mechanics Institution and making of sexual cultures, 38–50; ordering railway labor, 6–8
Swindon Advertiser, 27, 48, 49–50
Swindon Amateur Dramatic Society, 44–49, 45fig
Swindon Mechanics Institution, 38–50
sympathetic strike, 123, 156–57; Triple Alliance and, 14, 123, 125, 167
syndicalism, railways and, 121–22
The Syndicalist Railwayman (Watkins), 122

Taff Vale decision, 113, 118
Taff Vale Railway, 113
Tagore, Surendranath, 141
Taylor, Marion, 46
Temple, William, 80
Tilak, Bal Gandahar, 133, 141–42
Tillett, Ben, 125
The Times, 22
Titus Andronicus (Shakespeare), 98–99
Trade Disputes Act (1906), 118
trade unions, 2; early trade unionism, 8–9; EIR strike (1906), 13; *John Ingram: Or, Railway Life behind the Curtain* (Leahcimrac), 113–16; mass labor unrest (1905-7), 3; National Insurance Act (NIA) (1911), effect of, 14–16; reciprocal sympathy strikes, 14; social liberal approaches to governance and, 14; Triple Alliance, 14, 123, 125, 167. *See also* specific union names
transgender people, 70–71, 74–75
Trant, William, 106, 107
Triple Alliance, 14, 123, 125, 167
Trollope, Anthony, 42–44, 49–50
troop transport by railway companies, 23–24
Turkish baths, 40–44
"The Turkish Bath" (Trollope), 42–44, 49–50

unemployment insurance, 120, 127
uniforms, as badges of respectability, 82–83
unions, 2; early trade unionism, 8–9; Triple Alliance, 14, 123, 125, 167. *See also* specific union names
unions, Britain: all-grades unionism and gendering of railway labor, 113–18; benefit funds of, 84–85; making railway unionism in, 86–94; National Insurance Act (NIA) (1911), effect of, 14–16; national railway strike (1911), 122–26; politics of railway labor (1889–1914), 112–13; reciprocal sympathy strikes, 14; social liberal approaches to governance and, 14, 118–22, 167; social liberalism and rise of all-grades unionism, 118–22; union leaders as guardians of widows and children, 83–84, 164–65
unions, India: EIR strike (1906), 13; mass labor unrest (1905-7), 3, 134–35; nationalist-aligned unionism, 132–35; partition of Bengal, railway labor movements and, 145–49; revocable social benefits and suppression of strikes, 154–59; state intervention in wake of strike wave (1905-7), 150–54
United Pointsmen and Signalmen's Society, 113, 117
Urquhart, David, 42

venereal disease, 68–69, 70, 75, 185n55
vernacular press: conveying of labor grievances, 133–45, 165–67; coverage of GIPR worker strike (1899), 2; GIPR signal operator strike (1899), coverage of, 139–43; nationalist movement, 133–35; partition of Bengal, railway labor movements and, 145–49; rhetorics of railway masculinity, 10–11; surveillance of, 136
Victoria (steamship), 28
Victorian era: domestic life, 26–27, 38, 54; elasticity of marriage in, 6, 74; family law reform, 53–54; Matrimonial Causes Act (1857), 74; orphanages in, 90; polarization of self-help and charity, 84; print culture, 49–50, 94–100; respectability as cultural concept, 2–3, 50, 82; sexuality norms, 54–55
violence: against Indian passengers and Indian railway workers, 139; towards women, 136–37, 149, 185n54, 186n55; vernacular press reports of railway outrages, 136–39, 149
Viranwali, Mussammat, 149

Wacha, D. E., 141
wages, 2–3; benefit funds and, 119; contributory schemes and, 30–31, 95, 119; gratuity (retirement bonus), 14–15; labor-management conciliation boards and, 120–21, 165; labor migrants, contracts of, 103; national wage rate, demand for, 118; orphan fund payments and, 92; railway boards and settling of disputes, 87; respectability and, 138, 169; strikes over, 88, 113, 118, 122, 147, 168–69; Taff Vale strike and, 113
"Wake, Buds," 62
Wakley, Thomas, 29
"A Watchword," 62
Watkins, Charles, 122
Wedderburn, William, 1, 140–41
white British, racialized discrimination and, 1–2
white laborism, 100, 108
white supremacy, 100; India, racialization of paternal responsibility, 100–108, 105*fig*
widows: ASRS debate about the Orphans Fund and, 91–94; benefit funds for, 91–94, 164–65; as boarding house operators, 22–23, 27–28, 38–39, 49–50; Britain, mid-century contributory schemes and moralization of widows, 30–38, 164–65; compensation, right to, 28; economic fallout of workplace injuries, 21–22; payment of benefits to, 15, 28; as tenants in railway towns, 22–23
Willard, Emma, 60
Williams, Alfred, 41, 48–50

Winship, Henry, 59–67, 61*fig*, 64*fig*, 66*fig*, 75, 162–63, 183n28, 184n33
Wolverton, LBR railway town, 25
women: benefit funds, paternalist practices of, 9; economic fallout of workplace injuries, 21–23; India, vernacular press coverage of experience of women passengers, 136–37; male breadwinner, female domestic norm, 84, 85, 117, 162, 168–69; marriages between women, 74; violence toward, 136–37, 149, 185n54, 186n55. *See also* widows
Wood, Ellen, 95–96
workers' compensation: Britain, history of, 28–30; social liberalism and, 120
workhouse system, 84
working hours: labor-management conciliation boards and, 121; strikes over, 118
workplace injuries, 87; economic fallout of, 21–23; government regulations in response to, 94–95; increases in (early 1870s), 86–88; paternalistic institutions for employees and their families, 22–23, 28, 165–66; paternal railwayman in Victorian print culture, 94–100; unions, rise of, 87–88. *See also* benefit funds; widows
workshop employees: domestic life and, 5–6; ordering railway labor, 6–8. *See also* railway towns / colonies
World War I, as historical conjuncture, 12
Worsell, Leonard, 124
"The Worship of Wealth," 67
W.S. Smith & Son, 22

Founded in 1893,
UNIVERSITY OF CALIFORNIA PRESS
publishes bold, progressive books and journals
on topics in the arts, humanities, social sciences,
and natural sciences—with a focus on social
justice issues—that inspire thought and action
among readers worldwide.

The UC PRESS FOUNDATION
raises funds to uphold the press's vital role
as an independent, nonprofit publisher, and
receives philanthropic support from a wide
range of individuals and institutions—and from
committed readers like you. To learn more, visit
ucpress.edu/supportus.

www.ingramcontent.com/pod-product-compliance
Lightning Source LLC
Chambersburg PA
CBHW020813230426
43666CB00007B/987